Windo  es

A University F

DONALD S. MACQUEEN

www.studentlitteratur.se/windowontheunitedstates

Art. No 3466
ISBN 978-91-44-05052-2
Fifth edition
5:3

© Donald S. MacQueen and Studentlitteratur 2009
www.studentlitteratur.se
Studentlitteratur AB, Lund

Cover illustration: Shutterstock
Cover design: Werner Schmidt
Maps: Henrik Hast, Mats Ekman

Printed by Replika Press Pvt Ltd, India 2011

CONTENTS

FOREWORD TO THE FIRST EDITION

This is a basic book about the United States. It is intended as a survey of American social studies for non-native-American adult readers who are fairly proficient in English. It differs from American social-studies textbooks in that it does not assume that its readers are already generally familiar with the American form of government, system of education, and geography. The overview of these topics it offers is geared to relatively well-educated foreign readers and is thus often contrastive in nature. In other words, this book probably had to be written by a native American who was raised and educated in the United States but who has observed America from abroad over a number of years and who knows what non-natives often find puzzling about the United States. The author of a book like this one must know the United States both from the inside and from the outside.

I have not included specific references to my sources, partly because many of them are virtually untraceable and partly because source footnotes would unnecessarily encumber a book of this scope. Apart from regular visits to the United States for immediate impressions, my sources have largely been those available to everyone these days, the print and broadcast media. Especially *Newsweek*, but also *Time, The Economist* (with its excellent 'American Survey' section), *Business Week, U.S. News & World Report*, and *The New York Times* have provided me with much insight and many statistics, as have various publications from the United States Information Agency in Washington, D.C., and from the United States Information Service at the American Embassy in Stockholm, Sweden. Of course, a great many figures were taken from the authoritative *Statistical Abstract of the United States*, which is published annually by the

U.S. Bureau of the Census. With the advent of cable television, I have been able to benefit from the daily broadcasts of *The MacNeil/Lehrer News Hour* on the Public Broadcasting System (relayed abroad by Worldnet) with its in-depth discussions of current events. Cable News Network has also been a boon. The Voice of America's short-wave broadcasts have long been another important source of information. I have attempted to maintain an objective point of view in my presentation. In my choice of material I have tried to balance favorable and unfavorable traits of American society, and I hope I have succeeded in providing an honest and sober assessment of some of the many serious problems the United States is facing as the twentieth century closes.

I am indebted to many of my colleagues at the Uppsala University Department of English for their help and encouragement. I would like to single out my fellow foreign lecturers Richard Glover (who got me started on this project), Daniel Ogden, and Alan Shima for concrete advice about my presentation of many sections of the work. My Swedish colleagues Barbro Almqvist Norbelie and Margareta Westergren Axelsson helped me find a voice suited to my audience. Pia Hansen and Brian Guss of the USIS at the American Embassy in Stockholm were extremely kind in offering me the services of the photographic archives at the USIA in Washington. Thanks, too, to Jan Olof Nyman, librarian at the USIS in Stockholm. My brother William J. MacQueen of Birmingham, Michigan, has been a much-appreciated and invaluable source of information about current events in the US

I would be grateful for any comments or suggested improvements for future editions. Please write to me at Uppsala University, Department of English, Box 527, S-751 20 Uppsala, Sweden.

Donald S. MacQueen

Uppsala, June 1991

FOREWORD TO THE SECOND EDITION

The reception of the first edition of this book has been gratifyingly favorable. To judge from the numerous cards and letters I have received from teachers and students from many parts of Sweden over the years, I seem to have found the appropriate tone of address, amount and choice of detail, and depth of explanation as well as the right mixture of topics for university-level English courses. I would especially like to thank my colleagues Martin Warren, (formerly) Luleå; Patricia Shrimpton, Umeå; David Isitt, (retired) Göteborg; Nigel Musk, Linköping; and Richard Fisher, (retired) Lund, for their words of encouragement. Ric Fisher, in particular, has contributed a number of specific additions to the second edition.

For the last couple of years my cable provider and I have not had access to *The News Hour with Jim Lehrer* from PBS, but recently I have been able to receive quality news daily from National Public Radio's *All Things Considered* via Public Radio International and Radio 6 in Stockholm. Of course, researching this edition has also been hugely facilitated by the advent of the Internet, and I have included a number of Web sites for teachers and students to use in following up and updating points brought up in the book.

Another major source of information was an extremely rewarding two-week trip to New York, Boston, and Washington that I undertook together with an international delegation in connection with the US elections in October–November 1996. This professional visit was arranged by the Citizen Ambassador Program, under the auspices of People to People, and it made possible extensive substantive sessions with various scholars, public officials, and media experts who I would hardly have been able to gain access to working on my own. I thank the English Department at Uppsala University for granting me the time and the financing to take part in the trip.

One of the co-leaders of the US elections delegation was Dr. Erik Åsard, director of the Swedish Institute for North American Studies (SINAS) at Uppsala University, a friend and colleague whose expertise I have long valued highly and who has been of great help to me in preparing this edition. Another mainstay in this work has been my Uppsala department colleague, friend, and fellow Midwesterner Daniel Ogden, alongside the others mentioned in the first foreword, especially Richard Glover, a constant source of encouragement. I am also grateful to my brother Bill for his continuing help and support. My address remains the same as above. I would also be very happy to hear from readers at donald.macqueen@engelska.uu.se.

Donald S. MacQueen

Uppsala, May 1997

FOREWORD TO THE FOURTH EDITION

The third edition (2002) of *American Social Studies* became the first edition of *Window on America*, and this is now the second of the latter and fourth of the former. Apart from the new title—and, of course, a thorough revision of the text, the greatest change starting with the third edition is that there is now a dedicated Web site provided by *Studentlitteratur* where I will be able to update the material in the book apace with developments in the United States. I hope the Web page will also serve as a forum for readers—teachers and students—to exchange ideas with me and with each other.

Donald S. MacQueen

Uppsala, February 2005

FOREWORD TO THE FIFTH EDITION

This fifth edition of *Window on America* has been revised and updated throughout. A new section was written to cover the rapidly evolving conditions for same-sex couples in the US, a topic that has come to the fore in recent years especially. The book's dedicated Web site will continue to update issues covered in the text, and I hope readers will continue to e-mail me about these matters.

Donald S. MacQueen

Ann Arbor, Michigan, January 2009

SOME WEB SITES FOR GENERAL NEWS AND BACKGROUND

National Public Radio
www.npr.org

Public Broadcasting System
www.pbs.org

CNN/TIME
www.allpolitics.com

Thematic Hosted Gateway
www.about.com

Microsoft NBC
www.msnbc.com

CBS News
www.cbsnews.com

ABC News
www.abcnews.com

Time Magazine
www.time.com

New York Times
www.nyt.com

Washington Post
www.washingtonpost.com

USA Today
www.usatoday.com

Newsweek Magazine
www.newsweek.com

International Herald Tribune
www.iht.com

Conservative gateway
www.townhall.com

Mother Jones Magazine
www.motherjones.com

PART I

Places

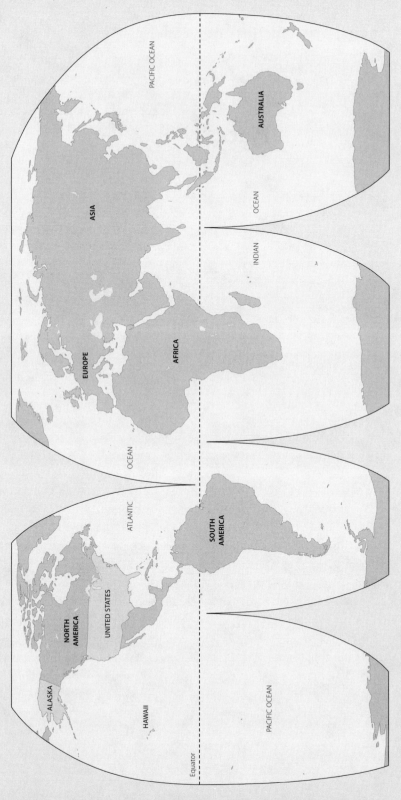

Figure 1.1 The United States in the World.

CHAPTER 1

The Lay of the Land

Bearings

Probably because of historical, cultural, and climatic affinities, most people on both sides of the Atlantic Ocean tend to think that New York City is located on a parallel roughly halfway between London and Paris. But New York is in fact somewhat south of Rome, on the same parallel as Madrid. London is due east of the southern tip of Hudson Bay in Canada, on the same parallel as Calgary, Alberta. Paris is in line with the long straight border between the US and Canada. The eastern seaboard of the US is roughly opposite southern France, Spain, Portugal, Morocco, and Western Sahara.

The north–south orientation of the United States is also commonly misjudged. People think that South America is more or less due south of North America. But if you fly straight southward from almost any point in the United States, you will wind up over the Pacific Ocean. Only some of the east coast states are directly north of parts of South America, namely Ecuador and westernmost Colombia and Peru. In other words, it is the east, not the west, coast of the US that is approximately in line with the west coast of South America.

Figure 1.2 Physical/Political Map the of United States.

Major Geographic Features

When most people, Americans included, think of the United States they tend to think primarily of the forty-eight **contiguous** states, sometimes referred to as the **continental** United States, although this concept is ambiguous in that it might be thought to include Alaska (usually it does not). Alaskans themselves often use the term **the lower forty-eight** to refer to the rest of the states (except Hawaii). In Hawaii the term for the rest of the states (usually excluding Alaska) is the **mainland states**. The shortened expression 'the States' is used almost exclusively outside the country. In America the abbreviation 'US' is the most common one; 'USA' is used for international mailing addresses and in official or patriotic contexts.

The United States is presently the fourth largest country in the world in terms of area, after Russia, Canada, and China. Back in the mid 1880s, increased railroad travel created a need for accurate timetables and standardized time zones, and the contiguous states now have four time zones: Eastern Standard, Central Standard, Mountain Standard, and Pacific Standard Time. Some states are split in two by time-zone boundaries.

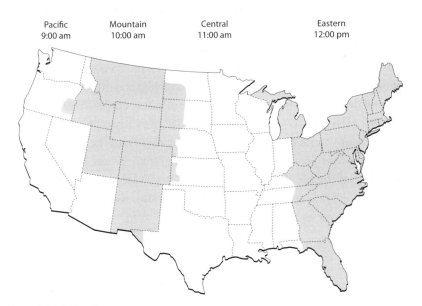

Figure 1.3 US Time Zones.

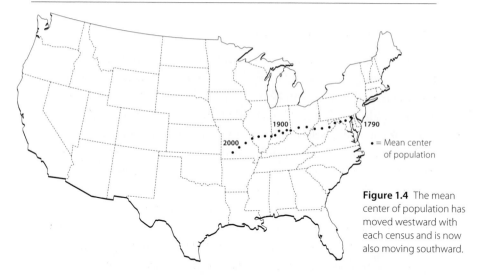

= Mean center
of population

Figure 1.4 The mean center of population has moved westward with each census and is now also moving southward.

Most parts of the country switch to Daylight Saving Time during the summer. Eastern Standard Time (EST) then becomes Eastern Daylight Time (EDT), for example. The four time zones mean that there is a three-hour difference between the two coasts. Hawaii and parts of Alaska are a further two hours 'later' than the west coast. If Puerto Rico and the Virgin Islands are included in the east and the farthest reaches of Alaska and various Pacific island territories in the west, then the US spans eleven time zones.

With more than 300 million people, the US is the world's third largest country in population terms, after China and India. Over the last two hundred years the center of population has moved steadily westward and, in recent decades, more and more to the south. It is currently southwest of St. Louis, Missouri, having crossed the Mississippi River during the 1970s.

Americans think of the Mississippi as the middle of the country, even though it is considerably east of the true geographic center, located near the middle of the Kansas-Nebraska border. If we turn the contiguous states on their 'side' and view them from the south, we can use the Mississippi River as a fulcrum:

Figure 1.5 Schematic Profile of the Contiguous States.

The high and rugged mountains to the west—the **Rocky Mountains**—are balanced by the older and worn **Appalachians** to the east of the fulcrum. The Rocky Mountains are part of a gigantic chain that extends with only minor interruptions from Alaska through the Sierra Madres of Mexico to the Andes in South America, reaching the southern tip of that continent.[1] In the contiguous United States this chain is broken down into the Coastal Range, the Cascades, the Sierra Nevada, and the Rockies proper, which have a number of peaks above 4,000 meters above sea level. The Alaskan Range contains **Mount McKinley**, the highest peak in North America, 6,194 meters above sea level. Between the Sierra Nevada of eastern California and the Wasatch Range of the Rockies in Utah, there is a broad, dry plateau called the Great Basin, covering the entire state of Nevada and parts of Utah. It is generally more than 1,500 meters above sea level and has occasional peaks above 3,000 meters. At the southern tip of the Great Basin, just across the California border, the plateau dips into **Death Valley**, the lowest point in the country at 86 meters below sea level. Just sixty miles (100 km) further into California, the highest peak in the contiguous United States, **Mount Whitney**, rises to 4,418 meters. In the east, the Appalachian ranges have different local names, such as the Allegheny Mountains, the Blue Ridge Mountains, the Smoky Mountains, the Adirondacks, the Berkshires, and the White Mountains.

Between the eastern and western mountain ranges the flat land around the Mississippi and westward consists first of the **Prairies** and then, at a slightly higher altitude, above four hundred meters, the **Great Plains**. Along the peaks of the Rockies at the western edge of the Great Plains runs the **Continental Divide**, the watershed line along which all water will ultimately flow either westward into the Pacific or eastward into the Atlantic.

The **Mississippi River** system, one of the world's major systems, drains the central parts of the continent into the **Gulf of Mexico**. The Mississippi is fed by the **Missouri** and the **Ohio** as well as a number of smaller tributaries. In the Southwest the largest rivers are the **Colorado**, which

---

1   This entire chain, from Alaska to Cape Horn, is known as the **Cordilleras**, although not many Americans are aware of this name. The term is also applied to the respective South American (more commonly) or North American complex separately.

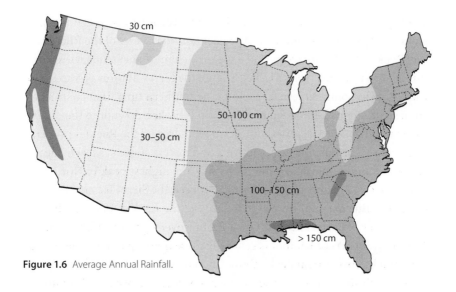

30 cm

50–100 cm

30–50 cm

100–150 cm

> 150 cm

Figure 1.6 Average Annual Rainfall.

runs through the **Grand Canyon** and into the **Gulf of California** in Mexico, and the **Rio Grande**, which forms a major part of the border with Mexico. The **Snake** and **Columbia** system dominates the Northwest, emptying into the Pacific at the Washington-Oregon border. In the Midwest the five **Great Lakes**, together the world's largest reservoir of fresh water, drain via the **St. Lawrence River** through Canada into the North Atlantic. In the 1950s the US and Canada developed this natural channel into the **St. Lawrence Seaway**, which allows ocean-going vessels access to industrial centers like Cleveland, Detroit, and Chicago and on to the mining district of Duluth, Minnesota, during most of the year (parts of it freeze over in winter). A smaller canal connects Chicago with the Illinois and Mississippi Rivers and thus with the Gulf of Mexico.

Of the fifty political units known as **states**, Alaska is both the largest and one of the smallest. It is by far the largest in terms of area,[2] roughly

---

2   Up to 1959, when Alaska and Hawaii became the forty-ninth and fiftieth states, respectively, Texans had always made much of their state's status as the largest in the country. People joked at the time that, out of pity for Texans, Alaska should be divided into two states before joining the union. However, (the joke continued) if Alaska had been split in two, Texas would now be the *third* rather than the *second* largest state in area.

one fifth the size of all the contiguous 48 states combined, but its population is tiny, around 675,000. The population of Wyoming, in the Rocky Mountains, is the smallest, at about 520,000, while the population of Vermont, in New England, is between that of Wyoming and Alaska. The New England state of Rhode Island (which is not an island, although it does include an island by the same name, about the size of New York's Manhattan Island) is the smallest in terms of area, not even the size of the island of Majorca. The state of California, which has the third largest land area among the United States, is a bit smaller than Sweden.

The largest state in population terms is California, with about 36.5 million inhabitants. California passed New York State in the 1970 census, and has since left New York, with its 19.4 million residents, far behind. In the mid 1990s Texas moved up to the number two position, now at over 23.5 million. Both of these shifts reflect the general tendency among Americans to move westward and southward over the last three decades. Over a five-year period, one tenth of the American population moves from one state to another.

California is not only the most populous state; it is also the leading industrial state as well as the largest and most varied agricultural producer. Its gross state product represents roughly 14 percent of the entire gross domestic product of the US. It should be remembered, however, that the major share of industrial production is still in the northeast, from the Great Lakes to the northeastern seaboard (the Chicago–New York axis), and the Midwest is still the agricultural heartland of the nation.

Fully 80 percent of all Americans live in **metropolitan areas**, that is, in or around big cities. This fraction has increased from just over half in 1950. The land area occupied by these metropolitan areas represents about twenty percent of the total area. The ten largest American cities, or rather their respective consolidated metropolitan areas, are as follows (figures in millions, in 2000):

TABLE 1.1 The Ten Largest Metropolitan Areas in the United States.

1. New York, New York	21.2[3]
2. Los Angeles, California	16.4
3. Chicago, Illinois	9.2
4. Washington, DC	7.6
5. San Francisco, California	7.0
6. Philadelphia, Pennsylvania	6.2
7. Boston, Massachusetts	5.8
8. Detroit, Michigan	5.5
9. Dallas, Texas	5.2
10. Houston, Texas	4.7

The northern half of the eastern seaboard is the most densely populated part of the country. The term **megalopolis** is sometimes used to refer to the nearly continuous series of conurbations from Boston in the north to Washington in the south, including the metropolitan areas of Boston, New York, Philadelphia, Baltimore, and Washington. This megalopolis, sometimes called 'Bosnywash', is home to about 45 million people. In the more distant future, this huge urban and suburban area could extend across New York State and Pennsylvania to meet up with another megalopolis stretching from Chicago in the west via Detroit and Cleveland to Pittsburgh in the east. A similar concentration of population is underway in southern California, although here it is still on a somewhat smaller scale and growth will probably be limited by lack of fresh water, a chronic and growing problem in the West (see Figure 1.6 "Average Annual Rainfall" p. 22 and California p. 52).

3   This figure for the New York City consolidated metropolitan area is larger than that for the entire population of New York State (including New York City proper), 19 million. The consolidated metropolitan area reaches into New Jersey, Connecticut, and even Pennsylvania.

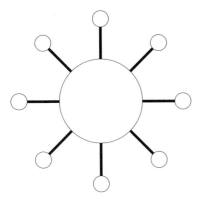

Figure 1.7 1950s City/Suburb Constellation.

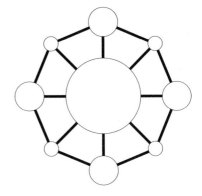

Figure 1.8 Urban Village.

The classic picture of a central city and its outlying suburbs that took shape in the first two decades after World War II was replaced in the following two decades by what was called the **urban village**. In the earlier city/suburb constellation traffic moved from separate **dormitory suburbs** (where people slept) via roads to the hub in the city (where people worked):

By the 1980s the suburbs had taken over most of the work places and shopping centers formerly associated with the downtown area.[4] A 1990 study showed that only about fifteen percent of the residents of Detroit's suburbs worked in the city of Detroit. Traffic patterns have changed to reflect this shift in most cities. Major highways now connect suburbs with one another, completing the wheel-like constellation of the urban village.

This growing independence of outlying nodes of metropolitan areas is clearly visible in most major cities. Many city centers have deteriorated markedly, and attempts to revitalize them by building luxurious hotels and shopping centers in former slums have often been only minimally successful.

---

4 In some American cities, 'downtown' has a more specific meaning than merely 'the center': in New York, for example, 'uptown' Manhattan is north of 'downtown' Manhattan. In most metropolitan areas, however, people say they go 'uptown' when they go to the local suburban business center and 'downtown' when they go into the central part of the metropolis.

The end of the 20ᵗʰ century found most of America's metropolitan areas in a new phase of decline, suffering from **urban sprawl**. As implied above, only 20 percent of all Americans live outside big city areas; 50 percent of the population lives in suburban areas surrounding cities, and the remaining 30 percent live in the cities proper. The loss of middle-class population and tax base that had earlier affected city centers started to spread to the 'inner ring' of suburbs, those first developed just after World War II. A third ring of housing developments, more and more self-contained and protected by security gates, 'leapfrogged' over the second ring of suburbs. These layers of suburbs are entirely dependent on roads and highways for cars and trucks and on expensive new water and sewage facilities further and further from the central system, all of which has placed a growing strain on metropolitan finances and threatens the very quality of life that people originally moved to the suburbs to find.

In response to this general tendency toward uncontrolled horizontal growth, a new way of thinking about urban life got underway in the 1990s, pioneered in places like Portland, Oregon. City planners started rethinking urban growth, coining the phrase **smart growth**. A key concept of smart growth is the coordination of local governments in a metropolitan area. Instead of each of dozens of small townships and 'villages' vying for benefits, businesses, and residents, a central **metropolitan council of governments**, working in conjunction with state authorities, takes a large view of the transportation and growth problems in the region. In Portland, and more recently in Grand Rapids, Michigan, the downtown area has been made attractive to young families with the construction of condominiums with shopping areas and leisure and cultural facilities within convenient walking distance. Local and state laws have consciously put a cap on further outward growth with an eye to rechanneling limited infrastructural resources into already existing urban and suburban areas to prevent them from becoming slums. State governments are beginning to provide financial support to farmers who are trying to resist the temptation to sell off their land to private contractors for residential development, offering so-called 'conservation easement programs' as an alternative. Instead of heavy investment in new road construction, light-rail and bus systems are being brought online to make transportation available to everyone in the metropolitan area, both

Figure 1.9 The Renaissance Center in Detroit, Michigan: An attempt at downtown renewal in the midst of urban decay. (Photo: Courtesy USIA)

into the city and out to the suburbs, where more and more of the jobs are now located. The uncontrolled centrifugal growth that has been encouraged by governments since WWII—through cheap, federally guaranteed mortgages for new homes, trillions of dollars in subsidies for highway construction, and low prices for land and gasoline—has started to be checked in a few urban centers, but most American cities have entered the 21st century with the same mindset that brought them many of their late 20th-century headaches.

CHAPTER 2

Regions

All countries can be divided into various regions on the basis of climatic, social, and historical differences. Americans tend to think in traditional terms of the **North**, the **South**, and the **West**:

The first two regions refer roughly to the opposing sides of the Civil War (1861–65), in other words the north*eastern* and south*eastern* geographical quarters of the country. The West means the 'rest' of the country, largely settled by Euro-Americans later, but representing well over half of the total surface area and exhibiting considerable differences within the region.

Another north-south dichotomy became popular in the 1970s. With unprecedented industrial and population growth in the (old) South and Southwest, the whole southern part of the country began to be called the

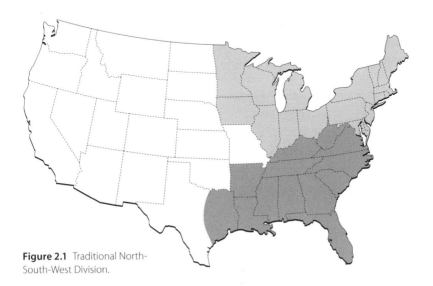

Figure 2.1 Traditional North-South-West Division.

Sun Belt. The term was associated not only with the sunnier and warmer climate of the south but also with innovative **sunrise** industries that contrasted with dying **sunset** industries like steel, for example, in the northeastern manufacturing centers. The northeast and Midwest came to be called, in contrast, either the **Snow Belt** for their cold winters or the **Rust Belt** for their decaying infrastructure and factories. Although these terms are still heard, slowed growth in the Sun Belt and rejuvenation of the old manufacturing centers in the northeast and Midwest has rendered them less common since the mid 1980s.

In the last couple of decades, the traditional 'North-South-Rest' picture has also been slowly supplanted by an east-west polarization. The United States is often seen as being **bicoastal**, with New York (flanked by Boston, Philadelphia, and Washington, DC) and Los Angeles (joined by San Francisco) cast as rival centers. This shift is the natural result of the rise in global importance of the Pacific Rim and the concomitant 'coming of age' of the West Coast, which shook off its earlier cultural inferiority complex in the course of the 1960s and 1970s. The **Bicoastal America** concept implies a huge void between the coasts, and New York–Los Angeles commuters refer to the rest of the country as **Fly-Over America**, the land mass you have to fly over to get to the other coast. The term launched by people in 'the middle' of the country to counter this thinking is **Heartland America**.

Beyond these basic generalizations, the United States is usually divided into a number of regions on the basis of climate, geography, dialect, and settlement history.

Figure 2.2 (below and right) Map of regions.

AK	Alaska	IL	Illinois	NC	North Carolina	SD	South Dakota
AL	Alabama	IN	Indiana	ND	North Dakota	TN	Tennessee
AR	Arkansas	KS	Kansas	NE	Nebraska	TX	Texas
AZ	Arizona	KY	Kentucky	NH	New Hampshire	UT	Utah
CA	California	LA	Louisiana	NJ	New Jersey	VA	Virginia
CO	Colorado	MA	Massachusetts	NM	New Mexico	WA	Washington
CT	Connecticut	MD	Maryland	NV	Nevada	WI	Wisconsin
DE	Delaware	ME	Maine	NY	New York	VT	Vermont
FL	Florida	MI	Michigan	OH	Ohio	WV	West Virginia
GA	Georgia	MN	Minnesota	OK	Oklahoma	WY	Wyoming
HI	Hawaii	MO	Missouri	OR	Oregon		
IA	Iowa	MS	Mississippi	PA	Pennsylvania		
ID	Idaho	MT	Montana	SC	South Carolina		

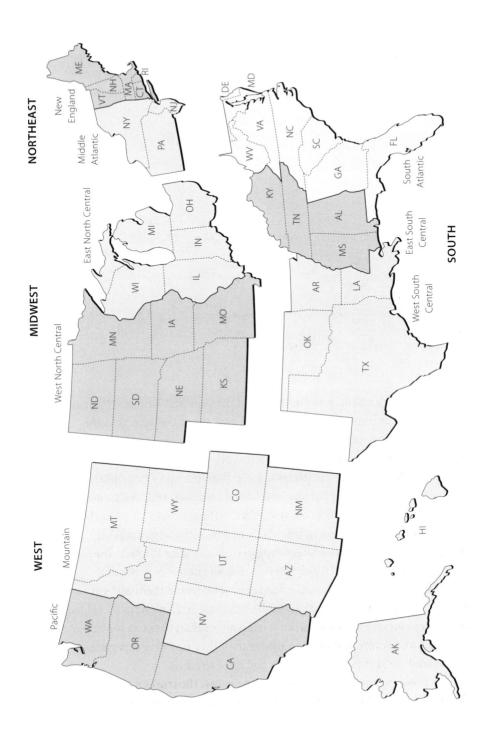

New England

CT Connecticut
MA Massachusetts
ME Maine
NH New Hampshire
VT Vermont

Figure 2.3
The New England States.

Although New England was not the site of the very first British settlement of America, it is common practice to start surveys of US regions in the 'upper right-hand' corner of the map. New England comprises six states: Maine (until 1820 a part of Massachusetts), New Hampshire, Vermont, Massachusetts, Connecticut (the middle 'c' is mute), and Rhode Island.

The English Puritan Pilgrims who first settled New England in 1620 had actually been granted a colony further to the south, in Virginia, but storms forced them to land in what became Massachusetts, and they decided to stay there instead, receiving permission after the fact. The land they farmed along the relatively narrow strip of coast was rocky and infertile, and when they moved inland they soon found themselves at odds with the indigenous nations (although these Indians actually helped the settlers survive the first few seasons). The contrast between the hot summers and severe winters was greater than they had ever experienced in England and Holland (where they had lived in exile).

For reasons of security and protection against the climate, they developed closely knit villages surrounded by fields. At the center of each

32

village was a church. Decisions were taken at town meetings where all men (not women) of property were allowed to vote. This tradition of town meetings, closely associated with the relatively egalitarian Congregationalist churches, is still alive in small New England towns, and picturesque white church steeples are still typical landmarks. Though place names that echo locales in England are found all over the US, they are especially common in New England.

There is a great contrast between (south)eastern and (north)western New England. The southern parts of the coast are densely populated, with Boston, Massachusetts, as the major metropolis, although some of the many medium-sized towns of Connecticut (the richest state per capita in the US) lean more toward neighboring New York City. Western and northern New England is hilly and sparsely populated, a popular resort area within easy reach of the millions of urban residents nearer to the coast. The rocky coast of Maine, with its many lighthouses, has a number of picturesque resort towns. Western Massachusetts and Vermont and New Hampshire are famous for the spectacular fall colors of the leaves in the mountains. The speech of rural New England is also known for its special accent, as is the accent working-class (non-African-American[1]) residents of the city of Boston, the upper-class version of which was on its way to becoming an American standard in the 19th century, but is now in some ways distinct from the so-called **General American** dialect, also known as **Network English** (used on national radio and television networks). General American is rooted in the so-called **Northern Tier** dialect, the Northern Tier stretching from New York State across the northern Midwest to the West Coast.

The early industries of fishing, whaling, shipbuilding, and slave-trafficking were replaced by shoe and textile industries in the early days

---

1 A majority of African Americans commonly speak a fairly homogeneous informal dialect regardless of where they live. This dialect has much in common with Southern dialects but is in many ways distinct, with possibly African creole traits. It used to be called Black English but is now termed AAVE, African-American Vernacular English. Another name for this speech, Ebonics, coined in the 1970s, resurfaced in 1996 in connection with a dispute over the official status of this dialect in the schools in Oakland, California.

of the Industrial Revolution. Boston's role as financial center of the nation was taken over by New York (following the construction of the Erie Canal in the early 19th century). New England's industrial base was slowly eroded by cheaper domestic and foreign competition, but its strength as an educational and scientific center placed it in good stead in the 1980s as a location for high-tech industries. Boston's Route 128 soon grew to rival California's Silicon Valley, partly as a result of lower property prices in the region. Connecticut has long been a major center of the American insurance industry.

Figure 2.4 A Church in Greenwich, Connecticut. (Photo: Rodney McKay Morgan, Courtesy USIA)

The Middle Atlantic States

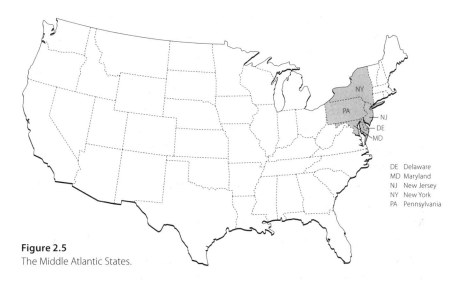

DE Delaware
MD Maryland
NJ New Jersey
NY New York
PA Pennsylvania

Figure 2.5
The Middle Atlantic States.

The term Middle Atlantic refers to the states of New York, New Jersey, and Pennsylvania, with Delaware and Maryland often but not always (see Figure 2.2 "Map of regions" p. 30–31) included as well. Maryland, from which Washington (see the District of Columbia p. 142) was carved in the late 18th century, is also often thought of as the northernmost 'southern' state (although it remained precariously neutral during the Civil War). What generally characterizes the Middle Atlantic states historically is the cosmopolitan nature of their settlement. The Dutch in New Amsterdam (later New York), the Swedes in New Sweden (later part of Delaware), and the Germans in the Quaker colony of Pennsylvania left their mark on the region. Maryland was ostensibly named after the contemporary British Queen, but the Virgin Mary was its true namesake; the colony was established as a shelter for persecuted English Catholics. Like its fellow Mid-Atlantic colonies, it too was open to many peoples and many faiths.

Settlement followed the gently rolling river valleys inland from the coast. Dutch names are still common along the Hudson River into eastern 'upstate' New York, a term used to distinguish the rest of the state from the city of New York. German names still characterize many parts of Pennsylvania. Philadelphia, on the Delaware River, grew to be the largest city of the early United States and the site of most of the political discussions that laid down the guidelines for the country. Baltimore, on Chesapeake Bay, is still a major port. The major cities of New Jersey cluster around New York City in the north and Philadelphia in the south. Called the 'Garden State', New Jersey has much more farmland than might be imagined from its position between two huge metropolises.

New York, Pennsylvania, and Maryland also have extensive gently rolling farmlands farther inland, although the Appalachian Mountains ultimately place a limit on major settlements. Across the mountains, western Pennsylvania has its major city in Pittsburgh at the beginning of the broad Ohio Valley. Pittsburgh, long the most important center of the steel industry, has now been transformed into a leading high-tech city, with Carnegie-Mellon University a prime innovator in the information industry. In western New York State, there are two industrial cities, Rochester, near Lake Ontario, the home of Kodak, and Buffalo, on Lake Erie. **Niagara Falls**, one of the great tourist attractions of the US, is located on the Niagara River between Lake Erie and Lake Ontario.

Like New England, most parts of the Mid-Atlantic area have four definite seasons, although winters are generally milder in the southern reaches. Summers are often hot and humid. Like Boston in New England, the metropolises of New York and Philadelphia have recognizably distinct working-class dialects that deviate from General American. The speech of upstate New York, and of most educated urban New Yorkers and Philadelphians, is considered uncolored by most, being the eastern edge of the standard Northern Tier dialect.

The South

AL Alabama
AR Arkansas
FL Florida
GA Georgia
KY Kentucky
LA Louisiana
MS Mississippi
NC North Carolina
SC South Carolina
TN Tennessee
TX Texas
VA Virginia
WV West Virginia

Figure 2.6
The Southern States.

As mentioned, the term **the South** refers particularly to the eleven states that seceded from the Union to form the Confederate States of America during the Civil War: Virginia, Tennessee, North Carolina, South Carolina, Georgia, Alabama, Mississippi, Louisiana, Texas, Arkansas, and Florida. The states of Kentucky and West Virginia[2], both of which did not join the Confederacy, are also traditionally called Southern states. As was pointed out above, Maryland is often seen as a Southern state: Maryland and Delaware both allowed slavery up to the beginning of the Civil War, and Maryland's border with Pennsylvania is the famous **Mason-Dixon Line** that divides North from South. South Carolina, Georgia, Alabama, and Mississippi are called the **Deep South**. Florida, which is in fact farther south than these states, has a somewhat separate history of Spanish colonization. Louisiana has both a Spanish and a French past. Texas, once Spanish, broke away from Mexico and was independent for nine years before it joined the Union in 1845.

2   West Virginia came into being as a result of the reluctance of the western counties of old Virginia to secede from the United States during the Civil War.

The coastal plain that was minute in New England but considerably broader in some of the Middle Atlantic states widens even more in the South. The various periods of settlement have given rise to names like the **Tidewater South** and the **Piedmont South,** the former referring to older European population centers along the coast and the latter to inland settlements on the plateaus and rolling foothills of the southern Appalachians.

The Virginia colony, named after 'the Virgin Queen', Elizabeth I, was the first British settlement in America, and as far as Britain was concerned it covered the entire continent, until France and Spain presented evidence to the contrary. The Carolina colonies were named for King Charles I and Georgia for King George II. Georgia was originally a penal colony, part of a progressive approach to the treatment of convicts (that also relieved some of the pressure on English prisons).

The warmer climate and the miles and miles of river valleys allowed early settlers to plant huge areas of land, especially in tobacco. When one field was exhausted, farmers needed only move on to new ones. Farming

Figure 2.7 Black Mountains, North Carolina. (Photo: Pressens Bild)

families thus tended to live farther away from each other than did New Englanders, and the cities that grew up along the coast, especially Charleston, were more like resort towns for well-to-do families. Although it is easy to exaggerate the differences, generally speaking, the South was a more 'aristocratic' society than New England or the Middle Colonies, and it maintained close ties with the mother country and its Church of England.

Agriculture continued to dominate the South, and with the invention of the cotton gin in 1797, cotton became the prime crop in the Deep South. Slave labor was closely associated with this surge in the market for cotton, since many farm laborers were needed to pick the crop by hand.

The cotton crop was also dependent on the abundant rainfall that characterizes the South as a whole. Precipitation maps show, however, that the state of Texas is roughly cut in half by the boundary of plentiful rain (see Figure 1.6 "Average Annual Rainfall" p. 22). This geographical fact turned out to be of great importance in American history: the Cotton Kingdom was envisaged by Southerners as ultimately covering the entire southern part of the continent, all the way to the Pacific. The Southern Empire was thus seen as keeping pace with the westward movement of the Northern states. Toward the middle of the 19th century, however, there was a growing realization that such a cotton empire would be impossible, owing to the lack of precipitation west of central Texas. This insight was a major factor in prompting the Southern states to decide to break away from the Northern states, to try to go it alone as a confederacy. This dividing line still makes eastern Texas a part of the South and western Texas a part of the (South)West.

Today Texas (like California) boasts two of the ten largest metropolitan areas in the US. Both Houston and Dallas grew tremendously as a result of the upsurge in the domestic oil industry in the 1970s. Manufacturing cities in the Midwest experienced substantial declines during the same period, and there was a mass exodus of workers to Houston and Dallas. When the price of oil went down again in the 1980s, these cities began to lose some of their newly gained population, often to the same Rust Belt cities—now revitalized—that had recently experienced hard times. This see-saw migration illustrates how the price of oil affects different parts of the country differently. Houston and Dallas are also major financial, chemical, and high-technology centers, however, and can expect continued growth.

Florida is different from the rest of the South in that the climate of its southern parts is sub-tropical and in that it has strong historical and present-day ties with the Spanish-speaking world. In the last decade Miami has grown into a major metropolis and will probably continue to grow as North and South America proceed toward closer economic cooperation. For several decades Florida has been a popular retirement haven for Snow Belt residents.

The South is still mainly agricultural, and some sections belong to the poorest in the nation. In most indexes of prosperity, Mississippi and Alabama rank toward the bottom, and many parts of **Appalachia** suffer from extreme rural poverty. The coal-mining towns of Kentucky and West Virginia have been declining slowly for decades.

On the other hand, the South experienced unusually rapid industrial development throughout the 1970s and 1980s. By the mid 1990s the South was the largest region in the country in terms of population. North Carolina is now a major manufacturing state, and its **Research Triangle** of three neighboring universities that cooperate with business to develop new products was one of the original modern 'research villages'. Atlanta, Georgia, now boasts one of the world's busiest airports, and it is a bustling hub of the communications industry. Interestingly, in the 1990s some Southern states started to capitalize on the less proud aspects of their past, attempting especially to attract black tourists by constructing museums and memorials to the civil rights struggles that took place there. New Orleans had long been a favorite tourist attraction, with its French Quarter and Creole culture, before Hurricane Katrina devastated much of the city in 2005, which is only slowly regaining a foothold as a cultural center. Another possible effect of global warming is the severe drought that has stricken parts of Georgia, including Atlanta, despite its location in a region that normally receives the most rainfall in the country.

The South is also separate in that most people speak one of a number of recognizable dialects that are different from 'standard' American. The variety of speech from the hill country of Tennessee has oddly enough become more or less the standard for popular music as a result of the importance of Nashville and Memphis in country-western and rock music history. Singers from all over the US, from Britain, and many other parts of the world commonly imitate this accent, often without even being aware of it. The rhythms and melodies of Southern speech are associated with a less hectic way of life than that of the metropolises of the North (New York City in particular). It has been pointed out, however, that the pace of Southern life is now approaching that of the North—a side effect of the widespread installation of air conditioning over the past three decades. The influx of people from other parts of the country has also moderated the distinctive features of non-African-American speech in the cities.

The Midwest

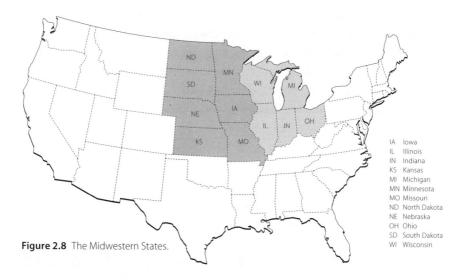

IA Iowa
IL Illinois
IN Indiana
KS Kansas
MI Michigan
MN Minnesota
MO Missouri
ND North Dakota
NE Nebraska
OH Ohio
SD South Dakota
WI Wisconsin

Figure 2.8 The Midwestern States.

The Midwest consists of two sections, the East North Central and West North Central regions in the divisions used by the US Bureau of the Census. The five East North Central states are roughly the old Northwest Territory from the period just after the American Revolution: Ohio, Indiana, Illinois[3], Michigan (with its Upper and Lower Peninsulas), and Wisconsin. This fertile and level or gently hilly region is naturally bounded by the Ohio and Mississippi Rivers and the Great Lakes. Although they are also major agricultural producers as well, these five states bordering on the Great Lakes are referred to as the **industrial Midwest**. Chicago, Illinois, 'the Windy City' at the southern tip of Lake Michigan, was also long known as 'the Second City' but is now the third largest in the country. It is the major metropolis in the region, having

---

3   The 's' in Illinois is mute and the 'ch' in Michigan is pronounced 'sh' (as is the 'Ch' in Chicago). These and many other deviant pronunciations are vestiges of the extensive French presence in the area prior to the Revolutionary War. For example, Detroit, on the straits between Michigan and Ontario, Canada, was founded by Antoine de la Mothe Cadillac in 1701; its French name was (*la Ville*) *d'Étroit*, '(city) on the straits'.

burgeoned in the latter half of the 19th century as a junction for the railroads, the site of stockyards for cattle and seat of the meat-packing industry, but now with a highly diversified industrial base. Detroit, Michigan, the second largest manufacturing metropolis in the region, has long been the automotive capital of the US, and the Detroit–Ann Arbor axis is one of the premier robotics and high-tech centers in the country. Cleveland, Ohio, the major port on Lake Erie, has many light and heavy manufacturing industries. The center of the US tire and rubber industry used to be in Akron, just south of Cleveland, and in southern Ohio, Cincinnati is a manufacturing hub on the Ohio River. With the exception of Chicago, which remains dynamic, these Midwestern cities have suffered greatly in recent years from the loss of manufacturing jobs to overseas countries such as China. High-tech and clean-energy companies are replacing the old heavy manufacturing industries, but not rapidly enough to stop population loss, especially in Michigan.

The seven West North Central states are generally called the **agricultural Midwest**. They are Minnesota, Iowa, Missouri, Kansas,

Figure 2.9 Kansas Wheat Field. (Photo: General Mills, Courtesy USIA)

Nebraska, South Dakota, and North Dakota. Parts of Minnesota were once a section of the Northwest Territory, and it has close affinities to the industrial Midwest. The Twin Cities of St. Paul and Minneapolis are a major focal point of the computer industry, among other high-tech fields. Another industrial center is St. Louis, Missouri, with its striking Gateway Arch (designed by Eero Saarinen). Many of the towns in Missouri, Kansas, and Nebraska grew up as gateways to the West; it was from here that the great overland journeys to the Oregon Territory and California started.

Apart from the minor Ozark Mountains of southern Missouri (plus northern Arkansas and eastern Oklahoma) and the Black Hills in western South Dakota, this region is strikingly flat. It is possible to drive for hours, even days, with only the rise and fall of telephone wires to break the straight line of wheat fields and the horizon. In the east the formerly grassy prairies were for years ignored by settlers, who assumed that land that did not support trees could not grow crops. But the prairies proved to be incredibly fertile, with deep layers of topsoil. The western parts of the region, the Great Plains, are drier and higher, but also excellent for crop farming and cattle grazing. The region as a whole is the world's leading producer of cereal crops and corn (maize), the **breadbasket** of the United States.

The entire Midwest has four distinct seasons, although in the southern sections they are of course less marked. Summers are hot everywhere and often humid as well in the central and eastern parts of the region. Winters on the northern Great Plains and Prairies can be brutally cold and windy, part of a truly continental climate. In the east, the Great Lakes moderate the four seasons considerably, but both hot and cold extremes are not unusual. The forests of northern Michigan, Wisconsin, and Minnesota rival those of New England for fall color splendor. With the many woodland rivers that feed them and their sandy beaches, dunes, and rock formations, the Great Lakes are a major recreational center, sometimes called the Third Coast. Michigan, nearly surrounded by the water, has the

Figures 2.10 (above) and **2.11** (below)
Two Faces of the Great Lakes:
Sandy Lake Michigan Dunes and Beach (above) and
Rugged Lake Superior Cliffs, Pictured Rocks National
Lake Shore, Michigan (below). (Photos: Courtesy USIA)

longest coastline of the 48 contiguous states and typically has more recreational boats registered than any other state.

The non-African-American speech of the northern urban Midwest, a part of the Northern Tier, shares most of the characteristics of Network English with the speech of New York State, the Rocky Mountain states, and the West Coast. The rural Midwestern dialects (in both sections of the region) generally have only slight variations from this standard, especially Minnesota, with certain Scandinavian features. Rural speech in the southern parts of Missouri, Illinois, Indiana, and Ohio is more closely related to dialects south of the Ohio River.

The Mountain States

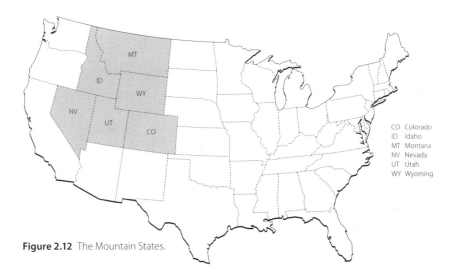

Figure 2.12 The Mountain States.

CO Colorado
ID Idaho
MT Montana
NV Nevada
UT Utah
WY Wyoming

At the western edge of the Great Plains the flat lands give way to the foothills and then suddenly some of the highest peaks of the Rocky Mountains. The Mountain States—Colorado, Wyoming, Montana, Idaho, Utah, and Nevada—are characterized by the various ranges of the Rockies and the sometimes rugged living conditions these mountains impose. This is the least populated large region in the continental United States. The 'Mile-High City' of Denver, Colorado, has become the major metropolis in the area, with Salt Lake City, Utah, ranking second. Both cities are major suppliers to the Department of Defense. The northwestern reaches of this vast area lean toward the cities of the Pacific Northwest.

Industry is dominated by forestry, mining, energy, and tourism, and agriculture by cattle and sheep raising. The spectacular mountain scenery of national parks like **Yellowstone** and the **Grand Tetons** attracts millions of tourists, and the ski resorts of Colorado, Utah, and Idaho are world famous.

In the 1990s the sparse populations of the mountain states made them attractive to tens of thousands of disenchanted Californians looking for

Figure 2.13 The Rocky Mountains in Colorado. (Photo: Courtesy USIA)

Figure 2.14 An Idaho Cowboy in Winter. (Photo: Courtesy USIA)

somewhere less crowded and cheaper to live. Natives of these states have tended to resent this influx of relatively well-to-do settlers, especially since their advent has often overheated the local economy, raising prices and 'crowding' formerly wide open spaces. Las Vegas, Nevada, was the fastest growing city in the US at the beginning of the 21st century.

The desert areas of the Mountain states and the Southwestern states are supremely suited for the construction of solar thermal power stations, that is, mirror-directed sunshine that boils water to create steam to drive turbines. It is estimated that a mere 150 square miles of desert would be sufficient to provide all the electricity used in the United States, although the transmission grid would have to be upgraded for this electricity to be distributed across the country. Several states are already working intensively to make this vision a reality in the next few years.

The Southwest

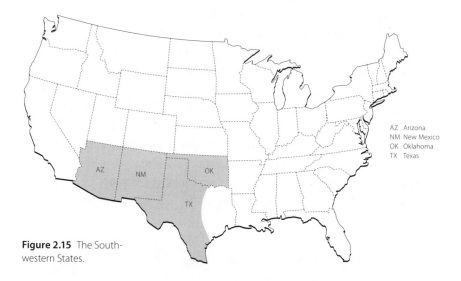

AZ Arizona
NM New Mexico
OK Oklahoma
TX Texas

Figure 2.15 The Southwestern States.

The Southwest can be defined as the part of the south that is not the South. Southern California is part of this region in many ways, but it is also a Pacific Coast state. Western Texas is the region's easternmost section. The southern tip of Nevada, including Las Vegas, belongs here as well. The state of Oklahoma, which has been left out as neither properly Southern nor decidedly Midwestern, does not really belong here either, but with its oil industry and dry climate it is similar to parts of Texas and could be squeezed into this region.

The first states people think of when the term 'southwest' is mentioned are the former Mexican territories of Arizona and New Mexico. They have been among the fastest growing states in the country for decades. Sprawling Phoenix, Arizona, is the most important city (if California and Texas are excluded), with burgeoning electronics, computer, and aerospace industries. Albuquerque, New Mexico, is rapidly growing, too, sharing with Phoenix a concentration on defense-related production. New Mexico, and half of Arizona, is dominated by the southern reaches of the Rockies, but the climate, like that of Oklahoma and western Texas, is extremely dry and warm. There are many arid and semi-arid desert areas, making artificial irrigation necessary for much of the region's agriculture.

Dry heat and nearly perpetual sunshine have made the Southwest a favorite area for retirees and for people with asthma and other breathing disorders from all over the country, but especially from the northeast. Tourism is also a major industry: the area contains historic and present-day sites of indigenous and Mexican cultures and has long attracted artists from all over the world. The **Grand Canyon**, in northern Arizona, is also a major attraction. As in western Texas and southern California, Mexicans and Mexican Americans play an important role throughout Arizona and New Mexico. While many natives of the area speak the clipped western form of southern dialect associated with Oklahoma and Texas, the general dialect is not significantly different from General American, owing to the tremendous influx of people from the northeast and other parts of the country.

Figure 2.16 Indian Cowboys on San Carlos Apache Reservation, Arizona. (Photo: Western Ways, Courtesy USIA)

The Pacific Coast

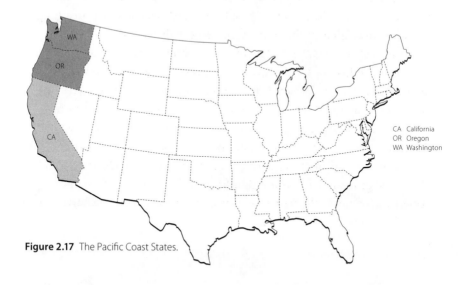

CA California
OR Oregon
WA Washington

Figure 2.17 The Pacific Coast States.

The Southwest (like Florida to some extent) is an area that has a Euro-American background that predates English colonization. The same holds true for the southern parts of the West Coast, especially California. Europeans populated the American colonies first along the two ocean coasts and the Great Lakes, and only later were inland sections settled, from both directions (although primarily from east to west). California and, further north, Oregon Territory, represented a dream within the 'American dream'. People made the greatest sacrifices to get to the incredibly rich and beautiful lands beyond the massive Rockies. Gold was discovered in California in 1848, the same year that the United States took control of the territory as a result of winning the war against Mexico (the US provoked this war after it annexed Texas in 1845). With its subsequent wave of 'forty-niners', California was qualified for statehood by 1850, decades before many states further east.

California is usually seen as consisting of a northern and southern coast, with a third division running the length of the state, the agricultural Central Valley. Southern California is dominated by Los

52

Figure 2.18 Hopi Indian Pueblo, Arizona. (Photo: Southwest Archeological Center, Courtesy USIA)

Angeles, the second largest city in the US, with its entertainment and aerospace industries. The climate is generally sunny and warm, with only minor seasonal variation. Extensive agriculture and urban growth are possible in this area only thanks to highly advanced water management, as the region is naturally dry. All sources of fresh water are already being exploited to, and often beyond, the maximum, and recurrent droughts often lead to drastic rationing among farmers. Unless a major breakthrough is made in the technology for desalinating sea water, the tremendous growth of the region will have to be curtailed. Plans to construct a pipeline to convey water all the way from the Great Lakes have been discussed, although the project would be virtually unfeasible, and the Great Lakes states are now firmly and formally united against the idea.

Further north, San Francisco is the dominant metropolis. Here rainfall is normally more abundant—although rationing of water is sometimes mandated here too as a result of occasional drought—and the climate more moderately warm most of the year. Here, as in Los Angeles, the Asian component of the population is a striking feature. Just south of San Francisco lies Silicon Valley, the cradle and still a major center of the computer industry. To the north the vineyards of Napa Valley have become famous in recent decades for their application of space-age technology to the ancient art of wine-making. Farther north there are vast stretches of surprisingly undeveloped coast and inland forests. Several sections of the California shoreline offer magnificent sights, and just inland national parks preserve Giant Redwoods, the world's largest trees.

A period of relative economic decline in the early 1990s led to a net loss of population of more than 400,000 people from 1993 to 1994 alone, many of them taking with them their savings and skills to the sparsely populated Mountain states for a fresh start. Though it remains the single

Figure 2.19 Irrigated Agriculture in California: A built-in weather station automatically regulates this traveling trickle system. (Photo: Courtesy USIA)

Figure 2.20 The Columbia River between Oregon and Washington State. (Photo: Josef Muench, Courtesy USIA)

largest industrial and agricultural state, California has been tested in recent years by economic downturns and state debt, as well as by fierce wildfires and mudslides in some parts.

North of California lie the states of Oregon and Washington, the **Pacific Northwest**. The spectacular coast continues into these states, and the moderate rainfall of northern California becomes the most plentiful in the nation. The Cascade Range, about 100 miles (160 km) inland from the coast, functions roughly as the Norwegian *fjell* do in Scandinavia or as the Andes do in southern Chile and Argentina: the mountains force the prevailing westerly winds coming in off the ocean to rise, cool, and pour down their moisture. People in Seattle, Washington, in the northwest corner of the continental US, say that it rains so often there that inhabitants do not tan in the summer, they rust.

Seattle is a center of the aerospace and other engineering industries, and has attracted numerous trained engineers and skilled workers from many parts of the world in the past few decades. The Puget Sound area, with its neighbor Vancouver, British Columbia, Canada, to the north, is a burgeoning industrial and cultural region, well positioned for further growth as the world enters the Pacific Century. Both Washington and Oregon are wary of growing too fast, however, and they hope to avoid some of the excesses of (especially southern) California, a process they refer to as 'Californication'[4] and which they feel would spoil the special quality of life they now enjoy.

Speech from the entire Pacific Coast area is basically standard General American or Network English, again owing to the great number of people converging here from all over the country, but especially from the Northern Tier.

---

4   Yes, the pun on "fornication" (sexual intercourse outside marriage) is intended. It is often pointed out that those who seem to be most worried about newcomers violating the Northwestern wilderness are the recent arrivals from California themselves.

Alaska

Alaska (AK)

Figure 2.21 Alaska.

Continuing the journey north along the western coast of North America, the traveler reenters the United States after some 550 miles (900 km) of broken British Columbia coastline. Alaska's coast is also heavily indented, with rugged mountains rising almost directly from the sea. Nearly half of all Alaskans live in the metropolitan areas of Anchorage, Fairbanks, and Juneau. Considering its latitude, the state's climate is surprisingly temperate along the Alexander Archipelago, which is warmed by the Inside Passage (just as the Gulf Stream tempers the climate of northern Europe). But farther north and farther inland the winters are extremely cold and the summers hot and brief.

The United States bought Alaska from Russia for $7.2 million in 1867, a purchase many people deemed a ridiculous waste of money at the time. In the 1890s there was a gold rush, however, and in 1968 oil was discovered in great quantities off the north shore. Over the protests of the Eskimo residents (about fifteen percent of the population is indigenous, by far the largest percentage of all states), a pipeline was built across the entire state, even cutting through national parks, to make possible year-round shipping to refineries.

In the late 1950s, prior to Alaska's becoming the forty-ninth state in 1959, there was a major influx of people, often teachers and other professionals, who were fed up with life in the lower forty-eight and who looked to Alaska as the last frontier in North America. When it comes to development issues, however, the private residents and the state of Alaska have often found themselves at odds with the federal government about land use. This is a problem that typifies much of the western half of the United States, where the federal government still owns roughly half of all land. The animosity is not alleviated by the fact that Washington, DC, is located a continent away. (On the other hand, many Westerners are glad that the national capital is not closer; they can do as they please.)

Hawaii

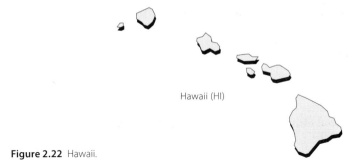

Hawaii (HI)

Figure 2.22 Hawaii.

The fiftieth state is also a region in itself. Located some 2,100 miles (3,400 km) southwest of San Francisco, the eight volcanic islands and numerous islets of Hawaii were probably settled by Polynesians in the 8th century. After a period of growing commerce with the United States and European traders in the 18th and 19th centuries, the islands became a US territory in 1900 and a state in 1959. About three fifths of the population of 1.3 million is of Asian origin, primarily Chinese and Japanese, while one third is white, there being only a small minority of Polynesians left. Pineapple and sugarcane are the main agricultural products, generally produced on huge corporate plantations, and food processing, tourism, and defense facilities are the major industries.

Although Hawaii lies in the tropics, its climate is temperate, owing to prevailing northeasterly winds. Its famous beaches and volcanoes attract visitors from all over the world.

This brief survey has shown that the United States contains a great variety of climates and land forms, from Arctic tundra to sub-tropical beaches, from towering mountain peaks to flat plains, from rainforests to deserts. Almost any type of geographic region can be found somewhere in the United States.

SUGGESTED WEB SITES

Library of Congress home page for states
www.loc.gov/rr/news/stategov/stategov.html

National Governors' Association
www.nga.org

Smithsonian Institution Resources
www.si.edu

or run a general search for the name of a particular state.

PART II

People

CHAPTER 3

Americans

At the end of a television program in English one sometimes wonders whether the production team was American, British, Canadian, or Australian. This can often be determined before the final production credit is given simply by reading the names of the camera operators, gaffers, and other crewmembers. If it is an American production there will be a greater number of 'non-English' names than if the program was produced elsewhere. Although Britain, Canada, and Australia are far from homogeneous countries—the latter two with proportions of foreign-born workers and residents that are actually about twice that of the US, they have not had mixed populations for as long as the US has. Even though English (and Celtic) names are very common in the US, Americans are likely to have just about any type of name in the world.

Americans are used to asking each other how they say or spell their names, and it is not too uncommon to find people who do not really know how their own names 'should' be pronounced; many people have names that are pronounced one way in the foreign country their family originated from and two or three different ways in English. While it was commonplace up to just a few decades ago for people to anglicize their foreign-sounding names (many Millers were once Müllers, and Kays were Kowalskis), today 'name ethnicity' is more widely accepted; indeed, Latino-sounding names—whether real or assumed—have grown in status in the last few years (see "Hispanic Americans" p. 88). Many Americans are proud of their name and ethnic heritage. On the other hand, many others cannot really say where their name comes from.

It is often said that the United States is a nation of immigrants. Most countries of the world, however, are nations of immigrants: after all, how many countries have been populated by the same people since, say, before the last Ice Age or since the birth of Christ? All of this is relative, of course, and it is clearly true that no other country has had so diverse a population as the United States for so long a time. On the other hand, the overwhelming majority of native Americans[1] do not feel that they are immigrants in their own country. It does not take very long for descendants of immigrants to feel that they have 'always been here'.

All native Americans obviously have American roots, but influences from 'the old country', wherever in the world that may be, often continue to make themselves felt in myriad ways. These influences might be subtle, as in parts of Minnesota and Illinois settled by Scandinavians where the Nordic and Lutheran heritage is discernible in people's moods and attitudes, or they may cause more palpable identity clashes, as in the case of young Chinese Americans in San Francisco's Chinatown whose grandparents speak only Chinese. The traditional picture of America as a 'melting pot' of different cultures is partly true, but so is the image of the country as a 'salad bowl' where different cultures are as recognizable as the ingredients in a tossed salad. The web of ethnicity and Americanness is incredibly complicated and will never be untangled by the thousands of scholars who have devoted their professional lives to studying it.

Thus, it cannot be overemphasized that although America has in many ways represented a fresh start for millions of people, they did not arrive in the country as *tabulae rasae*, as clean slates without a background. Far from appearing like mushrooms out of the ground, immigrants to America—including the first Europeans—brought with them complete cultural packages of language, knowledge, attitudes, and beliefs from their home countries. To take one example: the English language spoken in the United States is exactly—to the second—as old as the English language spoken in Britain. It merely changed geographical location in the early 17th century (as the language of the Angles and Saxons had done over a thousand years earlier) and continued to develop, though now differently from the English spoken in the old country.

---

1   This term is used in the conventional sense of 'born in America', not, as it has sometimes been used since the late 1960s (with a capital N), to refer to the aboriginal inhabitants of the continent.

This part of the book will start with a brief history of immigration to the US and then take a closer look at major minority groups and their special characteristics and problems. Much more space will be devoted to two groups with unique histories of oppression and decidedly different present perspectives, African Americans and American Indians.

CHAPTER 4

Immigration

The first Americans probably came from Asia via what is now the Bering Strait. They are generally thought to have migrated some 30,000 years ago, but recent findings in South America suggest a considerably earlier date.

Major European settlements of what was to become the United States were established by the British, French, and Spanish, in the early 17th century. Dutch and Swedish colonies were later subsumed by the British, but their colonists stayed on to leave their mark on New York and Delaware, respectively. Early Spanish settlements in the Southwest and California are still very much in evidence, and in the long view, the Mexican/US border is seen by many as a parenthesis in history. Spanish influence will be discussed more thoroughly below (p. 88 ff.).

By the mid 18th century the French settlers had been pushed by the British into what is now the Canadian province of Quebec. France also dominated the formerly Spanish area at the mouth of the Mississippi River, around New Orleans. French-speaking settlers of old Acadia in Canada found their way to their compatriots in Louisiana and to this day have their own Cajun (from 'Acadian') language and culture. Another node of French culture, though less evident today, is that of the Protestant Huguenots who fled from Catholic France in the 17th century and settled in British South Carolina.

The first non-European immigrants to enter the British colonies were African slaves. The very first slaves were brought to Jamestown, Virginia, by Dutch shippers who sold to the colonists the Africans they had kidnapped. The first slaves were 'indentured servants' just as many white colonists were, that is, they signed on for a period of usually seven years of free labor (apart from their keep—room and board) with a promise of a fresh start in the New World at the end of their term. In the period from

1640 to 1680 this servitude became life-long for Africans in the southern colonies, and their children were also automatically treated as slaves. More and more African people were brought over and sold by European and American colonial shippers until the importation of slaves was prohibited in 1808. After that year the Southern states 'bred'[1] their own slaves until the Civil War finally put an end to the use of human beings as chattel.

In the British colonies English was the standard language, and its saliency explains why this book about the United States is in English. William Penn's liberal colony of Pennsylvania welcomed large numbers of German-speaking settlers, however, and people still use 'Pennsylvania Dutch' (meaning German) expressions there. Substantial numbers of new immigrants came to the British colonies from Ulster in the mid 18th century. These are often called Scotch-Irish because many were Scottish Protestants who had migrated to northern Ireland and then on to America.

After the American Revolution the first major wave of immigrants came from Ireland in the 1840s as a consequence of the **Great Potato Famine** there. They settled largely on the east coast, especially in the cities of Boston and New York, and were often met with hostility by the local citizenry, especially as they were Catholics and peasants. In the first half of the 19th century Americans were intent on establishing some sort of national identity, and these new arrivals were the first, but hardly the last, major group to encounter truculent 'nativism', that is, strong nationalist feelings of hostility toward newly arrived immigrants, who are seen as outsiders. The Irish were very quick to learn nativist ways themselves: after one short generation they often made life difficult for the newly freed slaves who tried to enter the labor market after the Civil War.

The Irish were soon followed by large numbers of Germans and Scandinavians, who tended to move on beyond the east coast to settle lands being opened up in the Midwest in the mid 1800s. While many of these immigrants tried to pass on their languages to their children, they also soon realized that learning English was a key to success in the New

---

1   The very term reveals that these people were seen as animals and property. The words 'chattel' and 'cattle' (as well as 'capital') have the same Latin root, meaning 'head'.

World. Germans, both Protestant and Catholic, made up the largest single group of immigrants in the 19th century.

The construction of the transcontinental railroads in the 1860s was carried out with the help of large numbers of Chinese laborers, thus initiating the first major influx of Asians to the United States. By the 1880s the Chinese had become so numerous in San Francisco (about one sixth of the population) that they were attacked by 'natives'. Starting in 1882 a series of patently racist federal acts were passed to exclude the Chinese from further immigration. These **Chinese Exclusion Acts** were not reversed until 1949, the year of the founding of the People's Republic of China.

The Japanese, who started to immigrate in substantial numbers around the turn of the century, roughly one generation later than the Chinese, could not be so bluntly excluded: their home country had become a world power. When nativist riots erupted against Japanese immigrants on the West Coast, President Theodore Roosevelt appeased Californian whites by exacting the famous **Gentlemen's Agreement of 1908** from the Japanese government. They promised to voluntarily limit the numbers of people allowed to leave for America (much as the major Japanese auto companies would do in regard to car exports to the US in the 1980s).

At the end of the 19th century huge numbers of immigrants began to arrive from southern and eastern Europe. Poles, Russians, Greeks, and Armenians were numerous, but the largest groups were Italians and eastern European Jews. By 1930 three quarters of the population of New York consisted of first- or second-generation immigrants. New waves of immigration in the last decades of the century have led to continued high proportions: the number of immigrants in the US at the end of the 20th century was the highest ever, but the immigrant share of the population was only about 11 percent (a hundred years earlier the number was about 9 million, which amounted to about 15 percent). At the start of the 21st century, fully one third of all residents of New York City were immigrants, and children of immigrants made up another twenty percent—altogether more than half of all New Yorkers, and, in California, people of European descent assumed the novel position of being the largest single minority group in the state.

Native American fear that the country would be swamped by poor southern and eastern European immigrants led to the passage in 1924 of an Immigration Act which created a system of national quotas for future immigration. Quotas were devised for each country based on the number of people already in the United States from that country. This meant that eighty-seven percent of new immigration permits would go to people entering from Britain, Ireland, Germany, and Scandinavia. This principle regulated immigration until 1965.

At present no consideration is given to an immigrant's country of origin apart from the fact that only about 26,000 people are allowed to enter as immigrants from any single country each year. The number of legal immigrants reached an all-time high around 1990, nearly 2 million per year, but has since hovered around 600,000–800,000, roughly on a par with the early years of the 20th century. Of these, nearly 400,000 are given special priority to enter the country, roughly two thirds of them on the basis of family ties in the US and one third on the basis of special skills and education. The 600,000–800,000 figure also includes over 100,000 refugees. After one year of residence, refugees are eligible for immigrant status. An estimated 300,000 people also enter the country illegally or overstay their visitor's visas each year, and such people represent an ever larger number of those receiving legal immigrant status. They accounted for the record years leading up to 1990 after a general 'amnesty' was proclaimed regarding illegal Mexican immigrants who had put down roots in the US (see p. 92). In late 1990 Congress repealed a 1952 law that banned communists and homosexuals from immigrating to the US.

California is a state that has experienced huge numbers of immigrants in the last couple of decades. In 1996 *The New York Times* reported that the state accounted for more than half of all foreign-born people in the entire country. In the path of generally conservative political winds in the fall of 1994, a controversial measure was handily passed by the voters of California, Proposition 187, designed to close public services such as schools, non-emergency health care, and welfare benefits to illegal immigrants and in some cases even to legal immigrants who have not become naturalized citizens and to require authorities to report undocumented aliens applying for such services. As was expected, the new California law was immediately challenged and stopped in the federal courts as being unconstitutional (see the role of the federal courts in Part III). Partly as a reaction to this conservative wave in the states and to new restrictions on access to government services for legal but non-citizen immigrants under a new federal welfare law from 1996 (see p. 262), a record number of 1.1 million aliens across the country became American citizens in 1996 in order to ensure that they would not lose out on services. This was more than twice the number of newly naturalized citizens in one year than the previous record.

CHAPTER 5

Minority Groups

African Americans

HISTORY

Black Americans, nearly all of them descendants of people who were forcibly brought to America to work as chattel slaves, were long the largest but are now the second largest minority group in the United States, with about thirteen percent of the population, just behind Hispanic Americans, with roughly fifteen percent. First, some highlights of black history:

Even during the early decades of the 19th century there was much concern about integrating freed slaves in white American society. There were quite a few emancipated slaves in the Northern states and some people were starting to envision an end to slavery. Under President James Monroe the colony of Liberia was established in West Africa, and in 1817 the first of what was hoped to be a huge number of freed slaves were 'repatriated' there. By mid century only 3,600 African Americans had moved to the colony, however, which then became an independent country. President Abraham Lincoln also had advanced plans for deporting African Americans who would be freed by the Civil War. He too was convinced that blacks and whites could never live together in harmony, so he commissioned his secretary of state to investigate territories in Central and South America for a future black nation. These plans fell through, partly owing to dubious real estate dealings.

Under the protection of the Radical Republicans who dominated Congress after the Civil War, former slaves achieved considerable power in local politics in the South. This was accomplished at the expense of their former owners, who were often barred from politics. During this period of **Reconstruction of the South**, roughly from 1867 to 1877, the Union army occupied the vanquished South in a move to force the Southern states to comply with federal regulations which, among other things, aimed to promote black participation in society and politics. At the same time, this armed presence guaranteed Northern industrial and capital interests a chance to take a large share of reconstructed Southern businesses. It was during this period that white terrorist organizations like the Ku Klux Klan (probably 'ku klux' from Greek *kuklos*, 'circle', plus 'klan' for 'clan') arose.

After about ten years of federal protection, in 1877, African Americans in the South found themselves abandoned by their Republican Party. The Republicans had become the party of Big Business in the north and had reached a compromise allowing former white leaders to resume control of the South, while northern business interests indulged in the period of great industrial expansion now known as the 'Gilded Age' of capitalism. Almost overnight, blacks were ousted from their political positions and effectually disfranchised. Black codes, which were similar to pre-war slave codes, were passed in most Southern states, again legally limiting the rights of blacks. The former slaves and their offspring faced eighty years of *de jure* **segregation**, segregation by law (compare *de facto* segregation p. 85) in the South, a period that would end only with the Civil Rights Movement of the late 1950s and early 1960s.

In the Northern states there had always been a few blacks, but slavery had never taken hold because the economy was fundamentally different from that of the South, based on family farm units and industrial manufacturing. Many freed and runaway slaves lived as laborers and skilled craftsmen in the north, and there were (segregated) black regiments in the Union army during the Civil War. While there was little legal segregation in the North, African Americans were commonly discriminated against and harassed.

There was no mass migration of blacks from the South until World War I, when a combination of the mechanization of agriculture—which rendered much work formerly done by farm laborers unnecessary—and the great need for wartime industrial workers prompted hundreds of thousands of former farm workers to move north to manufacturing cities like Chicago and Detroit. An even greater surge of migration took place during World War II, with 1.6 million blacks leaving the South for northern city jobs. This exodus was reversed in the late 1970s when blacks moving 'back' to the South outnumbered those leaving. This return was the result of a transformation of the Southern economy and gains in civil rights, but, as mentioned above, the advent of air conditioning also played a major role in making life in the South more tolerable.

THE CIVIL RIGHTS MOVEMENT

Although there had always been protests of various sorts against discrimination of blacks, two major breakthroughs paved the way for what was to be called the **Civil Rights Movement**. One was the integration of the armed forces by order of President Harry Truman in 1948. African Americans had fought valiantly in World War II, but always in segregated

Figure 5.1 Rosa Parks sits in the front of a Montgomery bus, on December 21, 1956, as a Supreme Court ruling that banned segregation on the city's public transit vehicles took effect. (Photo: UPI/Bettmann News Photos, Courtesy USIA)

units, a fact that they vehemently protested against. The other breakthrough was the decision of the US Supreme Court in 1954 that 'separate but equal' schools for blacks (especially in the South) were inherently unequal. All American schools were ordered to be integrated, and a process was initiated that is still underway.

The beginning of the Civil Rights Movement is normally traced to December 1, 1955, when a black woman named Rosa Parks was arrested in Montgomery, Alabama, for refusing to give up her seat on a municipal bus to a white man. In reaction to this arrest, the National Association for the Advancement of Colored People (NAACP) organized a boycott of city buses, asking a 27-year-old Baptist pastor named Martin Luther King, Jr. to lead the action. The boycott lasted more than a year, and with the help of a US Supreme Court decision in 1956, it eventually ended segregation on buses all over the South. Blacks no longer had to go to the back of the bus.

Another feature of the Civil Rights Movement was the 'sit-in', a tactic devised by the Student Non-violent Coordinating Committee (SNCC, pronounced 'snick'). After careful training in non-violent reaction to

Figure 5.2 A.D. King (Martin Luther King's brother) participating in a lunch counter sit-in. (Photo: Lee Lockwood, Black Star, Courtesy USIA)

violence (inspired by Mahatma Gandhi in India, who, in turn, was a disciple of Henry David Thoreau, the 19th-century New England naturalist), volunteers would sit down at segregated soda fountains in drugstores and restaurants and refuse to move until they were served. Many of them were severely beaten, but in the end so much national attention was focused on the protests that segregation was ended.

Further methods used by King and others were protest marches and so-called Freedom Buses. Freedom Buses were filled with black and white volunteers from different parts of the country. With much publicity, they drove from one notoriously segregated town to another in the South, and a number of the volunteers were bloodied by local racists, often with the complicity of local and state law enforcement officers.

A major effort in the early 1960s was to get Southern blacks to register to vote. Since local and state authorities found infinite ways to avoid registering blacks, the federal government set up registration centers under the protection of federal marshals. Many white college students from the North joined local blacks and whites in voter-registration campaigns. A number of them were beaten and some were even killed by white supremacists.

There were showdowns between federal and state authorities over school integration. State governors in Alabama, Mississippi, and Arkansas actively opposed integration of their schools and universities, and the first black students had to be ushered to school through hostile white crowds by federal marshals sent by the Eisenhower and Kennedy administrations. The National Guard, normally a state-controlled militia, had to be mobilized under federal orders to maintain the peace in connection with school integration (for the distinction between 'state' and 'federal' see Part III, especially p. 135 ff.).

The Civil Rights Movement reached a climax of public awareness on August 28, 1963, when some quarter million people, blacks and whites, gathered in Washington. This was the occasion of King's famous 'I have a dream' speech. Under President Johnson the Civil Rights Acts of 1964, 1965, and 1968 outlawed discrimination on the basis of race, sex, and religion, echoing and more clearly focusing the principles laid down nearly a century earlier by the 13th, 14th, and 15th Amendments to the Constitution—the so-called 'Civil War Amendments'.

Figure 5.3 Martin Luther King, Jr. being arrested for participating in a sit-in.
(Photo: Charles Moore, Black Star, Courtesy USIA)

After the middle of the 1960s, with legislation in place to guarantee civil
rights under the law, African-American leaders turned their attention
to economic and social gaps between blacks and whites. Some leaders,
even King himself just before his assassination in 1968, were questioning
whether non-violence would always be the best approach to achieving
parity with whites. Massive 'long, hot summer' riots took place in Watts
(Los Angeles) in 1965 and Detroit in 1967, leading to several deaths and the
destruction of millions of dollars' worth of property. The immediate
causes of these riots were black complaints of police brutality at the hands
of predominantly white police forces, but the scope and vehemence of the
rioting must be traced to the pent-up frustrations among disadvantaged
African Americans regarding the slow progress being made toward the
realization of the promises of the Civil Rights Movement.

One militant group was the **Black Muslims** rallied by Malcolm X (born Malcolm Little). They were a black 'nationalist' movement, started by Malcolm X's mentor Elijah Muhammed in Chicago and advocating a separate African nation or nations under Islam. Their ideas of the location of these nations were usually vague, although certain Southern states were mentioned as possible localities. (Decades earlier, in the 1910s and 1920s Marcus Garvey, another black supremacist, had rallied thousands around a similarly vague 'Back to Africa' movement, even organizing a steamship line, but no one really went to Africa as a result.) Just before he was gunned down by Black Muslim rivals in 1965, Malcolm X was moving away from militant separatism. With their rigorous demands of a clean, drug-free life style, the Black Muslims are still today a major force in turning young African Americans away from lives of crime in city slums. The present leader, Louis Farrakhan, has attracted a great deal of public attention for his anti-Semitic rhetoric and militaristic discipline. At the same time he won considerable praise for calling a 'Million Man March' on Washington in the fall of 1995. Although the number of participants fell short of a million, the message of the march was felt by millions: far too many African-American men have been shirking their responsibilities as fathers and husbands and need to re-examine their own ideals and those they have been passing on to their children. Thousands of African-American men were inspired by the march to volunteer as mentors to black children and teenagers. Even Farrakhan's critics praised the initiative, although they were uneasy about some of the overtones of his rhetoric and ideology.

Another nationalist movement of the late 1960s was the **Black Panthers**. They based their analysis of American racism on Marxism-Leninism and created a program of Black Power involving a mixture of community involvement and, as a last resort, armed struggle to achieve a position in society. Their militancy led to a number of shoot-outs with police. The Black Panthers' 'Black is Beautiful' campaigns did much to bolster feelings of pride and self-respect among African Americans, and such feelings remain as a lasting result of their movement. Their attitudes also helped to inspire many whites who were disenchanted with America's war in Vietnam to 'drop out' of mainstream society in the early 1970s.

In the early 1960s it was argued that something more than legal guarantees of equal treatment was needed to redress the wrongs of hundreds of years of subjugation and discrimination. After all, laws prohibiting racial discrimination are of little help to a poorly educated black person seeking a qualified job; a well-educated person, probably white, will get the job. In a number of fields, the idea of **affirmative action** began to take form. This means actively helping culturally disadvantaged minorities and women to obtain positions that they are qualified for, even if they are not necessarily the best-qualified applicant. These efforts are seen as a temporary break with normal application procedures in order to make up for past discrimination which has rendered minority groups or women less qualified. In 1961 President John Kennedy issued an executive order mandating affirmative action programs within the federal government and for many companies that receive federal contracts, and President Richard Nixon later strengthened that order. Most state governments established similar policies. The Equal Employment Opportunities Act of 1972 set up a commission to enforce affirmative action, although the zeal of the commission to act has varied considerably, depending on the attitude of the President.

Critics of affirmative action call it 'reverse discrimination'. The most famous case, from 1978, was that of a white male student named Allan Bakke who was not accepted as a medical student at the University of California, Davis, because the university applied racial quotas in its admissions policy. He argued that a black student had been accepted even though he had lower qualifications than Bakke himself and that this violated Bakke's constitutional rights. The case went to the US Supreme Court, which found for Bakke, stating that he should not have been excluded on the basis of a system of numerical quotas. On the other hand, the court allowed that the university could select students to achieve a racial balance. Later decisions in the 1980s confirmed that institutions and employers may use so-called set-asides to correct *proven past discrimination* when hiring staff or admitting students. In a place like Los Angeles, with numerous minority groups, it has indeed become extremely difficult for a well-qualified, non-minority white male to be appointed, say, to the teaching staff of a college if there are qualified minorities or women available. At the same time, in the late 1980s a slightly more conservative

Supreme Court struck down local regulations giving priority to minorities over people with greater seniority (years of service) when decisions had to be made to cut down a staff of city firefighters, for example. In the mid 1990s the Court required federal and state programs to link affirmative action to specific and proven past discrimination. The Court is ambivalent on affirmative action, but tending toward restrictiveness, weighing one case at a time, but thus far stopping short of outlawing it outright.

In 1996 California voters passed Proposition 209, which banned any racial preferences in admissions to the state's universities among other places. Just as in the case of Proposition 187 (see p. 70), the new law was immediately challenged in the courts by opponents, but the federal Supreme Court ultimately upheld the law. Minorities representation declined at the University of Texas starting in 1996 as a result of similar state legislation forbidding discrimination in admissions. Soon afterward the University of Michigan was targeted for two lawsuits claiming reverse discrimination in its admissions policies, one for its undergraduate program and one for its law school, but the university fought back, winning support from a wide range of educational foundations and leading business corporations for its policy that student diversity in itself provides an educational advantage: a classroom discussion of racism will be more rewarding educationally if those discussing the issue come from different ethnic and racial backgrounds. In the Supreme Court's dual 2003 decisions, the university won the suit in the law-school case and lost the undergraduate one. Its law-school admissions principles were designed to provide "a highly individualized, holistic review of each applicant's file, giving serious consideration to all the ways an applicant might contribute to a diverse educational environment". Regarding undergraduate admissions, the Supreme Court asserted that although diversity is a compelling state interest that can justify the consideration of race as a plus factor in university admissions, the university's automatic distribution of a set number of plus points to students from underrepresented minority groups was not narrowly tailored to achieve that purpose.

In the November 7, 2006, election, however, Michigan voters approved a state referendum (see p. 184 for 'referendum') that makes it illegal to use most forms of affirmative action in college admissions and employment in the state. This means that the ruling from the US Supreme Court in 2003 allowing universities to achieve diversity in the classroom by factoring in applicants' cultural background when admitting students has been rendered powerless in Michigan by a new state law. Michigan now joins California and Texas in not permitting race, for instance, to be a factor in college admissions. Universities in these states are trying to mediate the effects of the new law by more actively recruiting fully qualified students among minorities.

PRESENT STATUS

With affirmative action, the number of blacks and other minorities in public employment rose dramatically. Though African Americans make up roughly 13 percent of the total population, they constitute 19 percent of all state and local employees and 17 percent of federal. In these federal jobs blacks have moved up the pay scale in recent years, but there are still nearly three times as many whites in top executive positions in relation to their respective total numbers of federal (non-postal, executive branch) employees.

In the professions African Americans have made inroads, but still lag far behind. They are severely underrepresented in all professions except counseling, dietetics, social work, and pre-school teaching. Only about 5–6 percent of America's lawyers, doctors, and engineers are black. In contrast, as recently as the mid 1980s African Americans still accounted for 42 percent of all private household cleaners and servants. By the 2000s, however, that proportion had dropped to roughly 20 percent, with Hispanics taking more and more of those jobs (about 40 percent, up from 12 percent in 1983, thus trading places with blacks over twenty years).

Among large corporations, high-tech companies tend to be more progressive than those in heavy industry when it comes to managerial careers for blacks. In the country as a whole blacks are still largely unrepresented among top executives of non-black firms.

Median family income (the *median* average ignores high and low extremes) for African Americans remains low but gained ground in relation to that of whites during the 1990s, rising from a previously stable 56 percent to 63 percent of white family income by 2003, but still the lowest percentage among minority groups. Mean per capita income (the mean average is affected by high and low extremes) for blacks is about

59 percent of mean white income. Median weekly earnings among black individuals working full time have risen slightly to about 80 percent of full-time white wages.

The picture is even bleaker if, instead of income, the accumulated wealth, or net worth, of black households is compared to that of whites. The mean net worth of non-white and Hispanic families is only one quarter that of non-Hispanic whites; in median values it is only one seventh. Even those African-American families whose money income places them solidly in the middle class have a median net worth that is less than half that of their white middle-class peers. Having more recently arrived in the middle class, they have not been able to save and invest their money to the same degree as whites, and they have less to fall back on if times get hard.

The late 1980s saw the rise of a new use of the boycott to attain black-white equality. PUSH (People United to Save Humanity), an organization started in Chicago by former Martin Luther King aide Reverend Jesse Jackson, declared consumer boycotts of companies that the organization felt were reaping huge profits from the business of their black customers without 'reinvesting' sufficient amounts in the black community. Such investments include jobs for African Americans, sponsorship of sports and recreation, and placement of funds with African-American-owned banks. Boycotts successfully 'reformed' the Coca-Cola Corporation, Coors Breweries, and the Burger King hamburger chain. In 1990 PUSH tackled the makers of Nike shoes.

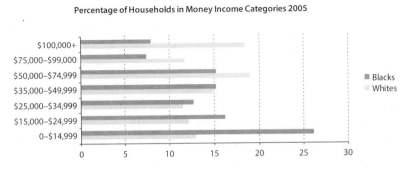

Figure 5.4 Percentage of white and black households in each income category.

They were startled to find that Nike not only did not comply with their demands, which the company claimed were unfair, but rather counterattacked, accusing PUSH of secretly being in the employ of a competing shoe manufacturer. The extreme popularity of Nike products among African Americans made it difficult for young people to honor the boycott, and the question is whether it was PUSH or Nike that came out of the conflict with more bruises. PUSH scored a major success in 1996 with its claims regarding discrimination at the Texaco oil company. Tape recordings of executives discussing black employees were made public, revealing racist attitudes in company management. This led to a major shake-up among executives, large cash payments to African-American employees, and a promise of fair treatment in the future.

Reverend Jesse Jackson, head of the National Rainbow Coalition, based in Chicago, has been the pre-eminent political leader among African Americans over the last three decades, with two relatively successful presidential election campaigns and high-profile international mediation missions. He has long served as a mentor to another African-American figure, Al Sharpton of Harlem, New York, founder of the National Action Network. Sharpton first attracted national attention in the mid 1980s in a bizarre case in which a young black girl accused white New York police officers of abusing her and smearing excrement on her. Sharpton came to her public defense, although she later admitted that the charges were false. In the time since then Al Sharpton has appeared on the scene wherever the civil rights of blacks have been set aside, at one point in 1991 even being accused of inciting people to riot during racial unrest in New York.

A new contender for the role of most prominent African-American leader burst on the scene at the national convention of Democratic Party in July 2004: Barack Obama, whose father is Kenyan, delivered an electrifying speech at the convention and went on to be elected senator from Illinois in the 2004 general election. He then went on to garner the Democratic nomination for the presidency and soundly defeated Republican John McCain to be come the 44th President of the United States. Throughout this entire process, however, he hardly ever accentuated his African roots, instead appealing to Americans in general.

Another extremely prominent African-American leader over the last several years is Oprah Winfrey. Through her daily television show, her book club, her magazine, and her extensive philanthropy, she has had a tremendous impact on Americans, especially women, but by no means only blacks. Her early support for the candidacy of Barack Obama may have been crucial in bringing him to the attention of voters. Both Winfrey and Obama are thus individuals of African-American heritage who are regarded as top leaders among the general public, not as leaders of the African-American community, unlike Jesse Jackson and Al Sharpton. Both, like Jackson, are also based in Chicago.

By the new millennium, although African Americans could point to considerable success in local politics, their political representation in Congress was nowhere near parity with their 13 percent of the population. The 111th Congress started work in January 2009 with only 40 black members (all Democrats) of the House of Representatives (out of 435, i.e. 9 percent) and one black senator: Barack Obama, only the third African-American member ever, was replaced by a black appointee.

In sum, the four decades that have passed since the assassination of Martin Luther King, Jr. have seen two salient developments. On the plus side, the black middle and upper classes have grown to represent a larger share of the African-American population than do blacks under the poverty line, although this progress was considerably eroded during the George W. Bush years. On the minus side, the people left behind by those who made it out of the slums are threatening to become a permanent underclass, with very small prospects of ever breaking out of the cycle of poverty (see p. 265). In 2005, some 25 percent of African-American individuals, and more than 34 percent of black children, were living below the official poverty line. The figure for children in poverty had improved from 46 to 30 percent during the Clinton administration, but rose again steadily under George W. Bush.

De facto segregation (compare *de jure* segregation p. 74), that is, spatial separation—as a matter of fact—resulting from economic differences, has become so firmly cemented in major cities that a University of Chicago sociologist coined the term *hypersegregation*. This term means that millions of blacks and millions of whites respectively can now live their entire lives without coming into substantial direct contact with people of the other race. Even the languages of isolated blacks and mainstream whites are growing farther apart. The University of Chicago itself presents a good vantage point from which to observe this phenomenon: it is an elite private university on a beautifully landscaped campus surrounded by the black slums of Chicago's South Side.

Even among the middle class, segregation is still the rule. There are some neighborhoods in the suburbs of major cities where black and white citizens live side by side, but the familiar pattern of white exodus—more recently an exodus away from metropolitan areas altogether, to small towns and the countryside—is still very much in evidence, despite more than three decades of fair-housing legislation at both state and federal levels. Whenever the proportion of black residents approaches the one-third level, the 'For Sale' signs start appearing on front lawns. Prices plummet, not because blacks are moving in, but because others start moving out. The circular argument has it that property values are going to go down, so it is time to sell while the house is still worth something. Each family (including black ones) that reasons this way accelerates the process by putting another house up for sale, thus lowering the prices of all houses in the area. It is obvious that most white Americans think of 'integration' as meaning having at the most a few black families in the neighborhood. Despite these patterns, blacks have slowly but surely increased their presence in the suburbs. Minorities now make up 27 percent of the suburban population, with the strongest growth among Hispanic Americans.

While many workplaces are integrated and there is much social interaction among blacks and whites at work, few people of either race count members of the other race among their good friends. Interracial marriages are rare, accounting for just over one half of one percent of all marriages at the end of the century, although the phenomenon is clearly on the increase (the man is black, the woman white roughly twice as often as vice versa). All in all, a century and a half after the freeing of the slaves, African Americans and whites are still in many essential ways living as nations apart.

At the outset of the 21st century serious claims began to be put forward for **reparations** to be paid by the US government for the centuries of slavery and oppression suffered by African Americans. These monetary claims were inspired by those recognized and paid by the German government and corporations who exploited various ethnic groups as slave workers during World War II. African Americans are clearly divided about the issue, with many maintaining that reparations would reinforce a sense of victimhood among American blacks and thus drain their own powers of initiative.

Figure 5.5 More African Americans belong to the middle class than live in poverty, but poverty grew under George W. Bush. (Photo: Getty Images)

Hispanic Americans

Americans of African descent, who until the late 1960s were generally called 'colored' or 'Negroes', have objected to being the only ethnic group categorized on the basis of skin color. 'Black' replaced 'Negro' in the 'Black is Beautiful' days of Black Power, and 'Afro-American' was often heard as an alternative. In the late 1980s the fuller geographical expression 'African American' came to be favored by most people (perhaps because 'Afro' had become firmly associated with a hairstyle). Another major minority in the United States is defined not in terms of skin color—they can be of several 'races'—or place of origin, but rather in terms of their mother tongue, Spanish. The term 'Hispanic' relates to people of many different origins who speak Spanish instead of or, usually, in addition to English. The expression 'Latino' is often used for these groups as well. The second fastest growing ethnic group (after Asians), Hispanics are now slightly more numerous than blacks, with about 15 percent of the total US population. Their numbers grew by 50 percent between 1990 and 2000. The new millennium promises to be one of ever rising Latino ascendancy: in its first few of years there were several cases of newscasters, for example, changing their Anglo or German names to Hispanic ones—whether or not they know a word of Spanish—with an eye to furthering their media careers.

CHICANOS

Although they are often lumped together as one group, Hispanics comprise several ethnic groups that are culturally distinct from one another. By far the largest group consists of people of Mexican origin, now usually called Chicanos (from Spanish *mexicano*). They make up about 60 percent of the Hispanic population. In the states of California and Texas, Hispanics constitute more than 36 percent of the total population, and most of them are from Mexico. New Mexico is about 44 percent Hispanic, and Arizona about 30 percent. Outside these four states, which share a border with Mexico, the Midwestern city of Chicago has the largest concentration of Chicanos.

PUERTO RICANS

The second largest Hispanic group consists of Puerto Ricans, people from the eastern Caribbean island that became a US territorial possession as a result of the short Spanish-American War of 1898. It became the Commonwealth of Puerto Rico in 1952, still a possession of the US, but not a state[1]. Puerto Ricans represent about 10 percent of Spanish-speaking Americans and are concentrated in the cities of the northeast, especially New York.

CUBAN AMERICANS

The third largest group of Hispanics is predominantly found in Florida, Cubans. Of roughly 2 million inhabitants of Dade County, which includes Miami, about 43 percent are Hispanics and only 39 percent 'Anglos', that is, English-speaking whites. The city of Miami itself is 63 percent Hispanic, 27 percent black, and less than 10 percent non-Hispanic white. Of the Hispanic plurality in Dade County, nearly 70 percent are of Cuban descent. In 1985 Xavier Suarez became the first Cuban American to be elected mayor of a major American city, Miami.

CENTRAL AND SOUTH AMERICANS

Nearly 5 percent of the Hispanic population consists of Central American and 4 percent South American immigrants and refugees. Until 2001 Nicaraguans made up the second largest Hispanic group in Miami, with the counter-revolutionary Contras organizing their resistance from there during the Sandinista period in Nicaragua. However, *Newsweek* reported in August 2001 that Colombians had surpassed Nicaraguans in number, partly as a result of the tremendous wave of cocaine entering the US via Miami starting in 1986 but more recently owing to a huge influx of well-educated entrepreneurs fleeing lawlessness in their home country. Refugees from El Salvador became a noticeable constituent of the

---

1   Puerto Rico sends non-voting observers to Congress in Washington, and its residents are allowed to migrate freely to the US.

Hispanic population of the southwest in the 1980s as a result of the civil war in their country. Not all of those seeking asylum were granted refugee status, and a controversial 'Sanctuary Movement' involving churches and other volunteer groups provided thousands of El Salvadorans with illegal shelter.

PRESENT STATUS

With the possible exception of Cuban Americans, Latinos have long been notoriously underrepresented politically. About two thirds of them tend to vote Democratic, although Cubans are usually staunch Republicans. As a group they have traditionally not been active in politics, often turning, rather, to the Catholic Church for shelter and a sense of community. As their numbers grow, however, the two major parties have been courting the Latino population, and traditional patterns of political passiveness were likely to be broken in the new millennium. Some Hispanics know little or no English, and their political participation is frequently limited for language reasons, although federal laws guarantee that ballots are printed in Spanish in heavily concentrated Hispanic areas. Their voter registration rates are generally 30–35 percent, and on average only about 20–25 percent of people of voting age actually vote, although the 2008 Barack Obama campaign activated record levels of Latino voters and swelled registrations. The low level of political participation is even more striking in relation to the size of the total Latino population, because high birth rates have led to an age pyramid with a broad base of politically ineligible children and adolescents, similar to that of many Third-World countries.

The great rise in the number of Spanish-speaking (and Asian) immigrants prompted the creation in 1983 of an organization called **US English** (USE), under the guidance of the conservative former senator from California S. I. Hiyakawa. Its ultimate goal is to amend the US Constitution to make English the official language of the nation, based on the fear that the Spanish (and Asian) threat to English could lead to political volatility similar to that evidenced in Quebec and Belgium, for example. Although not the first such movement in American history, it has been the most successful, at least initially attracting supporters from a broad political spectrum, including many prominent liberals. The organization supported legislation across the country making English the official language of nearly half of the American states by the end of the 1980s, and it has tried to steer bilingual education away from 'preservative' into 'transitional' programs, that is, foreign-language instruction which is designed to facilitate the learning of English, not to preserve the linguistic culture of immigrants. The latter types of programs are seen as being too costly.

Critics of USE (and other **English Only** or **English First** organizations) maintain that there is no serious threat to English as the language of the United States and that the movement is really an expression of mainstream America's unfounded fear of being overrun economically and socially by large numbers of culturally different new immigrants. The overwhelming majority of Latinos are eager to learn English, just as immigrants have always been in the past. Laws restricting the use of Spanish (and Asian languages) are seen as a provocation that has created much suspicion and ill will between ethnic groups. The largest organization specifically working against English Only is called **English Plus**; it argues for the view that other languages should be seen as a resource, not a problem.

Thus far the state laws making English the official language have had little practical effect since federal laws guarantee access to health-care, safety, and legal information in relevant foreign languages. Many attempts to amend the US Constitution to make English the official language of the country have failed over the last few years. However, popular support for such an amendment is very strong, according to polls, and might soon provide the thrust for Congress to place a proposed amendment before the states for ratification. Major general opponents of such a move are the National Council of Teachers of English, Teachers of English to Speakers of Other Languages, the National Education Association, and the Linguistic Society of America.

Economically, Hispanics as a group lag behind the national average. Median household money income in 2006 was 76 percent of non-Hispanic white income, which is nonetheless far better than for blacks (64 percent) that year. In 2005 some 22 percent of Hispanic individuals were living below the level of poverty. Mexican Americans and Puerto-Rican

Americans are generally poorer than the Latino average, while Cubans are richer: 'Little Havana' in Miami is a relatively prosperous area of Cuban entrepreneurship.

Latinos complete fewer years of formal education than average Americans, including African Americans. Fully 43 percent of all Hispanics over the age of 25, and 50 percent of Mexican Americans, have not finished high school (the corresponding figure for white Americans is 15 percent, and 21 percent for blacks). While roughly 27 percent of white Americans and 17 percent of African Americans have completed four years of college, only 11 percent of Hispanics, and 8 percent of Chicanos, have done so.

In 1986 a major piece of legislation was passed in an attempt to regulate the flow of illegal immigrants from Mexico and Central and South America. It was estimated in the early 1980s that there were some 8 million illegal immigrants in the country, mostly in the Southwest, close to the Mexican border, but also in major cities and working as migrant agricultural workers elsewhere. The controversial **Immigration Reform Act of 1986** was seen as representing a new departure in dealing with illegal immigration.

The 1986 act drew an arbitrary retroactive line at January 1, 1982. Aliens who could prove that they had been in the United States since before that date were given a residence permit if they applied for one before midnight of May 4, 1988. After that date any employer who was found guilty of hiring undocumented workers would be fined up to $2,000 per worker and $10,000 per worker for a third offense. Those granted amnesty by 1988 would eventually become eligible for US citizenship if they could pass English-language and civics tests. Owing to lack of information and incomplete understanding of the terms of the law and owing to fear of deportation because their continuous US residency would be difficult to prove, millions of Hispanics (and Asians as well as other groups) preferred to remain underground, and fewer than two million formerly illegal aliens applied for this special amnesty.

While it is now much easier for the government to monitor employers who hire aliens, Hispanics claim that in many parts of the country employers have become reluctant to sign on even American citizens of Mexican origin for fear that their documents have been forged (as indeed

Figure 5.6 Cuban Fruit Stand in 'Little Havana', Miami, Florida. (Photo: Courtesy USIA)

many have). At the same time, Mexicans and other Latinos desperate for employment continue to cross the long Mexican-American border in huge numbers. Faced again with up to 12 million new illegal Mexican immigrants, President George W. Bush proposed a controversial system whereby undocumented immigrant workers would be recognized as special work immigrants and be allowed to stay in the US, but only as long as their employer certifies they are needed. This Bush plan was severely criticized, and immigration was a major issue in the public debate before it was knocked off the agenda in the 2008 presidential election by the weak state of the economy. It remains an issue that the Obama administration will have to address, with public opinion about another round of amnesty highly divided.

As mentioned above, the United States/Mexican border is considered by many to be only a parenthesis of history. This view is supported by the formation of NAFTA (the North American Free Trade Association) in

1994, in stages turning Mexico, the United States, and Canada (and Central and South America may eventually be included) into more and more of a single market, partly in response to the growth and consolidation of the European Union. Also, every resurgence of separatism in Quebec prompts some (western) Canadian provinces to at least talk about becoming American states as an alternative to remaining in a future splintered Canada.

Asian Americans

Despite harsh and disrespectful treatment in the past (see p. 73 and p. 173) and some present discrimination, Asian Americans as a group represent a success story. The substantial numbers of Chinese Americans and Japanese Americans whose ancestors immigrated in the latter half of the 19th century have been augmented by new waves of immigrants and refugees from China after 1949, Korea after the Korean War in the early 1950s and again in the 1980s, and Vietnamese, Cambodians, and Laotians after the end of the Indochina War in 1975. While Asians live all over the United States, usually interspersed without racial problems in white communities, they are especially concentrated in the Pacific coast states and in special neighborhoods of major cities there and elsewhere, such as New York City. Los Angeles is believed to have the largest concentration of Filipinos, Vietnamese, Burmese, and Koreans outside their respective countries of origin, and San Francisco's Chinatown is the largest community of Chinese outside China and Taiwan.

Ethnic and historical differences among various Asian peoples are of course great. Chinese, Japanese, and Korean Americans are generally much more affluent than Filipino, Vietnamese, and Laotian Americans, for example. However, and again for cultural reasons, Asian immigrants are generally very ambitious and eager to succeed, with a deeply rooted work ethic to help them along.

This commitment to self-betterment and hard work sometimes leads to strife with mainstream American neighbors. In the 1980s large numbers of Vietnamese moved to Biloxi, Mississippi, on the coast of the Gulf of Mexico. The climate of the area was similar to that of their homeland, and by the mid 1980s they had bought and were manning more than half of the larger fishing vessels working in the Gulf. The success story for new Asian immigrants was marred, however, by numerous demonstrative acts of sabotage—including the burning of boats—on the part of the local fishermen who were being undersold and put out of business by the frugal Vietnamese family enterprises.

Asian Americans are famous 'over-achievers' when it comes to education. They are just above the national average (84 percent) for the percentage of people over twenty-five who have graduated from high school (about 87 percent), but when it comes to higher education, as many as 47 percent of Asian adults have completed four years of college. Among (Asian) Indians, college graduates constitute well over half of all adults over twenty-five. For the population in general, the figure is about 27 percent.

High rates of achievement in education even lead to problems for some Asians. Especially in California they dominate college campuses to the point where there is talk of limiting their numbers by quotas. Also, for average and below-average achievers among the Asian community it is a psychological burden to be constantly reminded of how well their fellows usually do in school.

Asians are exceptionally prominent in the professions, especially as physicians and engineers. On the other hand, they are underrepresented in business, with 1–2 percent of officials and managers. In 1990 Asian individuals started surpassing whites in regard to median income, an

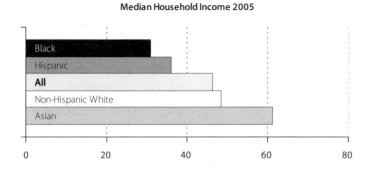

Figure 5.7 Median Household Income by Race and Hispanic Origin 2005.

impressive advance considering the fact that in 1960 they earned only 75 percent as much as whites. Median family income was 20 percent higher than the national median by the turn of the century and 30 percent higher by 2005. At the same time there is still considerable discrimination when it comes to top jobs in corporations—a so-called 'glass ceiling' is still in place. Asian women still work outside the home considerably less than average.

Owing to burgeoning immigration in recent years, Asian Americans have surpassed the Hispanics as the fastest growing minority, although they made up only 4 percent of the population in 2006. With the ascendancy of the Pacific Basin in world trade, Asian Americans can look forward to an ever stronger position in American society. In 1984, the year Los Angeles hosted the Olympic Games, US trade across the Pacific exceeded trade across the Atlantic for the first time in history. Just a few years later the rising influence of Asia was reflected in a major dispute, especially on the west coast, about the wisdom of basing American higher education so exclusively on the country's European (Judeo-Christian) heritage. Gary Locke, the son of Chinese immigrants, was elected mayor of Seattle in 1996, making him the first Asian-American mayor of a major city. In the 21st century Asian Americans will be instrumental in opening America's perspectives toward Asia (which, of course, is to the west, not the 'East'), just as Hispanics will play a key role in opening channels to the south.

Jewish Americans

Jews make up about 2.2 percent of the American population (2004). They come from many different European countries, and there are striking cultural differences among the various communities, some of which are highly integrated with American society while others are extremely conservative and stick to themselves. New York State has by far the highest concentration of Jewish inhabitants, about 8.4 percent in 2004.

The great wave of Jews from Eastern Europe in the first decades of the century led to anti-Semitism in many parts of the country. The revived Ku Klux Klan in the 1920s broadened its repertoire of hate to include, apart from blacks, Jews and Catholics, and expanded its field of action to include northern and western states. The Klan attained considerable political influence in some states during this period, even electing governors in Oklahoma and Oregon and totally dominating the political scene in Indiana. While the US cannot be compared to Eastern European countries, anti-Jewish feeling is still prevalent in many places. Residential segregation, where it occurs today between Jews and Gentiles[2], is not so much the result of economic disparities as a voluntary seeking out of kindred neighbors.

The mass migration of the 1910s and 1920s was followed by fairly large numbers of refugees from Nazi Germany in the 1930s and 1940s. These included many prominent artists, musicians, scholars, and scientists who found a haven at leading American universities. The international focal point of advanced science consequently shifted from Germany to the United States. In the arts, Los Angeles, in particular, attracted some of the world's greatest musicians during this period and into the 1950s, and Hollywood attracted leading directors, photographers, cinematographers, and actors.

Like Asian Americans, Jewish Americans are well known for their high levels of educational achievement, and Jewish names are common on the faculties of American colleges. There are also many prominent Jews in business, the professions, the mass media, and the publishing industry. Of course, not all Jewish Americans are wealthy or successful professionals, but their median income is well above the national average. Again, as was the case for Asian Americans above, the success of the minority group as a whole can be a burden for individuals in the group who are average or below-average achievers.

Jewish Americans are quite active in politics, although very few Jews have been elected to the Senate and there has been only one serious Jewish contender for the presidency, Barry Goldwater, the Republican candidate in 1964, and one for the Vice-Presidency, Joseph Lieberman, the Democratic contender in 2000. Jews tend to vote Democratic and hold relatively liberal views. The Jewish lobby in Washington has been

2   This is what Jewish people call non-Jews. It is also what Mormons call non-Mormons, including Jews.

extremely effective in guaranteeing US support for Israel, despite the relatively small size of the Jewish population in America. Although far from all American Jews are Zionists, those who are have played a key role in establishing and maintaining the Jewish State.

Arab Americans

Other Semitic peoples, from many different Arab countries, make up a minority about half the size of the Jewish population, roughly 3 million people. Nevertheless, by the 1990s they had managed to put together a considerable Washington lobby to counterbalance those supporting Israel in the Middle East. While there are small communities of Arabs in many American cities, the largest concentration is in the industrial suburbs of Detroit. There, as well as in some other metropolitan areas, Moslem mosques are also a characteristic feature of certain neighborhoods, and Arab-language newspapers and magazines are published. On the other hand, many Americans of Arab descent have been fully integrated in mainstream society for generations. Indeed, very many American Arabs come from Christian (often Lebanese) backgrounds and continue to attend Christian churches in the US.

American Indians

There is no adequate collective term for America's indigenous peoples. The standard name, Indian, is the result of one of the great mistakes of history, namely, Christopher Columbus' belief that he had landed in India by sailing westward from Europe. The word 'aboriginal' is accurate, but it is too closely associated with Australia for use elsewhere. In the late 1960s the expression 'Native American' was introduced, based on the distinction between colonizers and natives. The problem is that such a distinction can hold true for one generation only, since 'native' means 'born' and most modern-day Americans were born in America. Before the arrival of the European settlers, American Indians usually called themselves simply 'people' in their own languages. We are left with the misnomer 'American Indian' (as opposed to 'Asian Indian'), which everyone recognizes. This term is sometimes contracted to 'Amerindian'.

HISTORY

Like African Americans, American Indians have a unique relationship to the United States, and in order to understand their present-day position as a minority, it is essential to review the history of these relations. It is often assumed that blacks and Indians, as minorities of color, have the same goal—that of ultimately being integrated into mainstream society. But even a brief glance at Indian history will make it clear that integration is not the aim of most of the indigenous peoples in the US.

The North American continent was originally, that is, for tens of thousands of years, populated by the ancestors of today's Indians. Their numbers are estimated to have been between one and two million, most of them in the wooded eastern sections of the continent. Today the same continent is rather heavily populated by other peoples from all over the world. Thus it stands to reason that the basic pattern of Indian-white relations has always been that of the whites, with their more aggressive European cultures, acquiring Indian lands. The pattern has been repeated over and over again for nearly five centuries in the Americas, varied only when it comes to the means used by Europeans, later white Americans, to assume control of Indian territory.

In many cases, taking Indian land was like taking candy from a baby. Indians had no conception of what 'private' ownership meant and were often willing to 'sell' or 'give' land to European settlers, thinking that this merely meant allowing them to pass through or temporarily share the use of the land. When conflicts arose over what ownership really entailed, they were often ultimately settled by armed violence.

A good example of European shrewdness is offered by the story of how William Penn (Junior) acquired huge tracts of land in his father's Pennsylvania colony in the mid 1700s by arranging to acquire from a local nation as much land as a man could traverse in three days. Instead of pacing off or walking the distance, however, Penn had a series of runners in place to speed day and night across the land. The Indians reportedly complained afterwards that the men 'did not walk, did not sleep, did not hunt squirrels' on the way.

Almost without exception, this pattern of land acquisition included a fervent promise from the whites that the deal presently at hand would be the last one; in treaty after treaty, Indians were solemnly granted all remaining lands for their own use, without interference or harassment by white settlers. A long series of lines of demarcation were drawn across maps, starting with tiny areas for whites in New England and Virginia and expanding to President Thomas Jefferson's promise of a 'permanent Indian frontier' consisting of the entire US section of the 95th meridian in the huge Louisiana Territory that he purchased from Napoleon in 1803. All of these lines were almost immediately violated by the westward push of white settlers. Just a couple of decades after Jefferson's pledge, his enormous 'Indian Territory' had been shrunk to comprise roughly what became the state of Oklahoma after the turn of the 20th century.

The focal point of the Indian population was thus inexorably moved westward from the eastern seaboard. It became evident that the various nations would either have to learn the white man's ways or be annihilated. Ostensibly for the protection of the Indians, but obviously for less altruistic reasons as well, Congress passed the Indian Removal Act in 1830. The federal government spent several years rounding up Indians in the southeast, ironically including the five so-called 'Civilized Tribes': the Cherokee, Choctaw, Chickasaw, Cree, and Seminole nations had already taken to farming and had attempted peaceful coexistence with their white neighbors. After gold was discovered in the hills they inhabited, white harassment prompted them to appeal to the US Supreme Court for protection, and they received the Court's support. But President Andrew Jackson, a former army general and famous 'Indian killer', ignored the court decision and sent federal troops to escort the nations to Indian Territory, west of the Mississippi, hundreds of miles away. The Seminoles fled to Florida, but the other four nations were marched by force to new and completely different lands in an ordeal that was called 'the Great Trail of Tears'. Thousands of them died along the way as a result of the incredible hardships of the journey, largely because unscrupulous contractors who were paid by the government to supply them with provisions did not live up to their part of the agreement.

What we tend to think of as the period of 'cowboys and Indians'—an ethos largely created by Hollywood movies—was that of the Indian wars from 1860 to 1890. By the time of the Civil War, the only nations who still stood in the way of the so-called Manifest Destiny of the Euro-Americans to settle the entire continent were those who either inhabited or had been pushed into the prairies, the Great Plains, and the Southwest. With the discovery of gold in California in 1848 and the gold rush starting in 1849, thousands of people made their way across the continent via Indian lands. Most wagon trains were allowed to pass through peaceably, but when the continental railroads were completed, starting in 1869, extensive settlement along railway lines started seriously eroding Indian resources, especially the buffalo that were the prime source of livelihood for the Plains Indians.

Many nations fought uneven battles with the growing number of settlers and the US army that was mustered to protect the settlers. The Sioux, who had earlier been forced onto the Dakota plains from the Midwestern prairies and forests, took up arms to protect their holy Black Hills from settlers prospecting for gold. The Cheyenne fought similar battles just to the south, and in the Southwest the Apache and Comanche nations achieved notoriety as guerrilla warriors who refused to let themselves be rounded up by the US Cavalry. Farther to the northwest, the Nez Percé nation of Chief Joseph was involved in long wars with whites.

There were stunning Indian victories such as 'Custer's Last Stand' at the Little Big Horn River in Wyoming in 1876, where a whole company of cavalrymen who were planning to attack Sitting Bull's Sioux were themselves killed in a surprise attack at dawn. The victorious Sioux then escaped into Canada, but without the buffalo and other natural resources to support them, the Indians were doomed to famine and aimless wandering to avoid being removed to special reservations. By 1890 the last of the Indian nations, the remnants of Sitting Bull's once proud people, had turned themselves over to federal soldiers.

In December that year a final massacre of Sioux took place at Wounded Knee on the Pine Ridge Reservation in South Dakota. The nation had just lost their leader, Sitting Bull, who had been killed by Indian police for allegedly resisting arrest. They had let themselves be disarmed and were being marched by the army through the bitterly cold winter to their reservation. During the previous year they had been inspired by a nation-wide religious movement among Indians involving a Ghost Dance which it was believed would bring back the buffalo and their life on the plains. When they started to dance this Ghost Dance early one morning, the soldiers surrounding them in the camp, who ironically belonged to the same company of cavalry that General Custer had led fourteen years earlier, grew more and more nervous, and when someone (it is unclear who) fired a shot, they opened fire with their automatic Gatling guns from opposite sides of the gathered nation, killing over three hundred men, women, and children. The Indian Wars of 1860–90 are chronicled—'from the west looking east'—in a powerful 1970 book by Dee Brown titled *Bury My Heart at Wounded Knee*.

The massacre at Wounded Knee marked the beginning of a new phase of Indian-white relations. Government policy was executed by the **Bureau of Indian Affairs**, originally created as a part of the War Department in 1824, but transferred to the Department of the Interior in 1849. As early as 1871 Congress had decided not to sign any further treaties with Indian nations, but rather to regulate their activities by ordinary laws. In other words, the government abandoned the view of Indians as separate nations to be negotiated with in favor of a view of Indians as individuals.

Government policy was thus to assimilate the conquered Indians into American society by teaching them to live as farmers. Each family was given a 160-acre plot of reservation land (usually of inferior quality) under the General Allotment Act of 1887. It soon became apparent to some Indians, however, that this allotment policy would ultimately lead to the end of their reservations, and it was seen as yet another means to deprive Indians of their land. Since many Indians still had no thorough understanding of what was meant by private property, they were easily enticed by white businessmen into selling their land for a lump sum of money. By 1934, when the policy was abandoned and individuals were required to get the approval of the BIA and the tribal leadership before selling any land, more than half of reservation land was owned by whites. Indian land now represents about 2.5 percent of the territory of the US.

THE LEGAL BATTLE

Much of the struggle for Indian rights in the 20th century has been against what Indians call **termination**. This word refers to various attempts to terminate the special status of Indians as conquered peoples, to treat them merely as any other Americans without regard for their unique history. Just as affirmative action (p. 80 'Critics of affirmative action') can be seen as reverse discrimination, Indian claims for special status are often opposed by the surrounding community on the grounds that they violate the basic principle of the Constitution, namely, that 'all men are created equal'. Indeed, anti-Indian groups often assume positive-sounding names like 'Committee for Equal Rights and Responsibilities' in their attempts to have special treaties abrogated by the courts.

The prime battleground for Indian rights for the last few decades has been the courtroom. In the Northwest local nations were long ago guaranteed unlimited fishing rights in the rivers flowing through their lands. In the 1970s organizations representing the tourist industry, especially sports fishermen, claimed that the Indians were taking too many fish from the rivers, leaving too few for people fishing downstream. Some extremists even went so far as to ambush Indian fishermen with rifle fire when they went to empty their nets. The Indians turned to the federal district court and won its protection, despite inflamed local sentiment against the Indians.

In the Southwest, where water is chronically in short supply, Indians have seen the lakes on their reservations, which are often holy places in their religion, slowly shrink owing to drainage of the water table for irrigation of surrounding agricultural land. Valuable uranium and coal deposits on Indian reservations have earlier been exploited by outside corporations with only minimal compensation paid to the nations. Indian workers have also been employed for decades to extract uranium from the mines with a minimum of safety precautions, a fact which nations cite as a cause of cancer among Indians. In recent years, however, Indians have become far more sophisticated in business, often hiring top law firms to bargain for them.

In 1972 the first of a number of lawsuits was brought against the federal government to reclaim lands guaranteed to Indians by early treaties. In the New England state of Maine the Penobscot and Passamaquoddy nations demanded the return of nearly sixty percent of the area of the state, plus $25 billion in damages for past wrongs. In the end the nations accepted a much smaller cash settlement. In South Dakota the Sioux went to court to regain control of the Black Hills (including Mount Rushmore, with the sculpted faces of American presidents). They were granted a sizable sum of money instead, but continue to press for the return of their sacred mountains.

PRESENT STATUS

There are approximately 4 million American Indians[3] (including Eskimos and Aleuts) today, a figure which roughly corresponds to their estimated number when the first European settlers arrived. In 1890, at the end of the Indian wars, there were as few as 300,000 Indians left. American Indians have been full citizens of the United States since 1924. Roughly half of them live on reservations, the largest of which are found in the western parts of the country, and half in urban areas both in the east and the west. Most urban Indians have strong tribal affiliations and maintain regular contact with a reservation.

American Indians are caught in a bind between two worlds: they want many of the benefits created by modern industrialism, but at the same time they wish to retain their tribal values and traditions. Similarly, throughout the 20th century they have had a love-hate relationship with the federal government and its Bureau of Indian Affairs. On the one hand nations have enjoyed the protection of the BIA when threatened by hostile local communities and national politicians; on the other hand, the BIA has been accused of being paternalistic, 'looking after' Indians to the point where they have become helpless and lacking in initiative. This ambivalence toward modern society and its rights and responsibilities has often paralyzed nations and in many ways devastated their traditional culture.

Alcohol has been a major problem among Indians ever since European settlers introduced them to it. Although they had long used various drugs in religious rites, Indians were exceptionally vulnerable to alcoholism, and it still plagues them much more than it does the rest of society. On some reservations, up to three quarters of the residents are alcohol abusers, including many teenagers.

---

3   It is difficult to define 'Indian' since there is considerable intermarriage with whites. Many people of partly Indian descent sometimes hide and sometimes boast of their heritage, depending on the circumstances.

A system of boarding schools for many western Indians has aggravated the problem of cultural identity for young Indians. Because they are spread out over such wide areas, Indian children are often placed in boarding schools for weeks and months at a time. At many of these schools (and in city schools as well) they pick up sometimes subtle and sometimes not-so-subtle signals from white teachers and other pupils that the culture they have left behind them on the reservation is inferior to mainstream American society. When they return home, it is easy for them to feel like outsiders, and this alienation can easily lead to drug and alcohol abuse. The suicide rate among Indian teenagers is three times the national average. Among Indians over 25 years of age, only about two thirds percent have graduated from high school, well below the national average of 85 percent. Only 10 percent hold bachelor's degrees or higher, compared with 29 percent for the general adult population.

Living standards vary considerably from one reservation to another. The largest one is the Navajo reservation, which straddles the borders of three states in the southwest. It is also the poorest, with many dwellings that lack electricity and running water. Unemployment can be as high as 80 percent among the Navajo, which is twice the already high national average for Indians, about 40 percent. At the nearby Mescalero Apache reservation, the nation itself runs logging, cattle ranching, and tourist businesses at a profit, and housing is predominantly modern.

Productive investment of the $81 million awarded to them in their lawsuit against the federal government brought down unemployment among Maine's Penobscot and Passamaquoddy nations from 60 percent to under 10 percent by the late 1980s. The nations are now the largest private investors in the state and own tracts of land outside their reservation. They run profitable industries that produce frozen foods and wooden houses.

There are many other examples of nations that have exploited local resources to bring wealth to their reservations, but their pride over such material progress is nearly always moderated by nagging questions as to whether they are betraying their spiritual heritage by so actively participating in the capitalist market place. A case in point is the new and lucrative phenomenon starting in the 1980s and mushrooming in the 21st century: tribal ownership of gambling casinos in many parts of the country. The special status of Indians as conquered nations has been interpreted as entailing immunity to state laws forbidding the establishment of gambling facilities, and casinos have been a major source of tribal employment and income for a couple decades now.

Present Racial and Ethnic Strains

Most minorities naturally focus their struggle for economic security and social acceptance against the dominant groups in society. But as the sometimes diametrically opposed goals of African Americans and American Indians have made apparent, minority groups cannot be lumped together into a homogeneous mass. There is in fact substantial strife between certain minority groups.

Blacks and Jews have a long history of mutual animosity, especially in New York City. African Americans have generally felt that Jewish store-owners have taken advantage of them as customers and that Jewish employers have been slow to hire black help. Similar claims have been made by African Americans about Korean merchants in some urban neighborhoods.

The most worrisome expression of ethnic tension is found in the ongoing warfare between youth gangs in the largest metropolises. South Central Los Angeles is the most notorious neighborhood in regard to this violence. Two rival gangs—predominantly African-American—the Crips and the Bloods, started there and have branches with tens of thousands of members in many cities throughout the country. These criminal gangs not only attack and murder each other but also various Hispanic gangs.

In prisons across the country racial and ethnic tensions also run high, and white, black, and Hispanic inmates generally stick to members of their own racial or ethnic group for protection from brutal race-based attacks. Plans to integrate cells throughout the huge California state prison system starting in 2008 were met with considerable concern that there would be widespread violence.

During the 2008 election campaign it was not uncommon, especially in the South, to hear white Americans say that they could not bring themselves to vote for a black person for President. The fact that Barack Obama won the election by a landslide indicates that such thinking is limited in scope, but it is nonetheless still prevalent, nearly a century and a half after the emancipation of the slaves during the Civil War.

While tremendous progress has been made in race relations over the past few decades, it is clear that much remains to be done before the American goal of equal opportunity for everyone is realized. There are disturbing signs that some minority groups, especially sections of the African-American population, have lost ground in the first decade of the 21st century, ground gained in the last decade of the 20th century.

Same-sex Couples

Homosexual individuals in the US, as elsewhere in the world, have long been persecuted for their sexual orientation, and it has only been in recent years that their status and treatment by the surrounding community has begun to change. Discrimination based on sexual orientation has been banned in work and educational contexts for the last couple of decades under federal and state laws. In some American states, homosexual couples are allowed to enter into recognized partnerships and, in a couple of states, to get married, on a par with heterosexual couples. Social acceptance of same-sex couples is growing at an accelerating rate, though this has not taken place without struggle.

State laws forbidding what was called 'sodomy' were long universal in the US. Many states removed such laws from their books starting around 1970, and many others had stopped enforcing their own anti-sodomy laws much earlier than that. But more than a dozen states, mostly in the South, still had such statutes in 2003 when a US Supreme Court decision declared it a violation of the rights of an individual for a state to forbid sodomy.

Resistance to police action against gays first made the headlines in Greenwich Village, New York City, when a police raid of a gay bar called Stonewall led to violent rioting in 1969. The name of the bar became a battle cry for the gay rights movement. Another key event took place on the West Coast. In the 1970s the well-known liberal attitudes of the city of San Francisco began attracting gay people. A former New Yorker, Harvey Milk, was elected to the city Board of Supervisors, the first openly gay man to win a public election. In 1978 he and the city's mayor, George Moscone, were shot and killed in City Hall by a recent member of the

Board of Supervisors, Dan White. The relatively light sentence that White received when convicted of manslaughter (this was a result of the infamous 'Twinkie defense' that claimed White was temporarily insane because he had eaten too much junk food, including Twinkie cupcakes) led to what was called the White Night Riot in the spring of 1979. Later that year, in October, the first national gay rights march took place in Washington, DC, gathering roughly 100,000 supporters. In the 1980s, when HIV/AIDS began to ravage the gay community, the AIDS Coalition to Unleash Power, ACT UP, was formed, initiating the political struggle for homosexual rights.

In the late 1990s some states began instituting laws to allow same-sex couples to enjoy the same legal rights as heterosexual couples, though most stopped short of allowing them to marry. The Defense of Marriage Act of 1996 prohibited the federal government from recognizing same-sex marriages, leaving it to the states to decide such matters. Massachusetts was one of the some ten states allowing civil unions or domestic partnerships when a Massachusetts Supreme Court decision in 2004 declared that it was not sufficient merely to allow civil unions, only full marriage equality was constitutional. Massachusetts thus became the first state to recognize same-sex marriage. Neighboring Connecticut followed suit in the autumn of 2008 and Iowa and Vermont in spring 2009.

There has also been a considerable backlash to such challenges to the traditional concept of marriage. Michigan, Virginia, and Ohio all passed laws expressly forbidding same-sex domestic partners to receive state benefits intended for heterosexual spouses. Soon after the California Supreme Court ruled that same-sex couples could marry in that state in 2007, a popular proposal was put before voters in the 2008 elections to expressly outlaw gay marriage, and this referendum and similar ones in Florida and Arizona were passed. Thousands of legally married California couples suddenly found themselves in a legal state of limbo. However, the mounting pressure to accept same-sex couples on equal terms will no doubt ultimately lead to a reversal of the situation, probably starting in California, where the state Supreme Court will decide in the spring of 2009 whether the proposal accords with the California constitution.

One early indication of the national reaction to the passing of the anti-gay-marriage proposals in California, Florida, and Arizona was a federal district court ruling in Florida in late November 2008—just three weeks after the election—that declared that there is no constitutional or social scientific basis for the state of Florida to deny an unmarried gay couple the right to adopt a child that they had already been raising for years. The state of Florida will appeal this decision in a federal appellate court, and the legal process will probably be repeated in many states and end with a series of decisions in the nation's highest court. With the political sea change in Washington and across the country started by the election of Barack Obama and a Democratic majority in Congress, there may even be movement toward a federal law—perhaps even an amendment to the US Constitution—or, simply, rulings from a future US Supreme Court to guarantee marriage rights to homosexuals in coming years.

Before leaving this survey of groups of Americans, we should pause to look at, not another minority, but a majority, namely, women. Even though they represent slightly more than half of the total population, in many respects women can be seen as an underprivileged group.

CHAPTER 6

Women

A major socioeconomic shift took place between the late 1950s and the late 1970s, not only in the United States, but in most other industrialized countries as well. Families that could live comfortably on one full-time income up to the 1950s needed two incomes, or at least one and a half, by the 1970s to maintain the same relative standard (albeit at a higher absolute level). In other words, women entered the job market in huge numbers for the first time during this period. By the end of the century, three fifths[1] of all women over the age of sixteen worked outside the home, up from one third in 1960. The corresponding figure for men is three quarters. (In Sweden, by way of comparison, participation rates are 79 percent for women and 84 percent for men.)

Of all married mothers of children under eighteen years of age who are living with their husbands, as many as 70 percent now have gainful employment. The percentage of working married mothers with children under the age of six rose from about 30 percent in 1970 to about 60 percent in 2005, but this figure was down by three percentage points from 1999. These figures will nevertheless continue to rise, meaning that day care for infants and young children will continue to be an issue.

---

1   International comparisons can be difficult. OECD figures for 2003 differ from those provided by the US Census and Statistics Sweden and cited here: using the measure 'female labor force of all ages divided by female population 15–64', the OECD finds the Nordic countries, Switzerland, Luxembourg, Canada, and the US are the only nations where women's participation rates exceed 70 percent, with the US at 70.3 percent (down one percentage point since 1998), Switzerland at 78 percent, Luxembourg at 82.7.

Not surprisingly, the last couple of decades have seen a tremendous increase in the number of day-care centers. Most of these centers are run either by churches or by private companies, often in collaboration with corporate employers who find that they need to provide day-care facilities— often conveniently located on or near company premises—in order to attract qualified personnel to their firm. Before and after school care for young schoolchildren started to get under way in the United States in the late 1980s, which is witnessed by the lack of a name for it in English: it is referred to as 'before and after school care' or (more conveniently) 'extended day care'. Municipal day care is underdeveloped in the United States, but socioeconomic realities have brought increased demands for federal action to promote local expansion.

In the US there was no guaranteed maternity leave for women who work until 1993, when the Family and Medical Leave Act was passed. In other words, until then a woman who left her job to have a baby could not be sure of getting her job back. The 1993 law guarantees a parent up to twelve weeks of *unpaid* leave for child care (or to deal with sickness in the family) as well as the right to return to the same or an equivalent position. Thus American women normally receive no income during periods of childbearing and either have to give up working or make day-care arrangements to return to work very soon after childbirth. However, starting in the late 1990s, about half of the state governments began to compensate people who were taking this federal leave, often using funding from unemployment compensation.

The fact that women continue to assume the prime responsibility for raising children has clearly affected their lifetime income: women's median money income was only 59 percent of men's in 2005. Women work part-time to a much greater extent than men. A Bureau of the Census report from 1987 stated that roughly one fifth of the income gender gap is accounted for by loss of career momentum caused by interruptions for childbirth.

The number of American women who are self-employed roughly doubled in the 1980s and continued to soar into the new century. In the latest official business census from 2002, women owned about half as many firms as men did, with 28 and 57 percent respectively, while about 12 percent were owned by men and women and 2 percent were publicly owned. In 2004 companies owned by women of color were growing at six times the average rate for all companies. The failure rate for women's companies is 40 percent, roughly half of the rate for all new concerns. Female entrepreneurs are concentrated in service industries but also making rapid headway in such male-dominated industries as manufacturing, construction, transportation, and mining.

Businesswomen have traditionally had two major complaints: they have received only a tiny percentage of all federal government contracts, and they have found it difficult to get loans from banks. Recent measures to eliminate affirmative action programs for selecting government contractors suggest that the former problem will continue to hamper women-owned companies; women entrepreneurs will have to rely on regulations prohibiting discrimination instead, although discrimination can be difficult to prove in cases where contracts are awarded. The latter problem, on the other hand, underwent a dramatic change in the 1990s: even though men dominate upper management at commercial banks, women reported in a 1997 survey that they were largely satisfied with the treatment their credit applications were being given. This is true despite the fact that it is still not uncommon for bankers to require a woman to get a man—her husband or business partner—to co-sign her loan application.

Women often start their own companies because they have failed to be promoted in large corporations. Despite increasing numbers of female business-school graduates, women rarely climb higher than middle management, where they dominate many fields, like personnel, health administration, and even finance. Top executives of large American companies are still virtually all male, however, and women are rarely allowed to enter the informal 'old boys' networks that are so typical of the world of business. Feeling the need for an alternative of their own, many businesswomen have recently started setting up what they call 'new girls' networks.

In the professions women are not surprisingly over-represented in teaching (predominantly at lower levels), nursing, and library science, but underrepresented in medicine, law, architecture, and engineering. Women accounted for about 32 percent of all physicians and 33 percent of lawyers, but only 22 percent of all architects and 15 percent of all engineers in 2006.

Politically, American women have been allowed to vote since 1920 (although the state of Wyoming granted the franchise to women as early as 1869), and in 1986 they passed men when it comes to the number of people voting, but they are still grossly underrepresented in federal politics. Their position in local and state politics is somewhat better, though far from parity levels: women held about 22 percent of all county and municipal elected positions as well as 23 percent of all posts as state legislators in 2006, although this figure had more than doubled since 1975. Women state governors can be counted in single digits. In the 111th Congress convening in 2009, a record 17 out of 100 US senators and 74 out of 435 (also 17 percent) members of the House of Representatives are female.

The first serious woman candidate for the Vice-Presidency was Geraldine Ferraro in 1984. She was soundly defeated together with her running mate, Walter Mondale. Sandra Day O'Connor, a Reagan appointee, became the first woman justice of the US Supreme Court in the 1980s. She has since been joined by Ruth Bader Ginsburg, a Clinton appointee. After the 2006 election, Democrat Nancy Pelosi was chosen to serve as the first woman Speaker of the House of Representatives starting in 2007. In 2008 Hillary Rodham Clinton attracted roughly as many votes for the Democratic presidential nomination in 2008, and Sarah Palin was chosen to be the Republican vice-presidential candidate. Both of these women did a great deal—from opposing political sides—to increase the acceptance of women candidates at the top levels in US politics.

There are very few legal barriers to full participation of women in society. One of the last remaining bastions of male culture was brought down in 1988 when the US Supreme Court unanimously upheld a law in New York City banning discrimination against women in private clubs which have more than four hundred members and which earn money from serving the public. Smaller private clubs and any organizations formed primarily for religious purposes may still be segregated on the basis of sex.

Federal and state laws are stringent about sexual harassment in the work place. Employers are normally held liable for any sexual exploitation, discrimination, or offensive behavior on the part of one employee toward another. The responsibility therefore lies with the employer to inform all employees of pertinent rules.

Although most states and the federal government have far-reaching statutes prohibiting sexual harassment and discrimination, the women's movement pushed for an amendment to the Constitution in the 1970s to more firmly guarantee women's rights. The proposed amendment was called the **Equal Rights Amendment**, abbreviated ERA. Its fate presents an excellent example of the workings of the American political system (see p. 172 for the procedure for amending the Constitution).

The political climate was such in the early 1970s that the proposed amendment was easily passed in both houses of Congress by majorities of more than the required two thirds in 1972. The amendment, which would have been the twenty-seventh, was worded as follows:

Equality of rights under law shall not be denied or abridged by the United States or any State on account of sex.

The proposal was sent to the fifty states for consideration. Three quarters of them would have to ratify the suggestion within seven years.

By the end of the 1970s proponents of ERA had won ratification in thirty-four of the thirty-eight states needed to amend the Constitution. Realizing that the country's more conservative mood would make it difficult to swing another four states in the last year, Congress extended the ratification period by another three years in 1979. However, this extension was effected by a simple majority only, not by a two-thirds majority, and opponents of the bill were joined by many of its supporters in maintaining that this procedure was unconstitutional. Furthermore, two states which had previously ratified the amendment now proceeded to rescind their earlier decisions, raising another constitutional issue as to whether a state can change its mind about ratification. Both of the constitutional questions raised by ERA procedure remain moot, however, since the Equal Rights Amendment died in 1982, still four states short of ratification.

Opponents of ERA, both men and women, argued that a constitutional amendment would make any distinction between males and females illegal. The more vulgar arguments claimed that unisex rest rooms and even locker rooms would be mandated, and gentlemanly courtesy outlawed. The amendment was actively opposed by conservative women in organizations like the WWWW, that is, Women Who Want to remain Women. Even many people who sympathized with women's rights either opposed or were unenthusiastic about ERA, claiming that statutory (that is, based on regular laws passed by Congress) protection, combined with general human rights guaranteed by the Constitution, was sufficient.

The main supporters of ERA, such as NOW, the National Organization for Women, have promised to revive the amendment when the time is ripe. The key reason the proposal failed was the fact that state legislatures —where ratification battles are fought—tend to be conservative and overwhelmingly male dominated. NOW's long-term strategy is to see to it that more liberal women get elected as state legislators.

Another issue that the women's movement has given high priority is abortion. A clear majority of the American population think that women should have the right to choose whether they wish to follow through with an early pregnancy, and the Supreme Court found in the landmark 1973 case *Roe vs. Wade* that the Constitution implicitly grants women this right as an expression of their right to privacy (see discussion on p. 157).

Figure 6.1 Pro-Life Demonstrators outside Supreme Court in 1991. (Photo: Steve Halber, AP, AB Reportagebild)

People who oppose abortion on moral grounds have pressed their arguments forcefully ever since the *Roe* decision. Activist groups have picketed, blockaded, and occasionally even bombed abortion clinics, claiming that these institutions murder babies.

Five fatal shootings of abortion-clinic staff by fanatics between 1992 and 1994 were condemned by many, but not all, leaders of anti-abortion groups. Some of the latter leaders argued that these shootings of 'baby-killers' constituted 'justifiable homicide'. The shootings led to federal legislation forbidding demonstrations within a certain distance of clinics. Anti-abortion activists violated the law, however, claiming constitutional guarantees of the right to express themselves. They were repeatedly arrested and hoped to win support in the federal courts. Instead, the courts upheld the law protecting the integrity of the clinics, although the protected zone was established at only about five meters from the clinic entrances. A 1997 Supreme Court decision removed protection from clients outside the five-meter mark at the entrances and driveways. Anti-abortion activists commonly jot down license numbers of clients' cars outside a clinic with the aim of identifying the women and then approaching them at home or work to dissuade them from having an abortion.

In the American tradition of political groups' always being *for* rather than *against* something, anti-abortion forces prefer to be called 'pro-life'. Those who think women should be able to choose realize that 'pro-abortion' sounds bloodthirsty, so the preferred term here is 'pro-choice'. These activists maintain that pro-lifers are more concerned about the welfare of an unborn fetus than they are about women in difficult life situations, and they refer to their opponents as being 'anti-choice'. They also argue that if abortions are outlawed, they will be performed anyway, but either underground or by amateurs and quacks, thus increasing the danger to women's lives. A common symbol of the pro-choice movement is the American coat hanger (made of wire) crossed out, as on traffic signs. Before legalization, many women attempted home abortions using coat hangers and the like.

The close (five votes to four) *Roe* decision has long been under attack, and pro-life forces were pleased when the Supreme Court decided, again by a one-vote majority, in a 1989 case known as *Webster vs. Reproductive*

Services that the state of Missouri could impose certain restrictions on the conditions under which women are allowed to have abortions performed in that state, thus opening the door for other types of constraints. Other states soon followed suit, typically stipulating, for instance, that teenage girls must inform their parents of a decision to have an abortion (although these states must provide a judicial procedure for bypassing the law), or that women must observe a specified waiting period after first applying for an abortion. Many of these state laws will surely be challenged in the federal courts and ultimately be taken before the US Supreme Court for review.

In 1991 the court reached another landmark decision about abortion, again in a five-to-four vote. In *Rust vs. Sullivan* they found that it was constitutional for authorities to assume a policy of withholding tax-money support from any family-planning clinic that recommends or even spreads information on abortion as an option. The decision would force such clinics to carry on without financial backing from federal, state, or local authorities in places where the respective authorities wished to restrict abortions. At the federal level such a 'gag-rule' (prohibiting doctors from offering information) had been issued by President Reagan's Department of Health and Human Services in 1988. It has been highly criticized by the American Medical Association because it encroaches upon the doctor-patient relationship, and it has in fact never been fully implemented, owing to various legal challenges during the George H. W. Bush administration. In 1993 one of President Clinton's first acts as President was to issue an executive order countermanding any regulations limiting doctors' rights to counsel their patients. Generally speaking, however, the combination of anti-abortion agitation and of state and federal legislation in the last decade has made abortions far less accessible, especially in rural areas; well over 80 percent of all US counties have no abortion services available. At the same time, a major 1996 study showed that more than half of all American women have undergone at least one abortion. Interestingly the proportion was 30 percent higher among Catholic women than among Protestants. The United States has one of the highest abortion rates in the industrialized world, at least in part because of the lack of family planning services and sex education in many parts of the country.

In 2003 a federal law was enacted that expressly banned the use of rare abortion procedure, medically characterized as 'intact dilation and extraction' and generally called 'partial-birth abortion', the only federal act to prohibit a type of abortion. The statute explicitly allows physicians to perform such operations if the life of the mother is clearly in danger as a result of the pregnancy. In 2007 the US Supreme Court affirmed the constitutionality of the 2003 law in a five-to-four decision. Pro-choice advocates fear—and pro-life activists hope—that this unique federal law may be the beginning of a reversal of the basic reproductive rights established in *Roe vs. Wade*.

Pro-choice activists stress that the court did not overturn *Roe* in its 1989 and 1991 decisions, and they have won several victories in state legislatures where proposed restrictions were clearly voted down. The 2008 elections also went the way pro-choice people wanted: in three states voters clearly turned down proposals to limit access to abortions. The most far-reaching was a referendum in conservative South Dakota to ban all abortions except in cases of rape, incest, and serious risk to the mother's health. Two years earlier voters had rejected an absolute ban, and pro-life activists had hoped that the new proposal would be accepted. In Colorado, a referendum to establish legally that personhood starts at conception—a principle central pro-life arguments—was roundly rejected, and in California, for the third time, voters stopped a proposal to require that teenage girls notify their parents before having an abortion.

It is clear that the last word has not been said on this matter in the US. The situation can be summed as follows: Americans do not like abortion, but they want to keep it legal and available as an option. In the aftermath of the fatal shootings at abortion clinics, the two sides have attempted to reach out to each other, at least temporarily moderating the tone of the debate. Presidential appointees to the Supreme Court will continue to be put to a 'litmus test' regarding their opinion about *Roe*. The swing to the right, and right to life, in the composition of the Supreme Court that the George W. Bush appointees constituted seems likely to be halted and then reversed by Obama appointees in coming years.

CHAPTER 7

Religions

Religious Liberty

The abortion debate over the past couple of decades has been paralleled by tendencies in American religious movements. Born-again Christians and fundamentalist groups have been a driving force in what began to be called 'the New Right' in the early 1970s. While it might be argued that the movement has lost its dominant role in national politics—as witnessed by the limited numbers of keen supporters of vice-presidential candidate Sarah Palin in 2008, it remains very much a part of the mosaic of present-day American religion—as witnessed by the fact that candidate John McCain believed it would help him to choose her as his running mate.

Freedom of religion is one of the most cherished and jealously guarded pillars of the American republic. Freedom from religious persecution at the hands of the Church of England was the prime objective of the settlers of the early Plymouth and Massachusetts Bay colonies. Once established, however, these colonies made no distinction between church and state, and as a result they were quick to persecute heretics among their own numbers. Roger Williams was one of several early colonists to be forced out of Massachusetts in the 17th century. He later established a colony that would become the state of Rhode Island, basing it on the principle of religious freedom that is the true antecedent of the guarantee the Constitution provides present-day Americans. In fact, the state of Massachusetts did not abolish its laws favoring certain religions until 1933.

It is not easy to draw the line between church and state, however. Historically, the United States has always been a predominantly Christian nation, and despite the injunction against the government establishing any religion, there are many official signs of religiosity. The Pledge of Allegiance, for example, (see p. 216) includes the phrase 'under God', Presidents swear the oath of office with their hand on a Bible, sessions of Congress are opened with prayer, the currency is marked with the motto 'In God We Trust', etc. It used to be common for schoolchildren to be required to start the day with a moment of prayer or of devotional silence, but in response to protests from citizens advocating a clear separation of church and state the Supreme Court declared this practice unconstitutional in 1962. Many people have also objected, with varying success, to the use of public tax money to finance community manger scenes and other Christmas decorations of a specifically religious nature.

Alongside the abortion issue discussed above, the greatest clash of particular religious interests and the general public has involved the teaching of the theory of evolution in the schools. In 1925 a biology teacher named John Scopes was placed on trial for violating a Tennessee law by introducing his high school students to Darwinism. The case attracted national attention because both the prosecutor and the defense attorney were famous lawyers who volunteered their services. William Jennings Bryan, a former presidential candidate, argued eloquently as prosecutor that creation was literally described in the Bible, but Clarence Darrow, a famed legal defender, made him the laughing stock of the nation by putting Bryan himself on the witness stand and asking him common-sense questions. Scopes was in fact convicted (although the conviction was later overturned on a legal technicality), but Darrow largely carried the day on the national level. More recently, starting in the 1980s, advocates of biblical literalism have maintained that 'creation science' is just as scientific as the theory of evolution and should therefore be taught in the schools. In the latter half of the 1980s, the US Supreme Court struck down laws in a few states that mandated such teaching in public schools. The court argued simply that it was not the business of the state to regulate curricular content in such detail.

Despite this, in 1999 the Kansas state Board of Education undermined (but did not ban) the teaching of evolution in Kansas schools in by removing the theory from its state standard examinations. The decision turned out to be an embarrassment to the state, and voters threw out half of the members of the state school board in the 2000 election. The new board reversed the decision in 2001. At the same time a 2000 study showed that roughly one third of American schools did not teach evolution satisfactorily.

The First Amendment thus guarantees that while every citizen may freely exercise his or her religion, no religious group, not even that of a majority of the citizens, can dictate the beliefs of others. The government does promote religions in general by granting them tax-free status, but it is not allowed to show preferences for any particular faith. This was a major departure from the policies of European nations at the time, and it would become more and more important as the United States grew ever more pluralistic in religion.

Religious Diversity

At the time of Independence, the United States was overwhelmingly a Protestant country. After the settlement of the middle colonies and the revivalist movement of the 1740s, called the 'Great Awakening', the dominant Congregationalists of New England and the Anglicans (called Episcopalians after the Revolution) of the Southern colonies had been joined by Baptists, Methodists, Presbyterians, Quakers, Shakers, and many others. The Roman Catholics that established the colony of Maryland were a tiny minority in the new nation and welcomed people of other faiths from the outset.

The early 1800s saw a 'second Awakening' of evangelical Christian sects, especially as the country expanded westward. Toward the middle of the century the Catholic Church became an important fixture on the east coast with the arrival of millions of Irish and later German Catholic immigrants. With the annexation of the Southwest and California at mid-century, the Catholic culture of the former Spanish colonies also became a part of America. German and Scandinavian immigrants bolstered the Lutheran Church that had long existed in the middle colonies.

Small numbers of Jews came to the United States in the 19th century. They were primarily from Germany and represented a Reformed liberal branch of Judaism. Around the turn of the 20th century large numbers of Jews from Russia and Poland brought with them the traditions of Orthodox Judaism.

Islam is the largest non-Judeo-Christian religion in the United States, and it is growing steadily. The Muslim population of Michigan—where, as mentioned, many Arabs work in the industrial suburbs of Detroit—is estimated at 250,000.

American Indians are now generally free to worship their traditional spirits, although many of course converted to Christianity long ago, under pressure from American society. During the first half of the 20th century, when the US government actively pursued a policy of integrating them in mainstream society, Indians were often forced to conceal their traditional forms of worship, despite the guarantees of religious freedom expressly stated in the Constitution.

Although the United States is a highly secularized society, Americans remain a religious people. Gallup polls show that 90 percent of the population expresses a religious preference, and 70 percent are members of a local church or synagogue (down from over three quarters in 1947 but rising over the last couple of years). On any given regular day of worship, about 44 percent of Americans go to a place of worship. This figure has remained fairly stable over the last several decades, although it was at its highest in 1955 and 1958 (49 percent) and at its lowest in 1940 (37 percent). Roughly 80 percent of Americans feel that a person can be a good Christian or Jew without attending a church or synagogue.

Alongside its personal religious function in the lives of most Americans, the church fulfills a central social function, both for its active members and for other members of society. Church (synagogue, mosque) members spend a great deal of their spare time working and socializing in church-sponsored activities. These activities also include many programs designed to benefit social outcasts and people experiencing hard times. Volunteerism is a major strain of the American character (see p. 267), and churches are almost unfailingly on the front lines when it comes to helping persons in trouble, often providing care that citizens of other countries (and many Americans) feel should rightly be provided by authorities through official channels. President George W. Bush worked to increase the role played by religious groups by channeling more federal money through so-called 'faith-based' groups, and President Obama promised to continue to support such initiatives.

As mentioned above, the church has played a special role in the lives of two minority groups, African Americans and Hispanics. For the former, the church (normally Baptist) was the only place where blacks were allowed to congregate in groups of more than three in the days of slave codes and, after the Civil War, black codes in the South. For Hispanics, the Catholic Church provides a social framework almost to the exclusion of any political participation in society at large, although the 2008 Obama campaign inspired new levels of activism among Latinos.

One striking feature of Christian worship in the US, and one which accelerated in the 1980s, is the prominence of televangelism, that is, evangelism via television. Incredible amounts of money have been donated by individual television viewers (normally white, but not always) to help bolster the finances of a number of national evangelical churches, usually surrounding a charismatic preacher. The phenomenon probably peaked in the latter half of the 1980s, having been at least temporarily deflated by scandals involving two of the most prominent televangelists. In the wake of a sex scandal, Jim Bakker was sentenced to forty-five years in prison for fraudulent use of donations to his PTL (Praise The Lord—or, as critics had it, 'Pass The Loot') Foundation. Bakker was released in 1994. One of Bakker's most vocal detractors during the exposé of his extramarital relations with a secretary was his rival evangelist Jimmy Swaggart. Soon after the Bakker debacle, however, Swaggart himself was shown in highly compromising photographs together with a prostitute at a cheap motel. He was forced to resign as minister of his church. He soon returned to the pulpit, however. In 2006 pastor Ted Haggard, president of the National Association of Evangelicals, resigned when it was revealed that he had been paying a male prostitute for sex over a period of three years. He returned to his preaching in 2008, claiming that he had successfully undergone treatment to 'reverse' his homosexuality.

The relative size of the major religious groups is as follows:

TABLE 7.1 Religious Affiliation in the United States (2002).
(Source: Statistical Abstract of the United States, 2004).

Christian		83%
Protestant	55%	
Catholic	28%	
Jewish		2%
Other		6%
Non-affiliates		8%
		~100%

Within American Christendom, there has been a gradual erosion of the Protestant majority. In 1952 the Protestant dominance was greater by seven percentage points, 67 percent. Within Protestantism, there has been a shift from so-called 'mainline' denominations (Episcopalians, Lutherans, Methodists, etc.) to more conservative and fundamentalist groups. In the public arena this shift has led to attempts to merge religion and politics in a way that brings to mind the theocracies (where church and state are one) of early New England. The trend accounted for a major share of public support for Ronald Reagan as President (as for President George W. Bush in 2000 and 2004) and made televangelist Pat Robertson a prime contender for the Republican presidential nomination in 1988. To his credit, Robertson stepped down from the pulpit during his campaign and declined to mix religion and politics to the extent that many of his followers would have liked. President George W. Bush entered his second term under great pressure to pay back his born-again Christian supporters in the form of political action to promote religious issues, such as outlawing abortion and allowing school prayer and the teaching of creationism, and critics feared in 2004 that the separation of church and state might increasingly be weakened. Right after the 2004 election the same Pat Robertson launched a campaign to "de-liberalize" the US courts. One troubling phenomenon in terms of the separation of church and state was the often uncritical acceptance of probing questions concerning candidates' religious faith on some occasions in the 2008 presidential campaign, especially a televised joint appearance of candidates McCain and Obama in Pastor Rick Warren's southern Californian megachurch, Saddleback Church.

SUGGESTED WEB SITES

US Government, Bureau of the Census
www.census.gov

Organization for Economic Cooperation and Development
www.oecd.org

Urban Institute
www.urban.org

Economic Policy Institute
www.epinet.org

C-SPAN (Cable Producers' Network)
www.c-span.org/questions

National Immigration Forum
www.immigrationforum.org

Library of Congress, African-American exhibits
http://lcweb.loc.gov/exhibits/african/intro.html

American Association for Affirmative Action
www.affirmativeaction.org

Center for Individual Rights
www.cir-usa.org

American Life League
www.all.org

National Abortion Rights Action League
www.naral.org

Planned Parenthood Foundation of America
www.plannedparenthood.org

National Organization for Women
www.now.org

Small Business Administration
www.sba.gov

Center for Women's Business Research
www.womensbusinessresearch.org

Gay Rights Page
www.speakout.com/activism/gayrights

*American Civil Liberties Union page on Lesbian/Gay/Bisexual/
Transgender Rights*
www.aclu.org/lgbt

PART III

Government

CHAPTER 8

Principles

In principle, the United States of America is a **democratic republic**, that is, Americans govern themselves by choosing their own leaders by secret ballot, and these leaders in turn make the rules. Actually the words **democracy** and **republic** are almost synonymous: demo-cracy comes from the Greek for 'people power', and re-public means 'matter for the people' in Latin. In general usage, however, a distinction is made between the more general democracy—which can apply to monarchies with significant elements of rule by the people—and republic—which always refers to nations without hereditary heads of state. Although democracy is often taken for granted in liberal democratic countries, it should be borne in mind that such countries are still in the minority in the world community. In the historical perspective, democracy stands out as an even rarer luxury.

Although the United States is often thought of (even by its residents) as a 'young' nation, it is in fact the oldest democratic republic in history. Americans started 'governing themselves' as a nation on July 4, 1776, when the **Declaration of Independence** was signed in Philadelphia by representatives of the thirteen British colonies in North America. Breaking away from British rule entailed several years of violent conflict, during which the new states sent representatives to so-called **Continental Congresses** to coordinate their joint war effort. After gaining independence, these same states joined together formally in 1781 under a first 'constitution', the **Articles of Confederation**. That loose union of the states was replaced by the **Constitution of the United States of America** in 1789. This document—amended twenty-seven[1] times—is still the political foundation of the United States.

Being based on a **written** constitution, the American government is committed in principle to the **rule of law**. All countries are 'ruled by laws', of course, but the term rule of law is used in political science in contradistinction to **arbitrary rule** or 'rule by rulers'. Under the rule of law, citizens know what regulations apply because the rules have been agreed upon and then written down; under arbitrary rule, citizens are subject to the whims of individuals in power. Under the rule of law, those in power are themselves ruled by written laws and other conventions.

In theory, then, the people and their chosen leaders agree to submit to laws of their own making while retaining the right to change those laws. One of the basic problems of democracy, however, is what the French statesman Alexis de Tocqueville called the 'tyranny of the majority' after having visited the United States in the 1840s. There is a danger that the majority of the people might force its rules on minorities or individuals that have 'legitimate' claims not to follow such rules (an example would be the establishment of a certain religion as the only permissible form of worship). What distinguishes a democracy from unrestrained 'mob rule' is paradoxically the recognition of certain limits on the right of the majority to decide. Seen from the point of view of the minority, or the individual, this recognition translates into the establishment of certain 'legitimate' **human rights** that cannot be violated—not even by the will of the majority.

The American Constitution lays down a set of principles for achieving some form of balance here, between **personal freedom** and regulation for the **common good**, a balance that is the very essence of political philosophy. In the great debates surrounding the adoption of the new Constitution in the late 1780s, it became clear that many people—with memories of life as colonial subjects—were suspicious of the relative

---

1 The 27th Amendment—which prevents any pay raises for members of Congress from taking effect until there has been an intervening congressional election—was actually the eleventh of the original 'Bill of Rights', the first ten amendments to the Constitution (see p. 100), but it was not ratified with the other ten back in the late 1780s. It finally became part of the Constitution in 1992, when Michigan became the 38th state to ratify it, after more than two hundred years of dormancy.

concentration of power represented by the new document. Its promoters —who for various reasons wished to see just such a focusing of political power in a central government—realized that they would have to include express guarantees of personal and minority freedom in order to make the Constitution acceptable to a majority of the states. A compromise was arranged between supporters (the **Federalists**) of the new 'supreme law of the land' and their opponents (the **Anti-Federalists**): the latter would help **ratify** (approve) the new Constitution of 1787 (to take effect in 1789) in exchange for a promise of permanently guaranteed individual and group rights. This promise was fulfilled in 1791 when the first ten **amendments** (changes) to the Constitution, called the **Bill of Rights**, were adopted, guaranteeing the rights of free speech, a free press, freedom of religion, assembly, etc. Later on, notably after the Civil War in the 1860s, further amendments were adopted to explicitly extend basic human rights to the former slaves. All of these amendments still play a central role in American political life in a way that often surprises foreign observers. Indeed, 'constitutional issues' in general permeate American political discussions, and the term has a specific American meaning which British English has traditionally lacked, although in the last few years Britons have started seriously considering the adoption of some form of written constitution.

These brief comments on the underlying principles of American government must not be taken as a claim that the United States has always lived up to its own democratic goals or that these political principles can be fully understood in isolation from, say, economic and social factors or that the United States has the only key to problems of self-rule and should therefore be emulated in detail by all other countries of the world. Indeed, despite the system for problem-solving afforded by the Constitution, it cannot be denied that American history has been punctuated by blatant injustices and gruesome violence. Nevertheless, as the first and oldest democratic and republican nation in modern times, it is equally undeniable that the country has been relatively successful in accommodating—if not resolving—the various class interests and myriad individual wills of its citizenry from all over the world. The system has proven to be flexible and, above all, stable. Where it has failed, the principles mentioned above should be used to measure the extent of that failure. At the very least, understanding these principles and their specific corollaries, such as **federalism**, the **separation of powers**, and the system of **checks and balances**, which we now turn to, should help the reader to grasp why Americans approach problems the way they do.

CHAPTER 9

Structure

Before looking at the different features of government in the United States, certain peculiarities in American usage regarding words like **government**, **state**, and **federal** must be pointed out. In the US the word **government** does not have the specific meaning it so often has in British English, for example, where it can refer to the ministers that make up the executive in a parliamentary system (see Figure 11.1 "Executive Power" p. 177 for a comparison of parliamentary systems and the US system). Government is a much broader term in America, referring to the authorities in general, often including the legislative branch (Congress) and the executive branch (the President, the Cabinet, and various agencies).

The word **state**, on the other hand, has a specific American meaning denoting the fifty political units which make up the United States. In abstract discussions of political science, of course, Americans use **state** in the sense many other languages use it, to refer to a sovereign government or especially a **national** entity, but you should be aware that Americans (like Australians and Indians) can easily be confused if outsiders refer to their national government as 'the American state'. Americans wonder which of the fifty 'states' the speaker means: Pennsylvania? Idaho? Texas? This is indeed a confusing issue, because American states are sovereign states in a sense, but not **nations**. This fact is connected with the next tricky word, **federal**. We need to recall briefly how these words grew out of American history to understand their use today.

Having unilaterally declared their independence from Great Britain in 1776, the thirteen former colonies were suddenly independent and sovereign 'states'. There were considerable differences and substantial division among these states, some contributing much more than others to the war effort, for example. Some states promised to send money (they all had separate currencies, being sovereign states) and soldiers but never did. Even after victory had been won in the armed struggle, the Articles of **Confederation**, the original constitution of 1781, relied on the goodwill of the states to volunteer money to the weak central government (and this money was not always forthcoming). The central government was in fact destitute and thus more or less powerless to govern, since governments normally have to pay people to serve them. The movement for a stronger central government—with the power to tax the people, for one thing— came to be called the **Federalist** movement. Although the etymologies of **federation** and **confederation** are not significantly different—they both denote a league of sovereign states—federal came to be used to connote a strong central power to which the member states give up more of their sovereignty than in a confederation. It is not just a coincidence that the Southern states called themselves the **Confederate** States of America when they broke away from the **federal** union in the early 1860s.

To return to present usage, the fifty states are still sovereign in many ways: their territory is theoretically inviolable by the government in Washington, for example. In most parliamentary countries, all power resides in the parliament, and the various counties and municipalities exist and can be shuffled around only at the discretion of the central government. The American government has no such power over the states in the union. Of course, Washington was instrumental in deciding how to draw the borders in various territories as the country expanded, but extant states and new states, once established, are inviolable in principle. Regarding this sovereignty, the tenth amendment to the Constitution (that is, the last of the Bill of Rights) explicitly states:

> *The powers not delegated to the United States by the Constitution, nor prohibited by it to the States, are reserved to the States respectively, or to the people.*

Education provides a good example. There being no public education (anywhere in the world) when the Constitution was written, there is no mention of the subject there. As the industrial revolution created a demand for literate workers, universal education developed during the course of the 19th century. This development was left entirely to the respective 'sovereign' states, and education is still largely a matter for the state governments, who in turn delegate much of the responsibility for the schools to local authorities. It is not generally regarded as a **federal** matter.

This last sentence shows how the word **federal** is used, namely, to refer to the **national** government in the federal union of states. This may be confusing to the foreigner, so it might be a good idea to restate the source of confusion once again: to say that a country has a 'federal' system is theoretically to stress that power is to some extent **decentralized** in comparison with a more 'monolithic' or centralized power structure in another country. But in reference to America's partly decentralized or federal system, **federal** normally relates to the **central** government in that system. As we will soon see, the federal and state governments are separate entities that in fact are often at odds with each other in the United States.

Three Levels of Government

Having straightened out some common language problems involving American government, we can now turn to the three (or four) levels of government Americans elect and, in turn, are ruled by. They are:

- LOCAL < City
  County
- STATE
- FEDERAL

LOCAL GOVERNMENT

Local government can usually be further subdivided into **city** and **county** governments, although in rural areas the county is often the only local government. The word **city** is used much more loosely in America than in Great Britain, for example. Rather small towns often use the term 'city' in their names.

With some variation, city governments are usually of one of two basic types:

- Mayor/Council
- Council/Manager

Under the **mayor/council** plan, the mayor (either a 'strong' one with considerable power or a 'weak' one dominated by the council) and the city (town) council are elected separately, although in the same election. In small towns, mayoral and council elections are often non-partisan, meaning that the candidates do not represent the national parties. In the big cities, however, party politics does enter into the contest, and the mayors of the largest cities are often fairly well-known figures all over the country. (Being mayor of New York City is often referred to as the second hardest political post in the US, after the Presidency.) The mayor's job is similar to the President's in that the mayor is an executive (with varying powers) and a figurehead. The **city council** is elected either 'at large', that is, each **council-man/woman** (or sometimes **alderman/woman**) is elected by the whole city, or by 'wards' (or 'districts'), or by both methods. They determine policy, establish local laws, usually called **ordinances**, and control the city finances.

Under the **council/manager** plan, a **city manager** is appointed by the city council to be the chief administrator. The city manager is assumed to be a low-key 'professional' and not a 'politician' who might counter-balance the power of the council. Once hired, the manager is given fairly free rein to run the local government within guidelines set up by the council, with efficiency as a prime goal. In this system a mayor might also be appointed to act as the city's ceremonial leader.

The city government provides such services as police and fire protection (Police Department, Fire Department), trash and garbage collection (Sanitation Department), maintenance and cleaning of local streets and roads, sewerage, and parks and recreation. In order to finance these services, cities exact property taxes. In big cities these taxes are sometimes supplemented by a city income tax. Most big industrial cities in the Midwest and Northeast have experienced a concentration of poor residents in the inner city area, with a concomitant concentration of wealthier people living in the surrounding suburbs. Some big city governments have managed to alleviate their financial problems by imposing an income tax on people who commute from the suburbs to work in the city. New York City, for example, taxes the income of commuting workers even from other states, Connecticut and New Jersey, though at a lower rate than for New York residents. Washington, DC, on the other hand, has found it politically impossible to impose a similar tax on its commuting workers. Left with a 'tax base' consisting of poor residents—who are the very people most often in need of the city's social services, many old industrial cities are perennially short of funds. On the other side of the coin, municipal service is generally better in the suburbs. Some local authorities (for example, Miami) have experimented with **consolidated** city and county government, forming a single central unit for certain functions within a 'metropolitan area', that is, a big city and its surrounding suburbs. (These metropolitan areas are referred to either as, say, 'greater Chicago' or 'metropolitan Chicago'.) See also p. 26 regarding 'metropolitan councils'.

All cities are also in **counties**, and in rural areas the county government might be the only local government. In semi-rural areas a **township** might serve some of the functions of a municipality. The county is run by an elective **county board**, sometimes called a **board of supervisors** or **board of commissioners**. There is no chief executive. The county is responsible for county law enforcement (the **Sheriff**), maintaining county roads, providing some health service, and keeping birth records. Some counties also provide basic education and some offer free or low-tuition post-secondary education at community colleges (junior colleges). The role of the county varies considerably from place to place.

Before leaving local government, we should just mention the local court systems. At the lowest level, rural and semi-rural areas have a judge called a **justice of the peace** who hears both criminal and civil cases of minor importance. The same official is usually called a **magistrate** in cities, and the court is often called a **police court**. In both cases, their jurisdiction is limited to local ordinances. City and county judges are usually elected to office.

STATE GOVERNMENT

Each of the fifty states is independently responsible for all functions of government not explicitly given to the federal government in the Constitution. They are in this sense 'sovereign' states not to be interfered with by the federal government. In contrast, city governments are not 'sovereign'—cities are created or 'incorporated' by the state government, and they exist and exercise their powers only with the blessing of the latter. Although the federal government was originally involved in determining the boundaries of new 'territories' in the 1800s, once these territories had joined the union as states, they became as sovereign and inviolable as the original thirteen states.

This principle of 'states' rights' has been a salient issue throughout American history. The issue of slavery (paralleled a century later by the civil rights struggle) provides a good example of the concept. Any state which wished to support a system of human slavery—an issue which the writers of the Constitution conveniently skirted—could be construed to be within its legal 'state's rights'; such policies were simply none of the business of the other states. This legal aspect of the issue was clearly at odds with the moral aspect: should states be allowed to violate the basic human rights of some people (even though slaves were not citizens) in the name of state sovereignty? The Civil War decided the issue.

Notwithstanding their central role in the scheme of self-rule, state governments tend to be rather dull and fail to attract either the most talented leaders or the attention of the voters. State legislators are held in rather low esteem due to occasional scandals involving influence-peddling and corruption. State governors, on the other hand, sometimes attain national recognition; a state governorship is often used as a springboard to the presidency.

State constitutions, in stark contrast to the federal Constitution, are lengthy documents that codify procedures in detail. The structure of state governments largely mirrors that of the federal government:

- a bicameral legislature (usually called the **Senate** and **House of Representatives**)
- a chief executive, called the **governor**
- a three-tiered system of courts, headed by a **supreme court** (sometimes with a different name) all of whose members are usually elected rather than appointed.

Although all states have approximately the same governmental structure, their laws can vary considerably, a fact that often surprises visitors. A standard answer to questions about what American law says about some matter is that there is no single law about it. States have their own rules about, say, at what age young adults are allowed to drink alcoholic beverages and just how such beverages are to be retailed. Possession of small quantities of marijuana might lead to severe penalties in one state and be ignored in another. Marriage and divorce rules vary from state to state, as do rules regulating eligibility for voting and welfare benefits for people moving into the state, not to mention the tremendous differences in the size of such benefits. Educational standards and teacher qualifications may vary; Mississippi, for example, did not even have compulsory education until the 1990s. Until 1973 some states prohibited abortions while others did not, and at present restrictions on abortions vary considerably from state to state.

This variation can be troublesome: law schools of national caliber cannot teach only one set of state laws if their graduates are to practice in other states. Lawyers who move to a new state must pass that state's 'bar examination' to be certified to practice law there. There is a general movement toward uniformity, however, and various committees have been at work for some time trying to codify and standardize basic legislation. In the 1970s the voting age was standardized at eighteen by the twenty-sixth amendment to the Constitution, and Congress established a 'national' speed limit of fifty-five miles (ca. ninety kilometers) per hour, largely to conserve energy. The national speed limit offers a good example of how the federal government often exerts pressure without directly mandating a reform: federal funds for highway construction were made contingent on the respective states' maintenance of the new speed limit. Each state was free to establish its own limits, but only at the risk of losing huge amounts of federal money. In 1987 Congress moved to allow much more local discretion regarding speed limits.

THE FEDERAL GOVERNMENT

Since the federal government has the greatest impact on world politics and is therefore the level of American government that most people hear about, more space will be devoted to it here. Before looking more closely at its structure and functions, it might be appropriate to devote a paragraph to the place it is now located, **Washington**, the **District of Columbia** (DC).

The federal **capital** (the **Capitol** is the building which houses the US Congress) is not a part of any state, but rather 'neutral' ground, called the **District of Columbia**, after Columbus. The original idea was to create a capital in the middle of the country, between the rival northern and southern states. The choice of a site for the future capital—in a swampy area originally in southern Maryland and northern Virginia[1]—was a part of the extensive compromising that preceded the adoption of the new Constitution in 1789. (To follow the same line of reasoning today, the capital would have to be moved to, say, St. Louis, Missouri, near the population fulcrum of the nation. Incidentally, most of the states also consciously placed their capital cities in the middle of their territories; a state's capital is seldom its largest city.) For nearly two hundred years the 'city council' of the city of Washington was none other than the US Congress, with a mayor (properly 'commissioner') appointed by the President with the approval of the Senate. As of 1974, however, the people of the city elect their own mayor, city council, and school board, and they have their own courts, but all ordinances passed by the District must still be reviewed by Congress, and periods of mismanagement have led to temporary reversions to congressional government. The Twenty-third Amendment to the Constitution (1961) gave DC residents the right to vote in presidential elections, and they have been sending an observer (with no voting rights) to the House of Representatives since 1970. Congress passed a proposed amendment to give the District full voting rights in Congress in 1978, but very few states ratified it. So oddly enough, the citizens of the US capital have less say in their own government than do other Americans.

---

1 Virginia later (1846) reneged on the agreement, taking back its land. This explains why the District has a highly regular square shape on three sides but not to the southwest.

This logical, planned approach to establishing the new capital also permeated the structure of the government set up by the Constitution, which was obviously a product of the Age of Enlightenment (or Age of Reason). Many of the concepts of the American government can be traced to progressive thinkers of the 17th and 18th centuries, especially the Englishman John Locke (d. 1704). One of the most basic precepts of the American system was adapted from the ideas of the Dutch philosopher Spinoza (d. 1677) and, especially, the French jurist Montesquieu (d. 1755), namely the **separation of powers**.

Locke had envisaged a government in which the executive powers would be dissociated from the legislative powers. The writers of the US Constitution of 1789 followed Montesquieu's model rather, adding a third division, a separate judiciary. This third 'branch of government', as we think of it today, was not expressly empowered to be the equal of the other two branches; the founders merely established a Supreme Court for the country. But the founders clearly had Montesquieu in mind, and the court did in fact evolve into a potent countervailing force within just a couple of decades. The three 'branches' of the US government are thus (more or less in their original order of importance):

- LEGISLATIVE (Congress)
- EXECUTIVE (President)
- JUDICIAL (Supreme Court)

The major difference between this system and a **parliamentary** system is that in the latter the **executive** function is carried out by a 'cabinet' or 'government' created by the parliament and largely manned by its members. In the American system, the President is elected separately from the legislators and is more or less expected to be 'at odds' with them, acting as a countervailing force.

It is often remarked that this system—with its complex pattern of 'checks and balances' (see p. 159)—is inefficient, and, indeed, little legislation is actually passed, relative to the tremendous amount proposed. But it should be stressed that the system was *designed to be inefficient*. The former colonists feared the potential concentration of power inherent in a parliamentary system, where a strong majority for one party in the legislature can lead to a very 'efficient' and powerful executive government which is prepared to do the party's bidding. The original philosophy of the American Constitution was basically, as Thomas Jefferson put it and as H. D. Thoreau stressed in his tract *Civil Disobedience* some sixty years later: 'That government is best which governs least'. The idea was to create a popular government (that is, 'of the people') but to make it difficult for that government to make sudden changes. While the men who actively created the Constitution were radical for their day in many ways, they were basically afraid of any concentration of power—even in the hands of the people—and therefore created a form of government that was and still is conservative in essence.

This conservatism stemmed from the social and economic stature of the men who set up the Constitution. They were almost exclusively well-to-do landowners or merchants. In other words, they belonged to classes with vested interests who feared that too much direct popular influence—from the unpropertied 'rabble' of the day—might threaten those interests. This fear was manifested in two ways: the way in which officials were elected according to the new Constitution and the way in which the various states limited voting rights.

Originally, the only **direct** elections were those to choose the members of the House of Representatives. This close relationship between the House and the people at large was also underscored by the stipulation that all legislation dealing with **taxation** must originate in the House, the idea being that people would be reluctant to tax themselves. To ensure 'prudence' and 'balance' in the rest of the government, the Constitution set up indirect elections of the President and the Senate. The President is elected by a **college of electors** (see "Elections" p. 186), and until 1913 senators were chosen by the respective state legislatures. (Senators are now elected in state-wide direct contests.) The fact that Supreme Court justices and all judges in inferior courts are appointed, not elected, also reflects this striving for stability. The basic assumption underlying all of these devices for ensuring either indirect elections or appointments was that educated and affluent leaders would exert a moderating influence on the population as a whole and would tend to place in office other 'responsible' people like themselves.

Suffrage was originally granted by the various states to men (not women) who either owned a certain amount of property or could afford to pay a poll tax.[2] No women, poor people, or slaves could vote, but in an infamous compromise regarding the latter, called the federal ratio, the representation of the Southern slave-holding states was reinforced by counting slaves as three-fifths of a person when seats in the House of Representatives were apportioned. This extra voting leverage was of course exercised by the slave-holding males themselves.

Before looking at the way the various powers of the three branches of government balance each other in practical politics, we should briefly summarize those powers, taking each branch in turn.

Three Branches of Government

THE LEGISLATIVE BRANCH

The **Congress of the United States** consists of two chambers, the **Senate** and the **House of Representatives**. The two chambers, housed in opposite wings of the Capitol building in Washington, DC, are basically equal in power, though the Senate is generally regarded as the more prestigious, 'upper' house, having fewer members. The houses differ in the way they are constituted and in the length of terms served by their members. The Constitution also specifies a few differences in their roles.

Members of the Senate are called **senators**. There are **two** senators from each of the fifty states, thus an even **one hundred** senators as of 1959. Senators represent their **whole** state, and the states are equally represented without regard to population. Wyoming, the smallest state in population, is thus the equal of California, the largest state, and there is of course no distinction between new states and old states. Senators serve for **six years,** but elections are staggered so that **one third** of the seats are up for election

---

2   This fee to be paid for the right to vote at the polls should not be confused with the popular term for the 'community charge', the unpopular system for local taxation—based on each person rather than on property ownership—that ultimately toppled Prime Minister Margaret Thatcher in Britain in 1990. The use of the American type of poll tax was expressly forbidden by the 24th Amendment to the Constitution in 1964, a result of the Civil Rights Movement.

every **two** years. The two senators from each state are elected separately and normally not in the same election.

The Senate is specifically charged with advising the President in matters of foreign policy and in making major administrative and judicial appointments (see "Checks and Balances" p. 159). Through their prominent roles in promoting legislation or as chairs of various committees, about a dozen senators are usually fairly well-known public figures, and the Senate is a common stepping stone on the way to the Presidency.

Members of the House of Representatives are called **representatives** or, confusingly enough, *congress*men/**women** or *congress*persons, a term never used for senators. Congressmen represent the states on the basis of their population, each representative being elected by a district[3] of roughly 450,000 voters (600,000 residents). The number of representatives has been frozen at **435**, so the election districts are **reapportioned** (redistributed) every ten years after the official census. In 'the House', as it is usually called for short, Wyoming has only one representative, being such a small state in terms of population, while California has 53 (12 percent) after the 2000 census. Representatives are elected for **two years** at a time, and the **whole** House is up for election each time. The numbering of Congresses is based on this fact: there is a 'new' Congress every second year, and they are called, for example, the 111th Congress of the United States (2009–10, elected in 2008).

Each representative is expected to look after the interests of his/her own constituency, and only a few congressmen ever attain national prominence, one of them being the **Speaker of the House**, who chairs proceedings. The House is a common stepping stone to the Senate. The Constitution stipulates that all legislation regarding taxation must originate in the House of Representatives (and then proceed to the Senate).

Congress has the power to **legislate**, that is, to make laws valid for the whole country, but normally only with the signature of the President (see also Figure 10.5 "The Law-Making Process" p. 166). Other specific powers include the **regulation of commerce** between the states and with foreign countries (an important factor in unifying the various states into

---

3   These districts never cross state borders.

a nation) and the power to **declare war**. These and other powers will be discussed further in the section on "Checks and Balances" p. 159.

The procedure for ushering a **bill**, that is, a piece of proposed legislation, through Congress is initially similar in the two houses in that bills must first go through an appropriate committee. Most bills are shelved there and never reach the floor of the House or the Senate, making it necessary for sponsors to reintroduce the bill in the next session. Committee action often entails lengthy public **hearings**, in which experts and interested parties are called in to appear before the committee to give

---

CONGRESS has two chambers (or 'houses')
- **the Senate**
  members called 'senators'
  100 senators, 2 from each state
  senators represent the whole state
  senators serve 6-year terms
  1/3 of senators elected every 2 years
  must approve major presidential appointments
  must approve major foreign policy steps
  more prestigious than the House
  normally unlimited debate
- **the House of Representatives** ('the House')
  members called '**congress**-men/women/people/persons' or 'representatives'
  435 representatives, each representing a district (some 450,000 voters)
  districts are reapportioned every 10 years
  representatives serve 2-year terms
  all representatives elected every 2 years
  all tax legislation must start in the House
  less prestigious than the Senate
  limited debate

CONGRESS has the power to
- pass laws (with the President's signature)
- tax
- appropriate money
- regulate commerce (interstate and foreign)
- declare war
- impeach the President

Figure 9.1 Thumbnail Sketch: The Legislative Branch.

their opinions about proposed legislation. Committee chairs, who receive their positions more or less on the basis of their seniority within the majority party in the chamber, have considerable sway in determining what legislation will be put to the vote.

After committee referral the two houses differ: the House, with its 435 members, has strict rules for **limiting debate**, thus placing substantial power in the hands of the Speaker of the House, while the Senate's 100 members enjoy **unlimited debate**, unless three fifths (formerly two thirds) of the senators present vote for **cloture** (that is, to close the debate, allowing only one hour for each speaker). This open forum makes it possible for senators to **filibuster** bills, that is, to delay their passage simply by talking them to death. Senators have been known to read aloud from the Bible or even from a telephone book for days until the sponsors of the offending bill promise to withdraw it in order to let the Senate get on with its other business.

THE EXECUTIVE BRANCH

Executive power is vested in the office of the **President of the United States**. The President has the dual role of being the **chief of state** and the **head of government**. The chief of state is the ceremonial head of the country, usually the role of the monarch in modern-day monarchies or of figurehead presidents in some republics. The President's role as head of government corresponds to that of the prime minister in parliamentary systems.

It must be stressed that the President is *not* chosen from the legislature as in parliamentary systems. He/she is the only figure who can be said to represent the whole country, having been chosen separately in nation-wide elections, whereas members of the Senate and the House represent only their states or their districts respectively. The President is elected for a term of four years and may be re-elected only once.[4] The length of the President's term in office is halfway between the terms of representatives

---

4   Franklin D. Roosevelt broke a long tradition of one- or two-term Presidencies by being elected four times, which was motivated in part by World War II. The 22nd Amendment added the two-term limit to the Constitution in 1951. Any person who has served more than two years of another President's term—after the elected President's death, for example—may be elected only once.

and senators, creating an overlapping pattern of continuity in government (see Figure 9.5 "Clockwork Government" p. 152).

As the chief executive, the President is given considerable discretion in executing laws passed by Congress. In order to carry out these laws, the President can issue **executive orders**, which have essentially the same effect as laws. Some executive orders have had far-reaching effects: the Indochina War was carried out by a series of Presidents via executive orders, there having been no formal declaration of war by Congress (see "Checks and Balances" p. 159), and so-called 'affirmative action' programs (see p. 80), whereby companies and institutions with federal government contracts must guarantee that they take positive steps to hire more women and minority people, were first created by President Kennedy's, and later President Nixon's, executive orders.

The President is the **commander in chief** of the armed forces of the United States. This role is not merely ceremonial; the President actually gives the highest generals and admirals their orders. This was clearly exemplified during the Korean War (another war which was fought without any formal declaration of war, although in this case under the flag of the United Nations). General Douglas MacArthur, who headed the predominantly American United Nations forces, wanted to follow up a successful repulsion of northern Korean and Chinese troops by attacking China. President Truman did not want to provoke a war with China. When the tremendously popular MacArthur persisted in his plans, Truman summarily removed him from his post. In 1990 the head of the US Air Force was similarly relieved of his duties in the Persian Gulf for having spoken too freely with journalists.

The various members of the President's **Cabinet** (see Figure 9.3 p. 151) are also responsible to him/her and are expected to implement his/her ideas. The Cabinet **secretaries** are appointed by the President but their appointments are subject to Senate approval. This approval is normally just a routine 'rubber stamp' on the President's nomination, but occasionally there is opposition. President Reagan's appointment of Edwin Meese to the post of Attorney General was delayed for nearly a year owing to close Senate scrutiny of Meese's financial dealings. Once installed, secretaries can be asked to appear before various congressional committees to explain administration policies in their respective fields.

THE PRESIDENT
- is not a member of Congress
- is the chief of state
- is the head of government
- is commander in chief of the armed forces
- is the 'chief legislator' because he/she
    - indirectly proposes many bills
    - considers all bills from Congress and
    - signs them into law or
    - vetoes them
- issues executive orders
- appoints Supreme Court justices and all other federal judges (with Senate approval)

THE PRESIDENT is elected
- by the whole country
- for 4 years

THE PRESIDENT is assisted by
- the Cabinet, with its departments (see Figure 9.3)
- the White House staff
- independent administrative agencies

Figure 9.2 Thumbnail Sketch: The Executive Branch.

Cabinet departments have subordinate administrative **agencies** or **bureaus** for regulating activities or providing services.

Many Presidents have placed more trust in more 'unofficial' advisers than in the Cabinet. Presidents organize their own **White House Staff** to suit themselves, sometimes granting considerable informal power to, say, the **chief of staff**, who might determine who is allowed to talk to the President, for example. Critics of such reliance on informal 'kitchen cabinets' (as they have been termed since the F. D. Roosevelt administration) maintain that too much power is placed in the hands of people who are neither elected nor subject to the congressional oversight that Cabinet secretaries are.

The President also appoints the boards of a number of **independent agencies** and **regulatory commissions** that have been created by Congress and thus straddle the fence between the executive and the legislative branches. The Interstate Commerce Commission and the Federal Communications Commission, which licenses broadcast and other media, are long-standing examples; the Environmental Protection Agency is a creation of the 1970s. Once these agency heads and board members have been approved by Congress, they serve staggered full terms of several years that overlap presidential terms, and they are not subject to removal from office (except for malfeasance). The regulatory commissions and independent agencies are independent of Cabinet departments and are expected to report to various committees of Congress. They have the power to issue **regulations** that have the force of law.

The heads of the fifteen **departments** (never called 'ministries') are called **secretaries** (never 'ministers'). Some of them may need 'translation' (=) into international terms:

Secretary of State (= Foreign Minister) – Department of State

Attorney General (= Minister of Justice) – Department of Justice

Secretary of the Treasury (= Finance Minister) – Department of the Treasury

Secretary of Defense – Department of Defense

Secretary of Commerce (= Minister of Trade) – Department of Commerce

Secretary of Health and Human Services – Department of Health and Human Services

Secretary of Education – Department of Education

Secretary of Housing and Urban Development – Department of Housing and Urban Development

Secretary of Labor – Department of Labor

Secretary of Transportation – Department of Transportation

Secretary of Agriculture – Department of Agriculture

Secretary of the Interior (= 'resources') – Department of the Interior

Secretary of Veterans' Affairs – Department of Veterans' Affairs

Secretary of Energy – Department of Energy

Secretary of Homeland Security – Department of Homeland Security

(Ambassador to the United Nations)

The heads of these departments are expected to do the bidding of the President, and they continue to serve only at the President's discretion. They are assisted by **under-secretaries**. The Vice-President usually attends cabinet meetings as well.

Figure 9.3 The President's Cabinet.

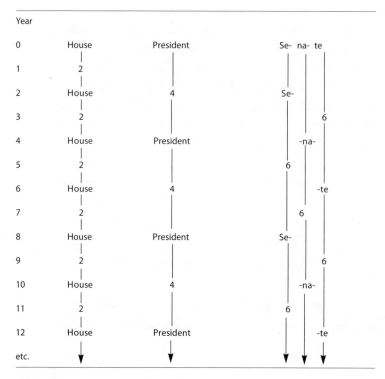

Year

0	House	President	Se- na- te
1	2		
2	House	4	Se-
3	2		6
4	House	President	-na-
5	2		6
6	House	4	-te
7	2		6
8	House	President	Se-
9	2		6
10	House	4	-na-
11	2		6
12	House	President	-te
etc.			

Figure 9.4 Staggered terms provide both continuity and renewal.

Figure 9.5 Clockwork Government: The 'machinery' of American government is driven by a 'gear' that takes two years to revolve once. Each revolution brings a newly elected House of Representatives and a partially (one third) new Senate. Every second revolution brings a presidential election.

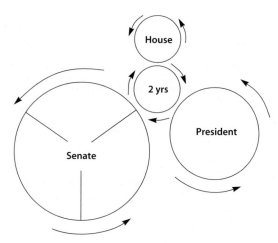

THE JUDICIAL BRANCH

The Constitution states:

> *The judicial power of the United States shall be vested in one supreme court, and in such inferior courts as the Congress from time to time may ordain and establish.*

All federal judges are appointed by the President and serve 'during good behaviour'[5], usually meaning for life. The fact that the judges cannot be removed from office—except for criminal behavior or malfeasance—makes them less vulnerable to political pressure than they would be if they had to depend upon politicians or the voters (as is the case in most local and state courts) for new mandates. Generally speaking federal judges have indeed lived up to the expectations placed upon them by the Constitution regarding independence. The federal courts are well known for making 'unpopular' decisions in the face of an enraged local majority of citizens: they supported voting rights for blacks in the South during the civil rights struggles of the 1960s and treaty rights for Indians in the Pacific Northwest in the 1970s, for example.

The main feature of this independent role for the courts lies in their power to interpret the Constitution. If the courts find that a certain law or executive order or regulation conflicts with the Constitution as the courts interpret it, then they can declare that rule unconstitutional and therefore 'null and void', that is, the law is no longer in effect. This prerogative has come to be called the **power of judicial review** and its exercise has rendered the American federal courts more powerful and prominent in the political arena than courts are in most other countries. This power is not exercised automatically, however: the law in question must have been challenged in the courts by someone who was victimized by i.

---

5   The American Constitution was written using a spelling system that was to become the British standard. American standard spelling, largely codified by Noah Webster, evolved in the first decades of the republic. The fact that the US and Britain were at war with each other twice in the half century between 1775 and 1825 influenced both countries in their adoption of national spelling standards.

When it comes to interpreting the Constitution, a distinction is traditionally made between **loose constructionists** and **strict constructionists**. The former favor a 'loose' or 'free' interpretation of the document, emphasizing the **spirit** of what it says. The latter maintain that the Constitution should be followed more or less to the **letter** and not distorted to mean things it does not expressly state.

Since there is no mention of education in the Constitution, for example, strict constructionists feel that the federal government has no power to get involved in schooling; schools are the domain of the states alone. Indeed the federal government did not even have a separate Department of Education until 1979, when one was carved out of the former Department of Health, Education, and Welfare. President Reagan, a strict constructionist, promised to dismantle President Carter's new Department of Education when he was elected in 1980, but never acted on the promise. Loose constructionists argue that universal education was simply not a part of the worldview of those who wrote the Constitution

---

THE **SUPREME** COURT
- was created by the Constitution
- has nine justices
  - a chief justice
  - eight associate justices
  - number of justices decided by Congress
  - appointed for life by the President (with Senate approval)
  - can be impeached by Congress
- reviews the 'constitutionality' of laws and executive orders when they are challenged

THE **INFERIOR** COURTS are
- 94 District Courts
- 13 Courts of Appeals
- created by Congress, with judges appointed by the President (with Senate approval)

ALL FEDERAL COURTS hear cases involving
- federal law
- state laws whose constitutionality is challenged
- the United States
- two separate states
- citizens of different states

Figure 9.6 Thumbnail Sketch: The Judicial Branch.*

and that it is natural for a modern-day central government to take some responsibility for the education of its citizens.

Advocates of a strict interpretation of the Constitution point to the express guarantee of 'the right of the people to keep and bear arms' in the Bill of Rights and defend the free sale of handguns and other weapons in modern America. Loose constructionists claim that this part of the Constitution must also be seen against the historical background in which it was conceived, namely a primarily rural 18th-century society which had just gone through a revolutionary struggle against a colonial power that had forbidden them to arm themselves. This interpretive context is supported by the words leading up to the clause so often quoted by proponents of the free sale of guns:

> A well-regulated militia, being necessary to the security of a free State, *the right of the people to keep and bear arms, shall not be infringed.* (Second Amendment)

The loose constructionists (and proponents of strong regulation of firearms) argue that the conditions of the late 20th century cannot be compared to those of the 18th century, and thus they do not take the Constitution literally on this point. The amendment is seen as referring to a state-organized militia, not an armed citizenry. In 2008 the Supreme Court decided that gun laws in Washington, D.C., were too far reaching and, for the first time, clearly stated that the Second Amendment does guarantee individuals the right to bear arms. At the same time, their decision left leeway for state and local governments to legislate and enforce 'reasonable' restrictions.

Another example: during the early part of the 1960s Civil Rights Movement, strict constructionists maintained that the federal government had no power to force, say, a private restaurant-owner to serve black customers. The Constitution prohibited discrimination, but only 'state action', that is, only discrimination practiced by a state was expressly forbidden, and it was assumed that individuals were free to make racial distinctions in business. In order to legislate against racial discrimination in restaurants, etc., Congress was forced instead to 'stretch' (with the tacit approval of the Supreme Court) one of the powers expressly given to it by the Constitution—the power to regulate interstate commerce. Any businessperson who benefited from interstate commerce (say, by buying meat that originated in another state) was obliged by new federal laws not to discriminate between races in providing services to the public.

The debate between loose and strict interpretations of the Constitution is of course central to the Supreme Court's power of judicial review. It is ironic that this extensive power is in fact not explicitly mentioned in the Constitution (although it was anticipated and discussed by the authors of the document). Instead, it was 'interpreted' by the Supreme Court itself as being essential to its role. Chief Justice John Marshall wrote in an opinion (decision) in 1803 that it is 'the province and duty of the judicial department to say what the law is'. Just a few additional examples from the 20th century will demonstrate how important the ramifications of this statement are.

During the Depression, when Franklin D. Roosevelt tried to 'prime' the national economy by involving the federal government in various business schemes and employment programs, the Supreme Court—which then consisted of mostly conservative members—ruled that one project after another was unconstitutional: the government had no formal power to get directly involved in the economy. Roosevelt had to threaten to ask Congress to change the construction of the Supreme Court (see p. 169) before the Court came around to allowing some government activism in the economy.

In 1954 the Supreme Court reversed an earlier decision (from 1896) that it was acceptable under the Constitution to provide separate schools for black children, as long as those schools were 'equal' to those for white children. The famous *Brown vs. Board of Education* (of Topeka, Kansas) decision stated that separate schools were by definition 'not equal' and thereby paved the way for the Civil Rights Movement of the 1960s. Obviously this decision was in response to decades of efforts on the part of blacks to improve their situation, and it should thus not be seen as the 'beginning' of a movement. Nonetheless the decision was the first clear response from the federal authorities in this question, and it should be noted that the Court took its stand a decade before Congress and the President did so. In 2008 a Supreme Court decision banned the use of race in determining who should attend which schools, based on cases in

Louisville, Kentucky, and Seattle, Washington. This is seen by many as putting an end to integration efforts, including busing children to non-neighborhood schools, that started with the 1954 Brown decision.

In 1973 the Supreme Court declared that no state could pass a law which deprived a woman of the right to have an abortion. In the *Roe vs. Wade* decision the Court loosely interpreted the Constitution as guaranteeing a right to 'privacy' which included the right for a woman to decide about her own body (thus assuming the embryo to be a part of the mother's body). On the other hand, a 1977 decision held that no state or local authority was required to provide abortion service free of charge, and a 1991 decision allowed authorities to withhold public funding from family-planning clinics that recommended or informed women about abortion (see also p. 118 ff.).

These few examples indicate some of the scope of the power of judicial review. It should be emphasized, however, that neither the Supreme Court nor the inferior courts review all legislation passed by Congress and the President. Judicial review is exercised only if a law is challenged in the courts, either by direct petition to the courts by someone affected by the law or in connection with a case where someone is arrested for breaking the law and that person's case makes its way through the court system, which we now turn to.

The trial court of the **first instance** or of **original jurisdiction** in the federal court system is called a **district court**. There are 94 districts throughout the country, populous states having more than one district, and populous districts having up to twenty-four judges. Cases are usually heard by a single judge in district courts, although for some questions they are required to sit in a 'commission' of three.

Decisions made by the district courts may be appealed to one of thirteen **courts of appeal**s, in eleven 'circuits' distributed among the states, one circuit for Washington, DC, and one 'Federal Circuit'. A court of appeals reviews the procedure and judgment of the original trial court and may reverse the decision if it is found to be faulty. Normally a panel of three judges hears cases, but sometimes a full court of nine judges is required to consider an issue.

In theory all cases heard by these appellate courts can be reviewed by the **Supreme Court**, with its **nine justices**, the **Chief Justice of the United**

States[6] and **eight associate justices**. But since nearly all decisions (the exception being 'emergency' stays of execution, etc.) are taken by the whole Court, it is in practice impossible for the justices to pass judgment on more than a tiny fraction of the cases that are appealed to it. In a sense, a refusal to hear a case does represent a decision of sorts, even though the Supreme Court may merely uphold the judgment of the court of appeals. The job of sifting through thousands of cases to find matters especially worthy of its attention represents a major part of the Court's work, but it has thus far not been considered fair to set up, say, a separate court to sift through the cases, as that would mean petitioners would be denied the right at least to have their hearing rejected by the highest Court itself.

The nine justices vote on each decision. One member of the majority is chosen to write the Court's **opinion**. Other members of the majority may wish to write separate **concurring opinions**, that is, they agree with the Court's decision but wish to emphasize some other aspect of the case. Any number of members of the minority may write **dissenting opinions** to explain why they disagree with the Court's official decision. The reasoning in a dissenting opinion sometimes resurfaces in the court decisions of another generation.

The **jurisdiction** (sphere of power) of the **inferior** federal courts is limited to federal **statutes** (written laws, not **common law** traditions), **executive orders**, and **regulations** and to aspects of state laws and regulations (or local ordinances) whose constitutionality is challenged by a citizen. Also, if two states are in conflict with each other, the 'neutral' federal courts will settle the dispute. No private citizen of one state may sue another state in a federal court, however. This jurisdiction was originally included in the Constitution but was canceled by the eleventh amendment to the Constitution (that is, the first amendment after the Bill of Rights).

Having presented the three branches of American government in broad strokes, we now turn to a schematic review of how the separation of powers was designed to work so as to avoid placing too much power in too few hands.

---

6 This is the official title. In everyday speech people often use the term **Chief Justice of the Supreme Court**.

CHAPTER 10

Checks and Balances

The 'inefficiency' of American government mentioned above (p. 143) is guaranteed by what is commonly referred to as the **system of checks and balances**. Most of the 'checks', used here in the sense of 'limits' or 'constraints', were deliberately written into the Constitution, but some have merely evolved as a part of an 'unwritten constitution' of tradition. The following series of schematic diagrams should help clarify the main features of the system.

The most powerful tool Congress has, and one of the most important 'checks' on the power of the President, is the power to **appropriate** money or, in other words, to set aside money for some specific purpose. This legislative power is of course essential to all government, since very little can be carried out without money to pay people for their services or products. For every **fiscal year** (from Oct. 1 to Sept. 30) Congress receives a proposed **budget** from the President, based on the perceived needs of the various departments of the administration and channeled through the President's **Office of Management and Budget**.

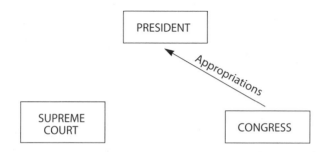

Figure 10.1 Checks and Balances: Appropriations.

There then ensues a battle for funds to finance various governmental programs, a battle referred to as the 'politics of appropriations'. Since the mid 1970s the Senate and House Budget Committees have been aided in their review of the administration's needs by a coordinating staff, the **Congressional Budget Office**. Like any law, the annual budget must be approved by both houses of Congress, the final draft being worked out in a **conference committee**, that is, by a 'joint' committee representing both houses of Congress, charged with reaching a compromise between the two versions of the bill. The President can then either accept or reject the whole bill based on his/her original budget proposal, which by then has usually been revised beyond recognition. Having signed the bill into law, the President must then restrict expenditures in the executive branch to those fields specified by the budget (see Figure 10.5 "Flowchart: The Law-Making Process" p. 166). Disagreement over spending in connection with the 1996 budget led to the federal government being largely closed down on and off for a couple of months, while President Bill Clinton and the Republican-dominated 104th Congress blamed each other for the budgetless situation (emergency measures created temporary funds to pay federal employees). The general public placed the blame squarely with Congress and voted accordingly in the 1996 elections.

Apart from this broad congressional control over the purse strings, Congress occasionally flexes its muscles on specific issues by limiting appropriations. The last years of the Indochina War provide a good example of this. Congress, peeved at the lack of progress toward peace and tired of being ignored in this major arena of foreign policy, expressly forbade President Nixon to spend any money for the bombing of Cambodia after a specific date. The President turned the tables on Congress by 'impounding' (putting aside, refusing to spend) money appropriated by Congress for civilian programs he felt were unnecessary. Congress turned to the Supreme Court and received a ruling that, once funds had been allocated by law for a certain end, the President was bound by his constitutional duty as the chief executive to carry out the wishes of Congress.

Another major check on the power of the President is the Senate's power of **advice and consent**. This means that the President is obliged to ask for the advice and consent of the Senate (not the House) on all major **appointments** and major **foreign policy** decisions he/she makes.

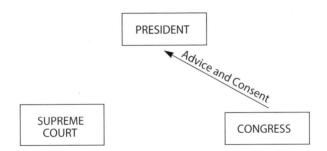

Figure 10.2 Checks and Balances: Advice and Consent.

As the chief executive, the President appoints thousands of people to administer governmental regulations and services. The most important of these appointments, notably the members of the President's Cabinet, new justices of the Supreme Court to replace deceased or retiring members, other federal judges, and members of administrative or regulatory agencies, are subject to the approval of the Senate. Controversial appointments are reviewed—and occasionally stopped—by the Senate after extensive public hearings have been held before a committee. Such a procedure is unnecessary, however, for the many routine appointments the President makes, so a tradition of **senatorial courtesy** has developed. The two senators from the home state of the nominee are expected to take a stand first, based on their supposed knowledge of the person's background, and the whole Senate then usually pays these two senators the 'courtesy' of agreeing with them. The system expedites routine appointments and enhances the influence of individual senators in their home states and in various bargaining situations.

Also as the chief executive, the President is basically in charge of foreign relations, but for major decisions, such as treaties, he/she is expected to ask the Senate to advise him/her. The classic example of the power of the Senate to influence foreign policy is the refusal by a Republican-dominated Senate to ratify the charter of the League of Nations, which was the brainchild of President Woodrow Wilson (a Democrat) to consolidate the Versailles Peace Treaty, which ended World War I. It is argued that the United States would have become a key member of the League if Wilson had only involved the rival Senate Republicans earlier in the peace process.

To declare war, the President must turn to **both** houses of Congress for their approval. The last time this was done was on December 8, 1941, when President F. D. Roosevelt asked a joint session of Congress for a declaration of war against Japan and Germany. Since then the United States has been overtly involved in two major conflicts, in Korea and in Indochina, but without any declaration of war. In the case of Korea (early 1950s), US military action was undertaken under the auspices and flag of the United Nations. In Indochina (Vietnam, Laos, Cambodia—early 1960s to 1975), military intervention was justified by a series of Presidents as being necessary for the protection of American interests at home and abroad and was undertaken by the Presidents in their role as commander in chief of the armed forces. Such extensive military action abroad without the consent of Congress in the form of a declaration of war has of course been challenged as unconstitutional, and Congress has attempted to curtail the freedom of Presidents to send troops abroad. The **War Powers Resolution of 1973** requires that Congress be informed within forty-eight hours if the President sends American troops into action abroad and that such troops may not be used for more than sixty to ninety days without a declaration of war or some other form of congressional authorization. This resolution has turned out to have little effect, however: the 'triggering' of its restrictive provisions lies with the President, and so far no President has deemed it necessary to inform Congress of military actions abroad, although many have in fact taken place. Furthermore, the Constitution does not give Congress the power to pass legislation without submitting it to the President, so there is really no force behind the threat of sanctions against the President for not complying with the War Powers Resolution. As a result, the 1973 resolution is virtually dead. Be that as it may, military technology has indeed rendered the Constitution obsolete in terms of 'declared' wars: the President can hardly be expected to convene a joint session of Congress before reacting to a nuclear attack.

Following the September 11, 2001, terrorist attacks against the World Trade Center in New York and against the Pentagon, Congress was quick to appropriate billions of dollars to enable President George W. Bush to take military and other measures to retaliate against the terrorists and to ensure the future security of the country. He immediately created a new Cabinet-level department, the Department of Homeland Security. His invasion of Iraq in 2003 was cast in terms of national security and carried out with the overwhelming support of both houses of Congress, although there was no declaration of war as such.

The President's major countervailing power in the legislative process is the power of the **veto**. The President must **sign** any proposed legislation before it becomes law, and his failure or refusal to do so can thus stop any bill (but see the next item about how Congress can overcome this obstacle). In effect, this means that the President can be seen as having a major 'legislative' role in the government, even though he is not a member of Congress and normally appears on the floor of Congress only once a year (to report on the **State of the Union**). His/her 'vote' is strong enough to overturn majority decisions of both houses of Congress.

It might be added here that much legislation also originates with the President, although the actual initiation of concrete bills is done by senators and representatives who support the President's policies. This informal but *de facto* initiation of much legislation by the President, together with the power of the veto, makes the **chief executive** the nation's **chief legislator**.

If the President is very much against a bill passed by Congress, he/she actively returns it to the Capitol with his/her written veto. If the President simply does not wish to be associated with a bill but does not feel that it is worthwhile to prevent it from becoming law, he/she can demonstrate this by using a so-called **pocket veto**. This means that he/she simply lets it lie on the desk for ten days without signing it or vetoing it, in which case it

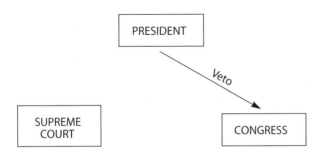

Figure 10.3 Checks and Balances: Presidential Veto.

becomes law without the President's signature (unless Congress should happen to adjourn during this ten-day period, whereupon the bill 'dies').

The President does not have a so-called **line-item veto** but rather a **blanket veto** only. This means that the President has to either accept or reject a bill in its entirety as it appears before him/her and is not been able to pick and choose among the various items included in it. Congress takes advantage of this limitation by appending so-called **riders**—nowadays usually referred to as '**earmarks**'—to bills, that is, pieces of legislation that are not necessarily related to other parts of a bill. This is common despite the fact that the House of Representatives has a rule that requires riders to be 'germane' (relevant) to the legislation. Influential members of Congress see to it that their pet projects are included as riders to bills favored by the President, leaving the latter with the choice of either approving their proposal or rejecting his own. Although the instrument of the President's blanket veto has long been seen as blunt to the point of being undemocratic, its tactical exploitation was so much a part of practical politicking in Washington that it was long considered unrealistic to expect Congress to change it into a line-item veto.

Yet, surprisingly, the 104th Congress passed legislation in 1996, to take effect with the 105th Congress in 1997, granting the President a choice among items in any spending bill placed before him/her for approval or a veto, in other words, a line-item veto. The law stipulated that within five days of having signed a spending bill into law, the President must notify Congress that certain items in the bill are unacceptable. He/she could not change figures, only reject them outright. Congress could then pass a new bill proposing those figures. If the President vetoed the new bill, then Congress needs to achieve a two-thirds majority to override the President's veto, just as in any other legislation. A similar power has been enjoyed by state governors in almost all states for years. The main effect was expected to be a shift toward less spending. However, as it came into force in early 1997, a group of six prominent senators and representatives challenged the constitutionality of the law in the federal courts, and a federal district judge declared the line-item veto unconstitutional in April 1997, thus forbidding its implementation. Upon appeal, however, the Supreme Court rejected the district court's finding, not because of any disagreement with the argumentation but rather because the six legislators who filed the suit were not themselves injured by the new law and therefore could not bring action. Soon afterwards the law was jointly challenged by state governments and business interests that claimed to have lost federal money as a result of President Clinton's 'unconstitutional' use of the line-item veto. The Supreme Court indeed agreed with the claimants that the new law represented a major shift in the balance of power between the executive and legislative branches as laid down in the Constitution. The short-lived line-item veto was thus declared unconstitutional and the blanket veto now prevails once again. The fate of these two legal challenges to the law offers an illustrative example of how judicial review works in practice.

Instead of vetoing bills, President George W. Bush made uniquely frequent use of a previously little known power presidents have occasionally used in the past. He issued 'signing statements' that outline the parts of the law that he does not feel obligated to execute. This is a type of statement that some presidents before him have made, but President Bush is the only president who used it well over a thousand times, most controversially in signing a bill from Congress forbidding the use of torture by the FBI and CIA, etc. He selected parts of this bill that he argued did not need to be honored by the administration and US intelligence agencies. These signing statements were seen as an underhanded attempt to expand the power of the executive over the legislative branch and went largely unnoticed until investigative journalist Charlie Savage of the *Boston Globe* drew attention to them in a book, which was awarded the 2007 Pulitzer Prize.

If the President returns a bill to Congress with a veto on it, the legislature has the power to **override** the President's veto by re-passing the legislation by a **two-thirds** majority in both houses. If such a majority can be mustered, the bill becomes law without the President's signature. However, since there is very little party discipline in Congress, meaning that individual senators and representatives vote as they like on each issue, it is usually extremely difficult to get two thirds of both houses of Congress to agree on anything, and vetoes are not often overridden. Nevertheless, before rejecting a bill, the President must consider the risk of being humiliated politically by having the veto overturned by a united Congress.

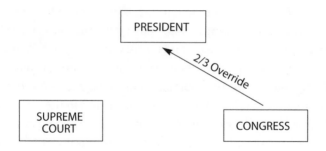

Figure 10.4 Checks and Balances: Congressional Override.

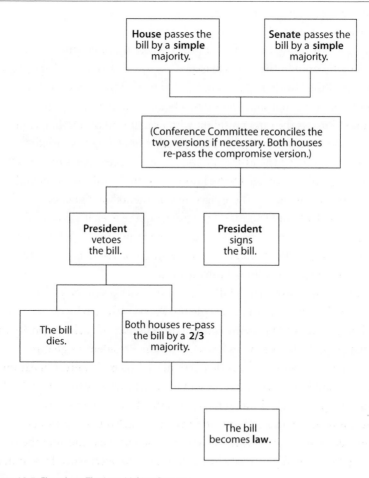

Figure 10.5 Flowchart: The Law-Making Process.

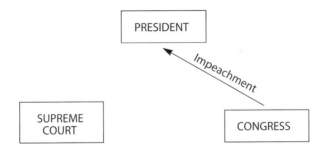

Figure 10.6 Checks and Balances: Impeachment of the President.

The Congress has the power to **impeach** the President. To 'impeach' does **not** mean 'to remove from office' but rather 'to place on trial' with the aim of determining whether or not the person should be removed from office. The President may be impeached for 'treason, bribery, or other high crimes or misdemeanors'. In other words, the President should not be put on trial or removed from office for political reasons; the President's job is not held merely at the discretion of Congress, and he/she is **not** subject to the **vote of confidenc**e that typifies parliamentarian democracy. But should the President be suspected of some serious form of malfeasance of office, he/she may be impeached by Congress according to the following procedure:

> Charges are brought by the **House of Representatives**, upon the recommendation of its **Judicial Committee** or a special *ad hoc* committee ('for that purpose'). If the House decides to prosecute, the President is tried by the **House** before the **Senate**, which must achieve a two-thirds majority of those Senators present to remove the President from office. The **Chief Justice** of the United States (i.e., of the Supreme Court) presides over the trial. Having been removed by impeachment does not imply that the President will not have to answer for any criminal actions before a federal court as well.

There have been only three impeachment processes involving Presidents. In the first of these, the whole process was completed, but the grounds for impeachment must be said to have been 'political' rather than 'criminal'. After the Civil War, President Andrew Johnson, a Southern Democrat loyal to the Union who had served as Vice-President under Abraham

Lincoln, was impeached by an opposition of 'radical Republicans' because of his conciliatory attitude toward the leaders of the recent rebellion in the South. Johnson won his impeachment by a single vote in the Senate and stayed on as President.

In the second example, the impeachment process was never carried through, although this time the President would in all probability have been removed from office for 'criminal' behavior. President Nixon was probably involved in trying to cover up the scandal in which people employed by members of the committee for his re-election were caught breaking into the offices of the Democratic Party at the Watergate Hotel and Convention Center in Washington in 1972. After weeks of hearings, more and more evidence pointed to the complicity of the President, and impeachment proceedings were initiated. When the House Judiciary Committee voted to recommend to the full House that charges be brought against the President in August 1974, he was persuaded to resign, realizing that his chances of winning an impeachment before the Senate were minimal. In a controversial move, his successor, President Gerald Ford, gave him a Presidential pardon from further prosecution by the regular criminal courts.

In the recent third instance, President Bill Clinton was impeached for his handling of the scandal arising from his sexual liaison with White House intern Monica Lewinsky. Two articles of impeachment were brought by the House before the Senate, one for perjury (lying) before a grand jury investigating his misconduct and one for obstructing the investigation. Chief Justice William Rehnquist presided over the proceedings. On the charge of perjury, 55 senators voted to acquit and 45 to convict (with 10 Republicans joining the Democrats); on the charge of obstruction of justice, the vote was 50–50 (with 5 Republicans joining the Democrats). In neither case was the necessary two-thirds majority reached, so President Clinton was acquitted. While most senators believed the President had committed both acts, the majority also believed that the behavior was to some extent understandable under the circumstances and was not in fact grave enough to warrant removal from office. A subsequent motion in the Senate to censure the President for 'shameful, reckless, and indefensible behavior' put forward by Democratic Senator Dianne Feinstein of California was defeated by a 56–43 vote.

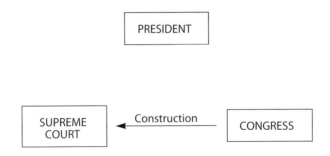

Figure 10.7 Checks and Balances: Construction of the Federal Court System.

It should be stressed that the President does not normally have to worry about being impeached. Rather, the power of impeachment is a vehicle for handling extraordinary situations of power abuse or criminality.

Turning to the relationship between Congress and the Supreme Court, we find that Congress has the power to determine the construction of the Court (and its inferior courts). Even though the number of justices has ranged from five to ten, the number has remained stable at nine since 1869. In theory, however, Congress can decide to change that number at any time, thus making it possible, for example, for a President to 'pack' the Court with justices of his own liking. As mentioned above (p. 156), President Franklin D. Roosevelt was constantly thwarted by a conservative Supreme Court in his efforts to involve the government in stimulating the economy during the Great Depression. Roosevelt had elaborate plans to get a presumably sympathetic Congress to allow him to appoint up to six new judges, one to match each justice over the age of seventy who did not retire after ten years on the bench[1]. As it turned out, Congress was reluctant to follow through with the 'packing' plan, feeling that it meant 'tampering' with the constitutional system.

---

1   Supreme Court justices have a way of hanging on into their eighties and nineties,
    sometimes to the disgruntlement of Presidents waiting to make new appointments.
    During the Gerald Ford administration in the mid 1970s, the ailing near-octogenarian
    Justice William O. Douglas, a liberal appointed by Roosevelt in 1939, was quoted as
    saying from his hospital bed that he refused either to retire or to die as long as Ford,
    a Republican, was President.

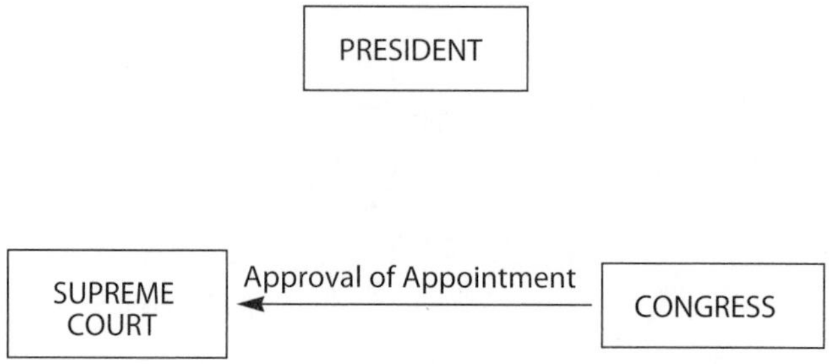

PRESIDENT

SUPREME COURT ← Approval of Appointment — CONGRESS

Figure 10.8 Checks and Balances: Senate Approval of Judicial Appointments.

Changes of heart on the part of the Court regarding legislation for economic recovery soon rendered the plan unnecessary anyway, and the number of justices remained at nine.

As mentioned elsewhere, the Congress has some say in who will sit on the Supreme Court bench, in that nominations made by the President must be **approved** by the Senate. Normally this is just a 'rubber stamp' if the nominee is basically competent, but the Senate occasionally balks at approving appointees who are deemed to be too 'extreme' in their politics. For such reasons, President Nixon had to withdraw the names of two nominees before the Senate gave their blessing to Justice William Rehnquist in the early 1970s. Rehnquist himself faced considerable opposition from civil rights groups in Senate hearings to confirm his promotion to Chief Justice by President Ronald Reagan in 1986. A year later appeals judge Robert Bork, a prominent legal scholar appointed by Reagan, was also thoroughly and publicly grilled about what many liberals felt were 'extreme' views that would 'upset the balance' of the Court. In the end, Reagan was forced to withdraw his nomination, choosing the less conservative Anthony Kennedy instead.

With this experience in recent memory, when he had his first opportunity to nominate a new justice in 1990, President George H. W. Bush went out of his way to find a candidate whose opinions were largely unknown. David Souter was coached by the White House for days on how to keep a low profile on issues like abortion. The strategy won him the Senate's confirmation and a seat on the Supreme Court.

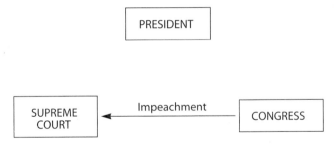

Figure 10.9 Checks and Balances: Impeachment of Justices and Judges.

President George H. W. Bush's next appointment, Clarence Thomas, a conservative African-American federal judge, led to highly publicized hearings involving charges from a former associate, Anita Hill, regarding alleged sexual misconduct on the part of Judge Thomas a few years earlier. In the end the Senate chose to approve the nominee.

Just as the President may be impeached by the Congress, so may justices of the Supreme Court (indeed, all civil officials, except members of Congress) be removed from office by **impeachment**. There have been about a dozen impeachments throughout history, five of them leading to the removal of the official. In all five cases, the person removed was a judge (most recently, in 1986, a district judge who was serving a prison sentence for tax evasion was removed by impeachment because he had refused to resign and continued to draw his salary in prison). Supreme Court justices are generally held in high repute by the citizenry, and if there is even a hint of any wrong-doing, as in the case of Justice Abe Fortas in the 1960s, the justice involved is expected to resign (as Fortas did) in order not to tarnish the reputation of the Court.

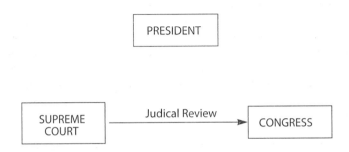

Figure 10.10 Checks and Balances: Judicial Review of Legislation.

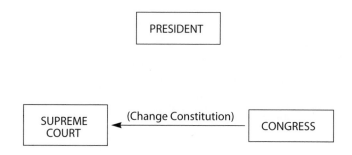

Figure 10.11 Checks and Balances: Constitutional Amendment.

The single countervailing 'arrow' of power aimed at Congress by the Supreme Court is the comprehensive power of **judicial review.** This has already been discussed above (p. 153 ff.), so there is no need to go through it again here, except to underscore once again the wide-ranging political consequences Supreme Court decisions may have, placing the Court close to the other two branches in influence. It should also be reiterated that this review of laws by the courts is not an 'automatic' part of the legislative process. Instead, cases challenging specific laws must be brought before the courts for a decision about their constitutionality.

This arrow in fig 10.11 is within parentheses because it represents a power that only partially resides with Congress. If the members of Congress find that the Supreme Court has interpreted the Constitution in a way which disagrees with their own fundamental views (or if they so wish for any other reason, of course), then Congress can initiate the process of **amending the Constitution** as follows:

> A majority of **two thirds of both houses** of Congress must pass the amendment. (Amendments may also be initiated by **two thirds** of the **states**, although this has never been done.) The proposed amendment is then sent out to the fifty states for consideration. As soon as **three quarters** of the states (thirty-eight of them) have **ratified** the proposed amendment, either by a popular **referendum** or, usually, by a vote in the **state legislature**, it becomes a part of the Constitution. This ratification must usually be completed within a stipulated period of time (typically seven years).

Looking at the relationship between the Supreme Court and the President, we find that we have already touched on all of the 'checks' they have on

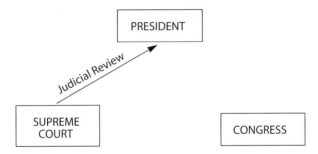

Figure 10.12 Checks and Balances: Judicial Review of Executive Orders.

each other's power. The power of **judicial review** applies to **executive orders** issued by the President as well as to legislation passed by Congress (and the President). One of the most controversial executive orders ever issued was Franklin D. Roosevelt's order at the beginning of World War II to round up all Japanese Americans on the west coast and place them in internment camps. Some 120,000 people of Japanese descent, many of them American citizens, lived in these camps for the duration of the war and were deprived of their jobs and property in the purported 'national interest'. (There was no corresponding rounding up of German Americans, who were, of course, less 'visible'. On the other hand, German Americans were often treated very harshly by other Americans during the First World War.) After the war this executive order was challenged in the courts, and the Supreme Court found that the action was in fact permissible in a time of crisis like war. It was also argued that the internment was for the 'protection' of the Japanese Americans. Much later, however, in the mid 1980s, many of these families, or their offspring, successfully sued the federal government before the Court and received some compensation for their wartime hardships.

The Supreme Court played an important role in the handling of the Watergate scandal. President Nixon claimed that the secrecy of tapes of White House discussions he had ordered was protected by so-called **executive privilege**, and he therefore refused to let Congress listen to them. Despite the fact that three of the justices had been appointed by Nixon himself, the Supreme Court ordered the President to give Congress access to the tapes. Nixon was forced to resign soon after the tapes were made public.

Judicial review of presidential executive orders came into play in connection with President George W. Bush's war on terrorism in the wake of the September 11, 2001 attacks on New York and Washington. When US and other armed forces attacked the Taliban in Afghanistan in pursuit of Osama bin Laden and his followers, they took hundreds of "enemy combatants" there and elsewhere prisoner and transported all of them to an internment camp at Guantanamo Bay, an American enclave in Cuba. These prisoners, including some US citizens, were held with no rights whatsoever, since President Bush declared that they were not traditional prisoners of war. They were not on American soil and not protected under US law or even by the international Geneva Conventions. The prisoners were held for several years without charge.

In June 2004 the US Supreme Court pronounced that these prisoners indeed had a right to be represented by attorneys and to take their cases before US courts, but, though some prisoners were released and returned to other countries during the second George W. Bush administration, very few of the remaining majority were charged and tried in court. The Obama administration is determined to close the Guantánamo facility, but is facing great difficulties in deciding what to do with some of the prisoners.

It has already been mentioned that the President **appoints** justices of the Supreme Court (and all other federal judges) with the consent of the Senate. Yet this does not necessarily mean that the President can expect the Court to do his/her bidding. In the first place, few Presidents ever have the opportunity to name more than one or two justices, if any, during their terms of office.

Second, **appointment for life** tends to make people independent—even of the person who put them in power. The best example of this is to be found in President Eisenhower's appointment of Earl Warren to be Chief Justice in 1953. The conservative Eisenhower was sure he had found a kindred spirit in the conservative former governor of California, but the President was shocked to find that he had in fact appointed a 'flaming liberal' who headed the most 'activist' court in American history, establishing the environment for the entire Civil Rights Movement and its

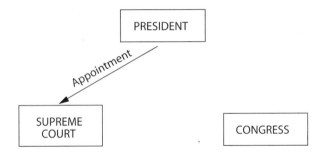

Figure 10.13 Checks and Balances: Presidential Appointment of Justices and Judges.

consequent reforms of the 1960s, among other things. Eisenhower later confided that the appointment of Chief Justice Earl Warren, who served until 1969, was one of the greatest mistakes he had ever made as President. During Warren's long tenure on the Court, ultra-conservative groups regularly campaigned (in the form of newspaper ads and roadside billboards, for example) for his impeachment as an 'un-American traitor', but to no avail.

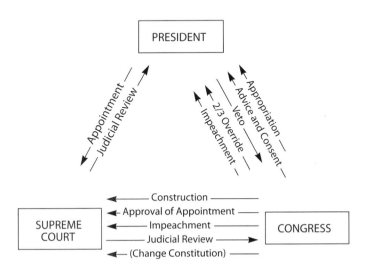

Figure 10.14 Review Chart: The System of Checks and Balances.

A mere six weeks after the September 11, 2001 terrorist attacks on New York and Washington, Congress overwhelmingly passed the **USA PATRIOT Act**, granting the President unprecedented powers to combat terrorism in the United States and abroad. The act was passed virtually without debate in a surge of patriotism, and most senators and representatives had not even read the 342-page bill that was enacted into law. Critics, including many senators and representatives after the initial rush of patriotism wore off, charge that the legislation violates basic civil rights and liberties guaranteed by the US Constitution and is edging the US toward a police state. Many go so far as to maintain that, by undercutting civil liberties, the act paradoxically does greater damage to the United States as a democratic nation than the September 11 terrorist attacks did. The federal courts have been a battleground for challenges to the constitutionality of the act's provisions and will be for some time to come, and the act will continue to put the system of checks and balances to the test. The act was largely renewed in the spring of 2006, but many of its key provisions are expected to be defused or reversed by President Barack Obama and the Democratic majorities in both houses of Congress.

CHAPTER 11

US Presidential
vs. Parliamentary Systems

With this sketch of the American system of separation of powers and its network of checks and balances in mind, it might be worthwhile to try to sum up the basic differences between this system and the parliamentary form of government familiar to Europeans and citizens of many other countries. Which is more efficient? Does either system lend itself to abuse of power more readily than the other? In order to address these questions we should first look at a schematic picture of the **executive branch** in each system:

In the American system, the President is clearly the central figure, and his/her Cabinet secretaries are expected to be largely extensions of the President. In parliamentary governments, the **prime minister** is usually seen more as a member of a 'team', the *primus inter pares* or 'first among

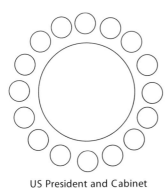

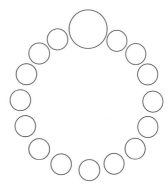

US President and Cabinet   Parliamentary Government

Figure 11.1 Executive Power.

equals'. Though each minister puts forward the various proposals most closely related to his/her domain, the whole government (or cabinet) is seen as being responsible for the decisions taken by it. The prime minister dominates the picture in varying degrees and is usually seen as being ultimately responsible for reshuffling or replacing the members of the government to accommodate new situations, always with an eye to the balance of power among the parties in parliament. It is not unusual for shifting coalitions to result in, say, a foreign minister taking over as prime minister.

Needless to say, such 'musical-chairs' situations are out of the question in the American system. The President is **the boss** and remains so throughout his/her term of office. The administration's policy either originates with the President or is at least made to appear to do so. Should any Cabinet secretary publicly launch an idea contrary to the wishes of the President, that secretary will usually be given a bawling out and/or be dismissed. Such decisions are not matters for the whole Cabinet to discuss: they are the President's business.

Thus far, the US President comes off as a more powerful figure, 'the boss' with his/her lackeys as opposed to 'the team and its leader' of the parliamentary set up. But if we add the legislative 'branch' of the parliamentary government, we get the following picture:

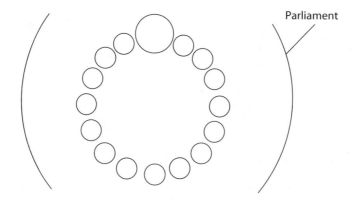

Figure 11.2 Parliamentary Executive a Creation of Parliament.

The cardinal principle of this type of government is that the cabinet is supposed to **reflect the current balance of power** between the parties in the parliament. The government is chosen from parliament to be its executive arm. This means that a parliament made up of many small parties will have to establish more or less temporary **coalitions** or **minority governments**, rendering the executive relatively weak (a situation typical of Italy, for example). Since the government is designed to reflect the wishes of the legislature, governments that fail to rally support for major legislation or suffer a **vote of no confidence** are expected to step down and make way for a new configuration. A government may also see a chance to improve its position in parliament by calling a new election (not possible in the US). On the other hand, if one party has a solid majority in the parliament, then the government can consist of members of that party alone, and this government can theoretically do anything it wants, relying on its party to support it in the legislature (although in practice attempts at creating a consensus are common, of course). While it might be argued that this constitutes 'unlimited' power, it can be countered that any party that can muster so strong a majority *should* be allowed to do more or less as it pleases when it assumes power; after all, it merely reflects the will of the majority of the people.

In contrast, the American picture looks like this with the legislative branch added:

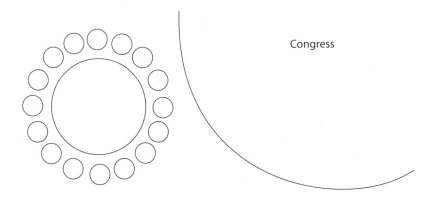

Figure 11.3 US President Elected Separately from Congress.

As the President is not a member of the Congress but rather is elected separately by the 'whole' nation, a fundamental rivalry is expected to prevail between the executive and legislative branches. Within the executive branch alone, the President is indeed more powerful than the typical prime minister, but if we take into consideration the separate role of the legislature, the President's power is placed in perspective. The President cannot simply rely on Congress passing bills he/she wishes to see enacted, not even if both chambers of Congress happen to be dominated by members of the President's party. This perennial rivalry is not only a consequence of the constitutional checks-and-balances system; it is just as much a product of the way American political parties function.

There is very little **party discipline** in the United States. In European-type parliamentary systems, political parties establish policy by majority decision *within* the party, and once a policy has been decided upon, party representatives are on the whole expected to vote with the party. American representatives, on the other hand, are seen as **free agents**, individuals who vote on every issue according to conscience even though the majority of the members of their party might vote differently. This makes American politics—and especially congressional decisions— extremely unpredictable. Even though there are differences between the Democratic and Republican parties, they are both sufficiently broad in their 'ideological' spectra to allow virtually constant cross-party coalitions on issues. In other words, liberal Democrats often find support from moderate or liberal Republicans, and conservative Republicans are often joined by conservative Democrats. Moreover, political issues are often so complex that it is impossible to categorize 'sides' in terms of 'liberal' or 'conservative' labels. On some issues, there are temporary alliances between archrivals at opposite ends of the traditional spectrum of 'left-right' within and between the two parties.

In this sense, then, the US Congress can be seen as a truly **deliberative body**: the debate taking place on the floor is a true debate in which participants are trying to persuade other legislators of both parties to vote for or against a bill at hand. (Indirectly, legislators are also hoping to convince the President of the merits of their arguments, since he/she can subsequently veto the bill.) In parliaments, on the other hand, the floor 'readings' or debates may indeed have a long-term effect on party policies (and on voters watching on television), but in regard to the bill at hand, the outcome of the vote is usually a foregone conclusion determined by party leaders or caucuses, and the executive government has usually already been involved in the decision—otherwise the bill would not have been proposed.

The lack of party discipline in the US also opens the door to **lobbyists**. This term comes from the original practice of interest groups stopping lawmakers in the lobby of the Capitol building in order to press their case for support on a particular issue. Individual legislators are easier for lobbyists to persuade than are entire political parties, and lobbying has developed into a major Washington industry, with highly professional companies offering their services to today's interest groups. At the same time, the rules regulating lobbying activities are comprehensive and complex, and lobbying firms spend a good deal of their time avoiding behavior that could lead to disciplinary action such as fines and even prison sentences for bribing legislators. New rules from 1995 even outline exactly what sorts of food a lobbyist may offer a lawmaker, for example— basically nothing more substantial than finger food, food at the end of a toothpick, or a bagel. No lunches or dinners are allowed to be bought for a legislator unless at least twenty-five people from an organization attend the meal, and expensive gifts are clearly illegal. All professional lobbyists must register with the government. A 1989 regulation stipulates that former elected and administration officials are not permitted to act as lobbyists within a year of leaving office.

Adding to the unpredictability of party politics the complexity of the legislative process—with the many committees of Congress chaired by persons of varying political ambition and prestige, we can see why any President might feel humbled by his/her antagonist in this ongoing 'war of attrition', the Congress of the United States. It will be recalled that the President is by no means expected to step down if a major legislative package he/she supported is defeated in Congress; after all, the President's term of office is regulated independently by the Constitution. But by the same token, the President does not have the advantage of being able to call for new elections in order to create a new parliamentary situation; elections are held according to the staggered schedule set down by the Constitution (see Figure 9.5 "Clockwork Government" p. 148). (The only power along these lines that the President has is the power to **convene** Congress should it be out of session, a power that is hardly ever used.) Suffice it to say, in summary, that nominal majorities from the President's party in both houses of Congress are no guarantee of frictionless relations between the two branches. In fact, a more or less chronic state of 'coalition government' (in the European sense) has evolved in—and was in a sense built into—American politics. (The President's power is circumscribed even further by the power of the judiciary, but we need no more than mention this here.)

THE PRESIDENT	A PRIME MINISTER
– not a member of Congress	– a member of parliament
– not subject to votes of	– subject to votes of no confidenceno confidence
– cannot influence election timing	– can call early elections
– the boss	– primus inter pares
– Cabinet reflects his/her wishes	– cabinet reflects wishes of parliament
– expects little party discipline	– expects party discipline

Figure 11.4 Brief Review: President vs. Prime Minister.

CHAPTER 12

Elections

Paradoxically, the United States might be said to have too little democracy partly because it has too much democracy. There is too little democracy in the sense that relatively few people take part in the elections that are so central to the democratic process as conceived by the founders of the country. While some countries—Sweden, for one—can boast typical voter participation rates of around 90 percent in their elections, the United States must shamefacedly admit that only about half of all people eligible to vote typically take part in presidential elections and only about a third vote in congressional elections between presidential contests. Even more alarmingly, fewer than 14 percent of all 18–20-year-olds voted in the congressional elections of 1998, for example. Even the enthusiasm generated by the Obama campaign in 2008 only produced just over a 60-percent turnout among voters, though the boost in activity was much greater among young people. One of the reasons for this low level of participation is voter 'burn out'—there are simply too many elections. There is 'too much' democracy.

Americans go to the polls to choose people for many posts to which people are appointed in most other countries. Local and state judges have already been mentioned as examples of elective jobs. County sheriffs are also elected, as are local and county prosecuting attorneys, which means that the criminal justice system is prone to direct voter influence at these levels (but not at the federal level). When voters cast their ballots, they have to pick and choose between two or more candidates for dozens of relatively minor jobs in the state and local administrations, including tax assessors and dog catchers.

Each visit to the polling booth also entails taking a stand on a number of state and local issues, such as tax rates, highway construction, the sale of firearms, etc. Voters in most states have the power of the **initiative**, which means that an issue that has gathered a certain number of signatures must appear on the ballot in a general election. Other issues are placed before the voters by the state legislatures in the form of **referendums**.

All of this is reflected in the barrage of campaign propaganda that arrives in the voter's mail before elections. Mass and direct mail circulars swamp homes, paralyzing voters with an excess of information about the candidates and issues. It is no wonder many eligible voters stay at home when election time rolls around once, twice, or more times a year. The dozens of switches to be turned or boxes to be marked inside the polling booth can be an intimidating barrier.

A further snag has long been the fact that registration rules often used to require repeated visits to the authorities for citizens to register as voters. In other countries this is something that is often done automatically once and for all when voters reach the voting age. During President Clinton's first year in office, however, the National Voter Registration Act of 1993 was enacted, providing potential voters with the opportunity to register conveniently at numerous state authorities in connection with other business they might have there, such as registering for welfare benefits or renewing their driver's license, the latter leading to the nickname 'motor voter' commonly used for the legislation. However, voters still need to renew their registration periodically, with the length of the period varying from state to state (Wisconsin allows voters to register when they come to the polling station, and North Dakota requires no registration). Michigan could boast in 2008 that the state had registered 99 percent of its eligible voters. It remains to be seen whether motor voter will change the generally depressing registration figures across the nation; the first decades have not had the impact its proponents originally imagined.

It is not merely that American voters do not pay much attention to who is running for minor offices. The 50–60-percent participation figure mentioned above goes in fact for *presidential* elections up through 2008, where it might be expected that voters would have had the time and opportunity to get registered and to make a choice between the candidates. Voter indifference seemed to be on the increase (figures were ten to twenty percentage points higher in the early 20th century) and was probably connected with a general lack of the strong identification with particular parties that is characteristic of voters in European democracies, for example. A third or more of American voters are independents, and as the presidential campaign reaches its close, the candidates tend to play for the center, that is, to tone down their differences or any extreme views they might have had. Half of the potential voters have simply perceived that it makes no difference who wins, and they vote 'neither of the above' or 'either of the above' by staying at home.

Voter participation is not high in international comparisons also because many voters are no doubt simply exhausted by the months, even years of exposure to the candidates for the Presidency. Even though the 'official' campaign is limited to a period from August through early November every fourth year, many campaigns are effectively launched two or three years before that. The Republican and Democratic state parties **primary elections** and **caucuses** arrange in the first half of the election year itself, often both parties simultaneously but sometimes separately.

These **primary elections** are not arranged by the federal authorities. Rather, they are contests set up by the respective parties in the respective states, and the parties themselves are not 'official' government entities but rather voluntary associations (see p. 192). The purpose of primary elections for state governor, senators, representatives, etc.[1] is to choose which one of two or more candidates will represent the party in the election proper. In the presidential election process the primaries are normally used to choose some or all of the delegates who will represent the state at the respective party's national convention. These delegates, in turn, are pledged in varying degrees to support certain candidates at that convention. In the last few decades—the period that saw the rise of state party primary elections and caucuses—the states of Iowa and New Hampshire have established a traditional privilege of being the first in the country to hold a caucus (Iowa) and a primary (New Hampshire). This focuses a great deal of national attention on these states and brings in

---

1   In local politics, especially in small towns where the national parties might not be represented in mayoral elections, primary elections are sometimes held to choose the two or three strongest candidates from a much larger field of hopefuls. The regular election is then a sort of 'run-off' contest involving the winners of the primary.

tremendous amounts of money in the form of visiting journalists, for example. In the 2008 election Democrats in Michigan and Florida challenged this order by going against Democratic Party's established order for caucuses and primaries, arguing that Iowa and New Hampshire are tiny in terms of population size and atypical in terms of race and ethnicity, both being largely white. This challenge led to Michigan having a primary that was boycotted by most candidates and to Michigan and Florida initially being punished by the party by having their delegates' votes count only for half at the party convention (though ultimately their delegations were fully reinstated). The rebellion led to a promise to change the order of primaries and caucuses, probably involving a rotating regional plan. The main idea is to have all of these contests, especially the earliest ones, reflect something closer to the national population than New Hampshire and Iowa represent.

Primaries are either **closed**, meaning that only party members are allowed to vote, or **open**, where any registered voter can take part. In open primaries there is the danger of members of the other party 'crossing over' and packing the ballot boxes with votes for the candidate they perceive as being easiest to beat in the official election. Some states hold caucuses instead of primaries. Party **caucuses** are more limited in that people attend local meetings and vote publicly by voice, though this is sometimes combined with a second round of secret ballots.

Strategies for winning presidential primaries and for the campaign in general are largely steered by the **winner-take-all** system of election. The Constitution stipulates that the President shall be chosen by a **college of electors** representing the combined number of senators and representatives in Congress (now **538**: 100 senators, 435 representatives, plus 3 electors from the District of Columbia). The states are thus represented in rough proportion to their representation in Congress. In the presidential election on the Tuesday after the first Monday[2] in

---

2   This odd stipulation from 1845 calls for some explanation. The original idea of having elections on a Sunday was seen as sacrilegious, so Monday was proposed. But in the 1800s it was very common for farmers and businesses to balance their monthly books on the first day of the month, meaning that 'the first Monday of November' would coincide with this essential duty. The 'Tuesday next after the first Monday' was the elegant solution.

November every fourth year, the winner of a simple majority of the votes in each state takes **all of the electoral votes** from that state. The loser receives **none**. This means that it is possible for a candidate to win the Presidency by getting a majority or a plurality of the electors even though he/she might have received fewer votes than his/her opponent nationwide (that is, simply counting the 'popular vote'—without regard for state boundaries). If a candidate wins the most populous states by one vote only, he/she can afford to lose all of the votes in the less populous states.

Although the above discrepancy has appeared a couple of times in distant American history, few Americans were fully prepared for what happened in the 2000 election: the loser, Al Gore, the Democratic candidate garnered some 550,000 more votes nationwide than the winner, George W. Bush. Bush won the electoral college by finally being awarded the 25 electoral votes from Florida after several weeks of disputing and recounting ballots, a scenario that involved the Florida state and county election officials, the Florida Supreme Court, and the US Supreme Court. The final word came from the US Supreme Court, which ruled that an ongoing recount of disputed ballots must cease. Al Gore conceded the election after this ruling, in the interest of maintaining stability in the nation. People were left reeling, however, to find that the balloting system was so vulnerable to confusion and that the usual rule-of-law procedures could so easily wear so thin that chaos and anarchy were clearly visible. A commission consisting of former Presidents Gerald Ford and Jimmy Carter was appointed to suggest ways to stabilize the balloting system. Their report proposed the modernization of voting technology and declaring election day a national holiday in order to make it easier to vote. Despite federal attempts to provide uniformity in the **Help America Vote Act**, by the time the 2004 elections came around many states still had a mixture of often questionable voting procedures, and there was considerable concern that some modern computerized systems would be easy to tamper with and difficult to monitor, even if there was a paper record of voting. No national holiday was declared. As it turned out, President Bush defeated Democratic contender Senator John Kerry by well over 3 million votes across the country and by 22 electoral votes, so the frenzy of recounting that was anticipated never came to pass. For the 2008 election very little progress had yet been made, with computer and ballot-design problems still plaguing many states. As in 2004, the 2008 victory for Barack Obama over John McCain was so overwhelming—53% to 46% of the popular vote and 68% (365) to 32% (173) of electoral votes—that there was no need to question state by state results and ballots. Nevertheless, the US election system is still in great need of reform in order to insure that the traumatic election of 2000 is not repeated in the future.

A more serious issue involves the sense among many Americans that, in his first term, George W. Bush did not really have a mandate as President. Gore's victory in the popular vote and what was perceived by many as partial behavior on the part of the Supreme Court undermined voter confidence in the election system. The US Commission on Civil Rights found that ballots cast by African-American voters in 2000 were disproportionately thrown out and recommended that the Justice Department investigate the matter. Black organizations provided evidence that the Republican Party used intimidation tactics in many places in 2000, such as placing official-looking white men in suits with bogus badges close to polling places in African-American neighborhoods and spreading false rumors that two or three types of identification would have to be shown at the polls or that voting rights would be tied to having paid child support. Also in 2000, newly elected New York Senator Hillary Rodham Clinton vowed to make the scrapping of the electoral-college system and the introduction of direct election of the President her first priority as senator, but no serious action was taken toward such a reform, and the clearer mandates that voters gave George W. Bush in 2004 and Barack Obama in 2008 rendered any major change in the system highly unlikely for some time to come.

Campaign Financing

Strategies for facing the long series of primaries have become even more complex in recent years as a result of efforts to limit and monitor candidates' spending. These reforms came in the wake of the Watergate scandal (see p. 168) and were part of an attempt to 'clean up' government by curtailing the amount of money spent on presidential candidates by wealthy donors. The rules are rather complicated and in a state of constant evolution, so we will only touch on the broad principles here. For the **primary elections**, all candidates who succeed in attracting at least $5,000 in each of twenty states in the form of individual contributions under $250 each (usually by arranging dinners and by direct-mail soliciting) qualify for **matching funds** of up to $250 per contribution, but there is a total federal spending limit for all of the primaries together. If candidates accept these funds (which must be taken from tax money that is voluntarily earmarked as available for this purpose by taxpayers when they file their annual income tax returns), they must follow a basic spending agenda through the spring primaries. Candidates who choose not to accept the funds, which would double their resources, are free to spend as much as they please (as some wealthy individuals indeed have). Individuals are not allowed to contribute more than $2,300 to any candidate, $5,000 to any national political action committee in support of a candidate or a cause. The number of these latter committees, abbreviated PACs, has skyrocketed as a result of the ceiling on individual contributions. Nearly all presidential candidates opt for the matching primary funds, but in 2008 Barack Obama (and Hillary Clinton and others) did not, and, once nominated, Obama decided not to accept federal funding for the **general election** either. His campaign, while including substantial amounts from big-money donors, was unprecedented in its ability to attract small donations from individuals: a total of roughly $750 million from as many as 4 million donors in the primaries and general election combined. The Federal Election Commission makes all records available to the public, relying on journalists and political opponents to keep tabs on candidates' contributions.

Until Obama in 2008, all major candidates opted to take the federal funding available, as John McCain did in 2008. A Supreme Court decision from 1976 established that right to spend freely is a form of freedom of expression and is thus guaranteed by the US Constitution. The success of Obama in soliciting financial support via the Internet suggests that this will be the model for the future. Originally the sum of federal money was $25 million per candidate in 1976 but by 2008 it was $84.1 million for the McCain-Palin campaign, owing to indexing. There are no guidelines as to how this money should be spent (most candidates concentrate on buying national television exposure).

A major reform was passed in 2002—the **Bipartisan Campaign Reform Act**, better known as the **McCain-Feingold Reform**, named after its congressional sponsors. It targeted the huge sums of so-called soft money that the parties spent alongside the hard money provided by the federal government. This money was supposed be spent to promote general party positions on issues and could not explicitly support the party's candidates, but these rules were often broken. McCain-Feingold outlawed this soft money, making it illegal for the parties to spend soft funds during the campaign proper. When first put to the test, however, in the 2004 campaign, a loophole was immediately found in the Act: so-called "**article 527**" groups were allowed to educate the voters about issues and to promote get-out-the-vote ads, but these groups—both Democratic and Republican—soon started funding television ads that not only blatantly supported one candidate over the other but also slung political mud against opponents. The 527s, as they were soon called, had no official connection to the parties, although on both sides informal ties were soon uncovered. Both candidates could sling plenty of mud and yet tried to claim that they were above the fray, that the dirt was coming from independent voters groups, the 527s. The 2004 election was thus one of the dirtiest ever, despite McCain-Feingold. While the 2008 campaign saw some political mud-slinging from 527s, especially in support of McCain, their effect was limited. The McCain campaign tried to make up for its limited funding from the government by relying on Republican Party ads focusing on issues.

The various generations of campaign finance reforms have thus been unsuccessful in keeping 'big money' out of presidential politics, and the individuals who reach positions from the level of senator and state governor up to the Presidency are still overwhelmingly individuals of considerable private wealth. Critics blame the predominance of prime-time television advertising for the astronomical costs of campaigning, adding that the medium itself—with its slick, 'soft-sell' packaging in thirty- or sixty-second shots—does not lend itself to responsible analysis and weighing of serious issues, but rather to eliciting emotional responses. In 1996 the networks experimented with new forms of 'free' airtime for slightly longer presentations of issues, but the impact of these spots was limited. Oddly, the 1996 Republican candidate, Robert Dole, did not even fill up the allotted free time given to him by the CBS network. That network initiative was not repeated.

It is also maintained that the short ads and occasional face-to-face encounters in televised debates have created a new kind of candidate, with blow-dried hair, suave stage presence, and a keen awareness of the best camera angles. John F. Kennedy's defeat of Richard M. Nixon in 1960 is often attributed to his more pleasant appearance during their TV debate. While the importance of that debate has probably been exaggerated (and it must in fact be countered that Nixon came back to win in 1968 and 1972), it is nonetheless true that Nixon never again let his 'five-o'clock shadow' (visible late-afternoon beard stubble) show on television. Nor can it be denied that the last two decades have seen a proliferation of politicians at all levels who could pass for stars of soap operas or anchorpersons on television news programs. The most telegenic candidacy to date was that of Ronald Reagan, a former movie actor, who was elected to the Presidency in 1980 and 1984. While it can be argued that politicians have always been masters of the communications media available to them and that these tendencies therefore do not represent anything radically new, it is disturbing that opinion polls taken during the Reagan administration showed that Americans very often strongly disagreed with the President's views on specific issues but supported him anyway, more or less because he 'seemed to be such a nice guy'. President Clinton showed consummate mastery of the 'citizens' forum' type of debate, handily beating his 1996 opponent, Bob Dole, not only with arguments but with stage presence and professional use of the TV medium in responding to questions from the audience. Being the better debater does not always help, however: Senator John Kerry was declared the winner of the three television debates in the fall of 2004, but he lost the election. Barack Obama clearly came across on TV better than John McCain in 2008, although McCain's controversial and surprising running mate, Sarah Palin, proved to be highly telegenic and was able to make up for McCain's lack of excitement, inspiring core Republican voters far better than the presidential candidate himself.

Political Parties

The Democratic and Republican parties have been such an integral part of American politics for so long that it is hard to believe that they, or at least a two-party system, were *not* ordained by the Constitution. The founders made no mention of parties, yet from the very outset US politics has been dominated by two parties, periodic attempts at establishing third parties (such as the Socialist Party in the first decades of the 20th century) and numerous splinter groups within the parties notwithstanding. Some observers view the two-party system with the distance of anthropologists and stress the basic sameness of the two parties. In this view the Democrats and Republicans take on the aspect of 'moieties', very much like the National League and American League in baseball. There is much to recommend this argument, which sees the groupings merely as an apparatus necessary for culling candidates but largely devoid of ideological content. From global and historical points of view both parties are relatively liberal bourgeois associations, yet there are some fundamental differences in emphasis when they are viewed from the American perspective. A brief look at their respective origins and histories, depicted in the very broadest strokes, might make it easier to grasp the differences between the two.

Even though the **Republican Party** (symbolized by an **elephant**) calls itself the Grand Old Party (GOP, a ubiquitous abbreviation), the **Democratic Party** (symbolized by a **donkey**) is the older of the two. It traces its roots to the grouping called the **Democratic-Republicans** from the very beginning of the country. The Democratic-Republicans (then most often referred to, confusingly enough from the modern point of view, as 'Republicans') preferred a decentralized form of government with more power for the individual states and less for the federal government. They basically envisaged an agrarian United States and their foremost spokesman was Thomas Jefferson, an enlightened landowner and architect from Virginia, primary author of the Declaration of Independence, and third President of the United States. During the controversy surrounding the adoption of the new Constitution, these people were called **Anti-Federalists**.

The opposite tendency was represented by leaders like Alexander Hamilton, the first Secretary of the Treasury, who was a **Federalist**—that is, a supporter of a strong central government and banking system. The **Federalist Party** represented the interests of the budding urban capitalist class and envisioned the United States as a strongly unified nation. American politics in the tremendously expansive period of the first decades of the 19th century was characterized by a rivalry between the Federalists and the Democratic-Republicans.

The latter party suffered a split in 1828 and became known as the **Democratic Party** with the rise of Andrew Jackson, the seventh American President. He was the first President of truly humble origins, having been born in a log cabin in Tennessee. He made his mark as a general and Indian-killer, and as President he rallied 'common people' against the propertied (either landed or commercial) classes that had held power in Washington until then (the 1830s). He is known for having dismantled the Bank of the United States (the American central bank, which had originally been established by Alexander Hamilton).

The three decades that led to the Civil War (1861–65) between the Northern and Southern states saw the rise of a series of new parties that challenged the Democrats. The **Whigs** (1834–1855) organized under the name of the liberal, anti-monarchical British party to show their opposition to Andrew Jackson, who they felt thought he was 'king'; the **Free Soil Party** (founded in 1848) based on opposition to the expansion of slavery into new territories; and finally the **Republican Party**, established in 1854 as an anti-slavery party in the Northern states. The election of the Republican candidate, Abraham Lincoln, to the Presidency in the 1860 election was the immediate cause of the secession of the Southern states from the federal union.

The Northern victory in the Civil War ushered in a long period of Republican dominance in national politics. The final three decades of the 19th century saw the rise of monopoly capitalism and industrial expansion, and the Republicans came to be associated with big business. For white Southerners, the humiliating defeat and subsequent punishment (the South was divided into five military districts under Northern generals during the decade of 'Reconstruction' after the war) at the hands of Republicans spelled unswerving loyalty to the Democratic Party for a century. For the former slaves in the South, the opposite was true: the Radical Republicans of the Reconstruction period protected them from their former owners and guaranteed them a say in politics which they have regained only in the last couple of decades. They responded by showing their loyalty at the polls.

However, the Republicans turned their backs on Southern blacks in the late 1870s and largely permitted 'business as usual' in the South. In concrete terms, this was the beginning of nearly a century of disfranchisement for blacks there. Blacks in the North shifted their allegiance to the Democratic Party during the Great Depression of the 1930s in response to F. D. Roosevelt's New Deal attempts to help the poor. Since then black voters—including the half of their number who were re-enfranchised as late as the 1960s in the South—have overwhelmingly supported the Democrats, though Abraham Lincoln is still a folk hero for his role in liberating their slave ancestors.

Southern whites maintained their antipathy towards the party of Lincoln, the Republicans, into the 1970s, even though the somewhat more conservative stand of the national Republican Party was often closer to their hearts than the more liberal Democratic stance at the national level. For many decades this peculiar split personality of conservative Southern whites was characterized by the concept of the Dixiecrat, meaning a Democrat from the land of Dixie, the South (the term probably comes from the French *dix* on ten-dollar bills issued in New Orleans, a former French colony). A sea change finally started to take place as a reaction to the Democratic Party's full support of racial integration in 1964. By the 1980s the conservative vote in the South was firmly entrenched in a revitalized Republican Party there.

Republicans suffered such humiliation during the Watergate scandal of the second Nixon administration that political commentators joked that America had a 'one-and-a-half party system'. Jimmy Carter, an unknown Democrat from the Southern state of Georgia, was expected to initiate a new dynasty of Democrats. Economic recession and what was perceived as a muffed Presidency turned the tables, however, and by 1980 the Republicans were back in the limelight, taking the Presidency and a majority in the Senate. Loyal black Democrats had been alienated by Carter's lack of interest in issues dear to them, but could not bring themselves to vote for the conservative Reagan. In 1984 liberal Walter Mondale could not shake off his background as Carter's Vice-President and thus could not mobilize black voters, despite his liberal platform. The result for blacks was unprecedented indifference to politics in 1980 and 1984. African-American voters and many others stayed at home in 1988 as well. The moderate Democratic candidate, Michael Dukakis, who was first predicted to beat George H. W. Bush handily, seemed unable, even unwilling, to defend himself in the last months of the campaign when Bush, given a new and tougher image by his campaign staff, ran a series of racially dubious ads calling for law and order. Bush came across as a worthy successor to Reagan and won hands down.

Four years later, in 1992, Arkansas governor Bill Clinton emerged as the Democratic nominee from a carefully prepared position in the Democratic Leadership Council, a very middle-of-the-road caucus within the Democratic Party. Occupying the middle ground, yet promising reforms attractive to more liberal voters, such as a national health-care system, he easily cast Bush, who had chalked up record-high popularity figures in connection with the Gulf War just a year earlier, as a figure of the past and robbed him of a second term (partly aided by the candidacy of the populist Ross Perot, who siphoned off a good share of Bush's support and took 19 percent of the popular vote). Ironically, Clinton came back from then record-low popularity figures he faced in the third year of his first term to beat the Republican Bob Dole (and Perot again) by a wide margin in 1996. His second term was marred by the scandal involving his sexual relations with a White House intern, Monica Lewinsky, and his impeachment (see p. 168).

The humiliation of Clinton's impeachment led Vice-President Al Gore, the Democratic candidate in 2000, to shun any support from his boss in his campaign. As the November election neared with Gore trailing Republican candidate George W. Bush (son of former President George H. W. Bush) in the opinion polls, more and more observers felt he should turn to Clinton for active support. As it turns out, Gore received more than half a million more votes than Bush, but lost in the electoral college in a uniquely contested election (see p. 188). It was generally felt that the independent candidacy of consumer advocate Ralph Nader, who received about 3 percent of the votes, tapped into the support for Gore to the point of robbing him of the Presidency.

The 2004 presidential election saw record number of voters registered, voter turnout reached roughly 60 percent for the first time since the 1968 election. This was probably due to a strong feeling of partisanship, with the country split basically in half between supporters of President George W. Bush and the others, who accepted Senator John Kerry as a candidate basically because he was "anybody but Bush". The Bush campaign succeeded even better than the Democrats in getting out the vote, primarily because the President was perceived as a stronger leader in the face of threats of international terrorism. Senator Kerry cast his campaign more and more toward the center and vowed to be just as tough as his opponent, but the voters chose Bush as the safer bet. In both 2004 and 2008 Ralph Nader culled only one percent of the votes and had virtually no effect on the outcome of the election.

In the 2008 election the Republicans tried to continue their claims that they were more patriotic and a safer bet in the struggle against international terrorism, but Americans seemed to have tired of such accusations from Republicans. John McCain, a former prisoner of war for more than five year in North Vietnam, won the nomination but actually lacked support from the most conservative Republicans, having been a notorious 'maverick' throughout his House and Senate careers. His surprising choice of Alaska governor Sarah Palin to be his running mate was clearly an attempt to appeal to more traditional Republicans and the religious right. The groundswell that surrounded the nomination of Illinois senator Barack Obama—after an extended and even battle with New York senator and former first lady Hillary Rodham Clinton—proved to be impervious to dubious Republican attempts to cast doubt about his basic American-ness, indirect appeals to racist tendencies among many voters to get them to turn against the first nominee of African descent, whose middle name is Hussein. On top of this, eight years of lax and often rolled-back regulation of banking and investment companies under George W. Bush—a laxity that in fact started in the centrist Clinton administrations—and the deflation of the huge bubble in house prices that this deregulation created led to the serious breakdown of the financial system since the Great Depression of the 1930s, just in time for the election, and John McCain seemed to have no idea how to handle the crisis. On top of this, Americans were tired of and frustrated with Bush's wars and uncontrolled spending on defense and clearly wanted some form of national health care plan, which Obama committed himself to providing. The balanced federal budgets and small national debt that Bill Clinton had handed over to George W. Bush had been replaced by deficit spending in the trillions, a stark reversal of the traditional roles of Democrats and Republicans. Obama won handily and got to work immediately to establish his credentials and his team to provide new leadership in the face of the deepening economic crisis.

There are no official 'party leaders' at the national level, though the incumbent President is the *de facto* leader of his/her party. Both parties also have national committees and chairs, but they are relatively weak. In fact the respective platforms (political programs) adopted by each party at the national conventions are often ignored by the chosen candidates themselves in the campaign. Most activity and influence is found at the state level. It is here that delegates to the national conventions are chosen, and, as has been mentioned above, it is up to each state's respective parties to decide in what fashion these delegates are to be chosen (primaries, caucuses, appointment). At the local level, in some of the biggest cities, parties have been known to establish party machines, meaning a system whereby politicians trade city jobs for votes in separate precincts, often 'delivered' by leaders of various ethnic groups in different neighborhoods. While there had never been a serious black contender for the Presidency before Jesse Jackson in 1988 and then, of course, President Barack Obama in 2008, most of the very biggest cities (New York, Los Angeles, Chicago, Philadelphia, Detroit, Atlanta, Washington) now have or have recently had black mayors, a fact which reflects the size of the black communities there.

Who then votes Democratic and who votes Republican? There is no simple answer, but certain basic tendencies are clear. With many notable exceptions, the Democrats are the party of the lower-to-middle rungs of the social ladder, the Republicans of the middle-to-upper rungs, or often people who like to identify with those who are economically successful. Organized labor often (but not always) publicly endorses a Democratic candidate (but it should be remembered that only one of every five or six working people in the US is a union member), while owners and management in big business are predominantly Republican. White 'ethnic' groups (the term is usually used to refer to recognizable communities such as the Irish, Poles, Italians, Jews etc. who are outside the northern European establishment of British, German, and Scandinavian origin) tend to vote Democratic, as do people of color (increasingly including Asians) and of Latin American origin (except older Cuban Americans—younger ones supported Obama), although in 2004 George W. Bush attracted larger than usual numbers among Hispanics. Latinos were strong supporters of Obama and the Democrats again in 2008. Women vote predominantly Democratic, and since 1986 more women than men have voted in elections.

These groupings reflect the different emphasis placed on the role of government, and especially the federal government. Since F. D. Roosevelt's New Deal, Democrats have favored government intervention to moderate the economy (Keynesian economics shared by liberal and social-democratic governments in Europe) and to achieve more equitable distribution of wealth through social programs and educational and occupational opportunities for the disadvantaged. This is of course a far cry from the decentralized society of independent farmers envisioned by Jefferson and the early Democratic-Republicans. The crisis that finally flared up in the fall of 2008 prompted a majority of Americans to advocate a greater role for government in stimulating the economy and helping society's weakest members.

The Republicans have also made a 180-degree turn from their beginnings as an anti-slavery party. Stopping the spread of slavery involved the federal government (and the Union armies) in what Southern Democrats considered the proper business of the individual states. But after their success in the 'Gilded Age' of capitalism, the Republicans held, with Thoreau and (ironically) Jefferson, that the best governments govern least, and when the Great Depression broke out in 1929, many of them felt that the economy would cure itself if left alone. During the 1950s, 1960s, and 1970s Republicans were often as 'liberal' as the Democrats when it came to government spending, but in the 1980s Republicans started taking advantage of the crisis that had shaken such traditional 'social liberalism' and Keynesian economics since the oil shocks and 'stagflation' of the late 1970s and early 1980s, advocating, if not cuts in federal spending, at least a halt to increases. However, conservative Republicans like Reagan have also supported increased spending for defense, which ironically led to the largest budget deficits in history in the last years of the Reagan administration—surpassed only by Republican George W. Bush's spending excesses. Probably partly owing to opposition from Congress, President Clinton—a Democrat—spent much less than his predecessors and finished his second term, as mentioned, with declining national debt and major budget surpluses. After one term as President, George W. Bush—a Republican—had incurred new record levels of budget debt on top of huge deficits in the balance of trade. In other words, at the national level fiscal responsibility has ironically been a hallmark of the Democrats rather than the Republicans for the last quarter century.

The fate of health-care reform in the first Clinton administration illustrates the difference in emphasis between Republicans and Democrats. Bill Clinton's wife, Hillary Rodham Clinton, seen by many as more liberal than her husband, took on the main responsibility for shepherding their plans for a sort of national health service through the public debate and through Congress in the first Clinton administration. Polls had shown that such a reform was the number one issue for most Americans. She was generally lauded for her competence early on in the process and even received an unprecedented ovation from members of a Senate committee after her testimony to them on the subject. However, her continued piloting of the issue was marred by misjudgments and, according to critics, even arrogance on the part of the First Lady. The tide turned when Republicans aired TV commercials suggesting that Americans would not be allowed to choose their own physicians under the proposed legislation. Almost overnight the specter of Big Government frightened away most support for the most promising attempt ever at establishing basic health care for all citizens on a European or Canadian model.

This ground-swell of conservative thinking led to the election of the first fully Republican-dominated Congress in many years in 1994 (see next paragraph) and launched Georgia congressman Newt Gingrich as Speaker of the House. On a roll, the Republicans presented a 'Contract with America', a list of conservative measures to cut back government which they proceeded to put through Congress. The histrionics and hyperbole of Speaker Gingrich ultimately slowed the momentum of this movement, but only after a majority of the items on the list had been realized. By the summer of election year 1996, President Clinton was so buffeted by conservative winds that he signed a bill from Congress that would eliminate major features of the welfare system (see p. 262). Having done so, he turned around and promised to see to it that most of the cuts would not affect welfare recipients, a promise he took with him into his second term, seemingly wanting to have his cake and eat it too.

In a sense American voters also seem to want to have their cake and eat it, too. From 1980 to 1992 they split their votes between Republican Presidents and a predominantly Democratic Congress, apparently hoping to achieve social responsibility in legislation and fiscal responsibility in the execution of these laws. President Clinton worked with a Democratic Congress for his first two years, but in 1994 both houses of Congress were taken over by Republican majorities in a sweep of conservatism. And despite his painless re-election in 1996, both houses remained in the hands of the Republicans, though they were nominally weakened. The Republicans regained the White House in 2000, kept a majority in the House of Representatives and control of Senate committees, despite a 50-50 split. Apparently total Republican dominance was surprisingly upset half a year later by a decision by Vermont Senator James Jeffords to leave the Republican Party and become an independent. The Senate committee chairmanships shifted to the Democrats in the 50-49-1 Senate. Other moderate Republicans, disenchanted with an aggressively conservative Bush agenda let it be known that they too may leave the Republican fold. Americans often seem more comfortable with this balance of power between Congress and the President. The 2004 election left President George W. Bush with strong Republican majorities in both houses, but growing disillusionment with Bush policies and wars placed both houses of Congress in Democratic hands in the 2006 elections. In 2008 Democrats controlled both the presidency and both houses of Congress, although the Senate majority was just short of a 'filibuster-proof' 60 out of 100 (see p. 148 about 'filibusters').

In the broad view, then, the parties are actually more similar than different. Both are still champions of basic social security for senior citizens, for example, and of many other very costly federal programs that have come to be taken for granted. Republicans and Democrats have solemnly vowed to work together to make the Social Security (pension) system financially viable in the future despite worrisome underfunding over the last two decades. President George W. Bush tried to introduce private investments to bolster this funding, but his national campaign in his second term failed miserably. Despite Bush's un-Republican spending and accumulation of debt, both parties as a whole do at least try to walk the narrow path between social responsibility and fiscal responsibility. In this and in other matters they are certainly fraternal—not identical—twins, and, as has been pointed out above, almost all legislation is ultimately the result of temporary coalitions of 'independent' senators and representatives from both parties. Recalling the etymologies of the words discussed at the beginning of this chapter, it should not be surprising that the Demo-cratic and Re-publican parties have become a perennial (some would say 'chronic') feature of politics in the American democratic republic.

SUGGESTED WEB SITES

The White House
www.whitehouse.gov

Library of Congress
www.loc.gov

Official Federal Government Web Sites
www.loc.gov/rr/news/fedgov.html

US Legislative Branch
http://thomas.loc.gov/links/

Thomas: US Congress on the Internet
http://rs9.loc.gov/home/thomas.html

Federal Courts Home Page
www.uscourts.gov

State governments
www.loc.gov/rr/news/stategov/stategov.html

about.com, Hosted Gateway
www.usgovinfo.about.com

National Governors' Association
www.nga.org

Federal Election Commission
www.fec.gov

PART IV

Education

CHAPTER 13

Introduction

Opening the 1990 annual meeting in New Orleans, the president of the American Association for the Advancement of Science quoted: 'If an unfriendly foreign power had attempted to impose upon America the mediocre educational performance that exists today, we might well have viewed it as an act of war'. He was reading from a report titled *A Nation at Risk: The Imperative for Educational Reform*, presented to the US Secretary of Education seven years earlier by the National Commission on Excellence in Education. It is typical of the ever more drastic expressions American educational and cultural leaders have used since the mid 1970s to shock the general public and politicians into improving the country's schools. It might be argued that teachers and their allies are merely speaking in their own interest, hoping that more money for education would largely wind up in their pockets. But the chorus of alarm has been joined by others, especially business leaders, who go so far as to say that the quality of schooling in America is jeopardizing the nation's future as an industrial power. This was also the conclusion the National Commission drew in 1983, and there was cause to echo it in the 1990s, since improvement had been slow. President George H. W. Bush's Secretary of Education, Lauro F. Cavazos prefaced his first 'report card' on the nation's schools in 1989 with these words:

> I regret to report that this year our students' performance has been stagnant. [...] We are standing still, and the problem is that it's been this way for three years in a row. [...] We must do better or perish as the nation we know today.

As the discussion at the end of this chapter will indicate, by the turn of the new century substantial progress had been made as a result of the 1983 report, although there is still considerable room for improvement.

Below we will briefly sketch the history of schooling and then turn to the basic structure and content of elementary and secondary education. This will be followed by a discussion of colleges and universities. The chapter will be rounded off with a closer look at some of the problems facing the schools today and some of the proposed remedies for these problems.

Elementary and Secondary Education

CHAPTER 14

History

Historically, education is associated with New England, especially Massachusetts. The Puritans who settled there in the 1620s and 1630s were anxious that every member of their religious community be able to read the Bible, so parents were required to teach their children to read. By the 1640s the Massachusetts Bay Colony had established two important and pioneering principles: that the state (that is, the public authorities) could require children to receive instruction and that the state could tax its citizens to pay for public schooling. The rationale behind this revolution was in fact narrowly religious rather than democratic, and actual compliance with the rules was patchy, but the fact remains that tiny New England was on the road to universal education by the middle of the 17th century.

It took nearly two centuries for these ideas to penetrate the rest of the American colonies (and most of Europe for that matter). The middle colonies were much less homogeneous, and schooling was sporadic and uneven, usually left to local churches of various denominations or to families. Language differences (Dutch, German, Swedish, etc.) also made it difficult to establish common schools here. The southern colonies were more traditionally European in their attitude to education, seeing it as a matter for the aristocracy and the wealthy and directly opposing the use of tax money to provide public schools. This latter attitude was typical of the South, where individual freedom and local control were paramount and the issue of 'states' rights' versus the federal government led to the Civil War.

Even before the present US Constitution was ratified in 1789 the American government passed a law that would have far-reaching ramifications: the **Northwest Ordinance of 1787** stipulated that every future township in the Northwest Territory (which later became the states of Ohio, Indiana, Illinois, Michigan, Wisconsin, and part of Minnesota) must set aside one square mile (of the thirty-six square miles making up a township) of land to promote education. Similarly, in 1862, during the Civil War, the **Morrill Act** gave to every state that established an agricultural college 30,000 acres (12,000 hectares) of federal land for every senator and representative that state had in Congress. This led to the establishment of some seventy 'land-grant colleges' still operating today, now as state universities.

The Northwest Ordinance and the Morrill Act were early examples of federal involvement in education, but it should be reiterated (see p. 136 and p. 141) that schooling is seen as basically a state and local matter in the United States. The federal government provides only about seven percent of all funding for elementary and secondary schools (see Figure 14.1 "Financing Public Schools" p. 210) and the Department of Education, which was carved out of the old Department of Health, Education, and Welfare by President Carter in the late 1970s, generally has only advisory and service functions. Some educators would like to see an enhanced role for the central authorities in raising national standards of education, while others prefer local solutions.

With the rise of industrialism in the early 19th century, it soon became apparent that the work force would need to be able to read written instructions. The United States was quick to realize the connection between education and industrial growth, and schooling was made available to the masses earlier than in most European countries. New England again took the lead when it came to universal elementary education, establishing the first state board of education in 1837. In the decades that followed, elementary schools were made available to virtually all children, boys and girls, across the country, with the Southern states lagging behind somewhat as a result of their more agrarian society. In the Midwest (the old Northwest Territories and other land acquired from France in the Louisiana purchase) education was given high priority from the outset despite a reliance on agriculture, largely owing to settlement by former New Englanders and by immigrants from northern European countries, where mass literacy was also getting underway in the mid 19th century.

The next step was the establishment of secondary education on a massive scale. American schools at this level during the colonial period were originally, as in Europe, designed for a tiny elite. They were called 'grammar' schools and prepared boys (only) for divinity studies at colleges such as Harvard and Yale. Scientific education entered the scene in the early 18th century in the form of 'academies', but these too were for very small numbers of males. Some few academies catered to girls (only), but they usually limited their curricula to the 'refinements' of a 'finishing school'.

The first public 'high school' was established in Boston, Massachusetts, in 1821. It was still only for boys, but its curriculum was clearly oriented toward practical as well as theoretical subjects, and, unlike the old grammar schools and academies, it was free of charge. This example was rapidly followed by many cities in the northeast and then elsewhere. By the end of the 19th century, free high school education was available all over the country, though only small numbers of students attended. Almost all high school graduates went on to college.

More and more American pupils attended high school as the 20th century progressed, and upper secondary education became commonplace in the US a couple of decades before it did so in many European countries. In 2006 over 85 percent of all people (but 81 percent of all blacks and 59 percent of Hispanics) over the age of twenty-five had completed high school. It should be borne in mind, however, that the comprehensive American high school covers a much broader range of subjects, including vocational and practical ones, than does its more theoretical and often more rigorous northern European counterpart, for example.

Control and Financing

As has been mentioned elsewhere, education is seen as a state, rather than a federal, matter in the US, and American elementary and secondary schools are run by locally elected authorities, so-called **boards of**

education or, informally, **school boards**. They are bound to follow broad guidelines from an elected state board of education, but most decisions are made at the local level, meaning either the county or township in rural areas and either the city or the school district in urban areas. At the head of the school board is a professional administrator or educator who is usually appointed by the board, the **superintendent** of schools. (This constellation is similar to the city manager type of local government described on p. 138.) A forum for contact between schools and pupils' homes is provided by a voluntary and unofficial organization called the Parent-Teacher Association, or PTA, sometimes called Parent-Teacher Organization, PTO.

Public schools have traditionally been financed by predominantly local money, traditionally taken from a special property tax called 'millage'. But since the late 1960s state supreme courts in many parts of the country have declared such systems unconstitutional in that they make the quality of students' schooling dependent upon the wealth of their immediate neighborhood. States have turned more and more to other tax sources, such as sales tax, and to profits from state lotteries to pay for schools (cumulatively, some 56 percent of all proceeds from state lotteries were used for education between 1964 and 1995). By the 1990s a shift had taken place whereby the state as a whole pays for somewhat more than local government does, about 48 percent and 43 percent respectively, thus ensuring somewhat greater uniformity at least within each state. The federal government funds about 7 percent of public schools, while fees charged for books, transportation, and food ('other' in the pie chart) account for about 2–3 percent of funding.

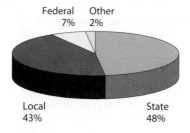

Federal
7%

Other
2%

Local
43%

State
48%

Figure 14.1 Financing Public Schools.

In 1990 the New Jersey Supreme Court ordered one of the most drastic reforms of financing to date: the state would be responsible for making up *any* difference in funding between the state's richest and poorest school districts. If a wealthy school wanted to spend more local tax money, the state of New Jersey would have to match those funds in all other schools in the state. In 1996 New Jersey passed the Comprehensive Education Improvement and Financing Act to level out differences across state school districts, and other states have taken similar measures. The New Jersey Supreme Court and state educational authorities are still working out the details of what equal educational opportunity means, and other states are making similar attempts to level out local differences, though they are fighting an uphill battle owing to the facts of local economies.

New Jersey is already a very progressive state when it comes to educational spending. Looking at the nation as a whole, however, we find major discrepancies from one state to another. Teachers' salaries in 2005 in states like California, Connecticut, New York, New Jersey, Illinois, and Michigan, for example, were 50–55 percent higher than in states like North and South Dakota, Mississippi, and Montana. These great differences are moderated somewhat by the higher cost of living in wealthy states, and the differences are in fact down from 100 percent five years ago, but the gaps are still huge. In 2005 New Jersey spent twice as much on schools per capita as did Tennessee.

At the elementary and secondary levels about 90 percent of all students attend public schools.[1] The remaining 10 percent go to private schools, with about half of these students attending institutions which are run by the Catholic Church, although the number of such schools has been steadily declining over the last three decades. The federal and, to a lesser extent, state and local governments contribute indirectly to the finances of private elementary and secondary schools by including their pupils in general programs for school busing, remedial learning, and student health and nutrition, but about 86 percent of all funding of private schools at all

---

1   These are 'public' schools in the true sense of the word, that is, they are run by the government for the general public. The term should not be confused with the traditional British expression for certain exclusive independent schools in England.

levels is actually private. Tuition[2] is typically around $4,300 per year for parochial (that is, parish) secondary schools run by the Catholic Church, $5,000 for other religious schools, and $8,000–$10,000 and upwards for non-religious private schools.

There have been repeated, and often successful, challenges to the constitutionality of any public funds going to church-affiliated schools, on the grounds that such spending violates the principle of separation of church and state. Any programs that do provide money to parochial schools are normally justified as being generally targeted to benefit schoolchildren in general, not any particular institution. In the mid 1980s President Reagan supported income-tax deductions for tuition payments made by families sending their children to the growing number of private (non-religious) academies, especially in the South and in suburbs all over the country, in the wake of the controversy over busing (see p. 243), but he was forced to back down on this issue. His position was seen as lending support to segregation.

The doctrine of separation of church and state cuts both ways (see p. 123). It not only means that the government is not allowed to promote any particular religion but also that the government must not interfere with the establishment and exercise of any religion. In the educational system this means that religious schools are free to lay down their own curricula, as long as they meet certain minimum educational requirements stipulated by the state. Catholic children who attend parish schools thus receive instruction in the catechism as a part of their normal school day. Catholic children who attend public schools often attend after-school catechism classes provided at a Catholic school.

A further category of schooling that is relatively small but growing is **homeschooling**. This means that one or both parents provide instruction in the home instead of sending their child to school. In 1999, 1.7 percent of all students between kindergarten and upper secondary school ages were homeschooled, girls slightly more often than boys, and by 2003 this figure had risen to 2.2 percent and it has continued to grow since then. As many as 2.4 percent of all kindergarten-age children are schooled at home. The

---

2   In American English this word is usually thought of as meaning 'the fee paid to attend a school', though it originally meant (and still can mean) 'instruction'.

practice is twice as common among white Americans as among blacks and Hispanics, and it is more common in families with college-educated parents. Some universities have special entrance procedures for homeschooled applicants to guarantee that certain prerequisite knowledge and skills have been acquired.

Structure

By the early 20th century there had evolved a basic pattern of eight years of **elementary** school (then often called **grammar** school—a term not to be confused with the early American colonial secondary schools by that name or with the traditional academic secondary schools in Britain—or **grade** *school*, a term still in use) and four years of secondary school (high school). This 8 + 4 system was often modified later to involve three schools, the eight-year grade school being replaced by a six-year grade school and a two-year **junior high school**.

In urban areas this 2 + 4 **junior and senior high school** shifted to 3 + 3 by the middle of the century. In other words most American school systems had the following plan: a six-year **grade** school, a three-year (grades 7–9) **junior** high school, and a three-year (grades 10–12; the numbering of grades is continuous) senior high school[3]. Though this constellation still occurs, social and demographic factors in the late 1960s and 1970s prompted a return to the 8 + 4 system in many places, though now with the eight-year grade school usually divided into **primary** (usually grades 1–5 or sometimes 1–4) and **middle** or **intermediate** school (usually grades 5–8 or sometimes 4–8). A major reason for reintroducing the full four-year high school in urban areas was the fact that ninth-grade students (especially boys) had become so rowdy and disruptive as the oldest cohort (fifteen-year-olds) in junior high that it was deemed advisable to put them at the bottom of the social ladder as **freshmen**. Freshmen are thus 9th-graders, with **sophomores** (10th-), **juniors** (11th-), and **seniors** (12th-graders), to keep them in line. This terminology echoes that of the four years of college in the US.

---

3   The standard international terms in English for these last two levels are **lower** and **upper secondary school**, respectively.

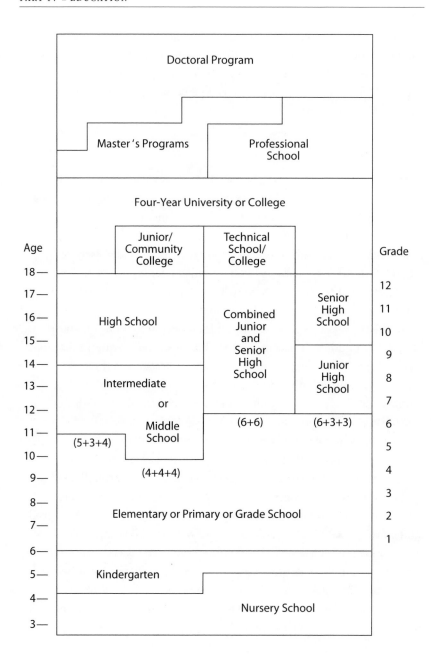

Figure 14.2 The Structure of Education in the United States.

The length of compulsory schooling is determined in each state, but all states now require students to attend school until the age of at least sixteen. This upper limit means that almost all American students at least start high school. The typical lower limit of six is misleading in a sense, since almost all American children go to **kindergarten** from the age of five. Children attend half-day sessions basically to learn social skills and prepare for first grade. First grade is still sometimes referred to by its old name, **junior primary**. (In American English 'grades' are never called 'forms' as in British English.) Before kindergarten many American children go to nursery school for a few hours a day.

Curricula and Activities

American pupils usually have only one teacher for all subjects for the first six years of school, but that teacher is often a different individual for each grade or even half-grade. The first semester (term) of a grade is (rather illogically) called 'B' and the second 'A', for example, '4A'. This nomenclature is especially useful in schools where pupils who were born

Figure 14.3 Children o f many races and cultural backgrounds attend American schools. (Photo: Susan Lohwasser, Courtesy USIA)

in the winter half of the year start in January instead of September (and graduate in January instead of June), although this practice is increasingly rare. In such schools there will be a class of 4A's and a class of 4B's attending at the same time. In rural areas there are tendencies in the other direction, namely, to combine two or more grades in one classroom.

In grade school the emphasis is of course on the so-called 3R's— Reading, wRiting, and aRithmetic. It is often argued that children in English-speaking countries need to start school at the age of six instead of seven because English spelling is so difficult to master. These basics are supplemented with training in social skills and creative activities, like art and music. Students take part in supervised physical activities either in the school gym(nasium) or on the outdoor playground. There is usually a morning and afternoon break, called **recess**, for free outdoor activities. Grading of student achievement is usually limited to **report cards** for pupils to take home with comments such as 'satisfactory' and 'unsatisfactory' in various subjects, including social skills such as 'citizenship'.

One peculiarly American phenomenon that surprises many foreigners is the 'Pledge of Allegiance' sworn daily by elementary school pupils in about half of the states. Every morning the class is asked to stand next to their desks, turn toward the flag, place their right hands over their hearts (or, if they are boy/girl/cub/brownie scouts, to salute), and recite:

> I pledge allegiance
> to the flag
> of the United States
> of America
> and to the republic
> for which it stands,
> one nation,
> under God,[4]
> indivisible,
> with liberty
> and justice for all.

---

4 This phrase was added in 1954 despite protests that it violates the constitutional principle of separation of church and state.

Children whose religion forbids them to take such oaths are allowed not to participate in the ceremony.

Corporal punishment is still permitted in just under half of the states, largely in the southeast and southwest, although the issue is highly controversial and there have been a number of civil lawsuits involving abuse by teachers. The paddle is used at least through junior high in connection with physical education classes or by assistant principals in charge of disciplining students sent to their office by teachers. Although rates of physical punishment have been dropping for the last couple of decades, President George W. Bush supported the passage of federal legislation titled the Teacher Liability Protection Act that may well bring back corporal punishment in many states that have banned it, by shielding teachers anywhere from legal action if they paddle children.

At the junior high school level instruction is given by more specialized teachers, and the students move from one classroom to another for different classes. The day often starts with a brief session in a home room with a home-room teacher who is responsible for a certain class. Toward the end of junior high school students are often 'tracked'[5] into classes, for example 9B-1 or 9B-3, on the basis of their performance on a number of standardized aptitude tests and their classroom work. Ninth-graders can start to choose some of the courses they take, and although most classes are still taken by everyone, there is already some 'voluntary' differentiation of those who will probably pursue academic, 'vocational', or 'general' subjects respectively. Starting with seventh grade, achievement is reported using a five-point scale:

A = Excellent
B = Good
C = Average
D = Poor
F (or, more logically, E) = Fail

---

5   This 'tracking' is called 'streaming' in British English.

These grades can be more finely tuned with the addition of pluses and minuses. In averaging overall grades mathematically, an A is worth four points, a B three points, and so on. By adding up all the grade points and dividing by the number of grades, students arrive at a **grade point average**, or GPA.

The American high school is typically a comprehensive institution, meaning that several different curricula are gathered together under one roof. Students are helped by student counselors to put together their own programs on the basis of their interests and their results on a battery of standardized tests. Thus academically gifted students are advised to select a 'college prep(aratory)' curriculum with more advanced English and mathematics, a foreign language (usually Spanish, French, or German), science, and social studies. In some schools the most ambitious students may even sign up for extra 'zero-hour' classes, that is, classes held early in the morning before school normally starts. Students with weaker academic results are advised to take 'vocational' and 'general' curricula, with more basic English and math[6] courses combined with a number of so-called 'shop' (short for 'workshop') courses for practical training in electronics, machinery, and crafts. Should a student change his/her mind about future careers, it is possible, within limits, to change curricula. If such a change is made late in a student's school career, complementary summer or night school courses might be necessary, or the student may be able to make up for certain gaps by taking remedial courses at the junior-college level after graduation from high school. About 65 percent of all American high-school graduates go on to some form of higher education within twelve months of graduating from high school.

Extra-curricular activities

American high schools are well known for the large number of so-called **extra-curricular activities** that are offered, that is, activities that take place outside the regular program of instruction. The most common form is sports. Every high school (and junior high, for that matter) has its

6   Cf. 'maths' in British English.

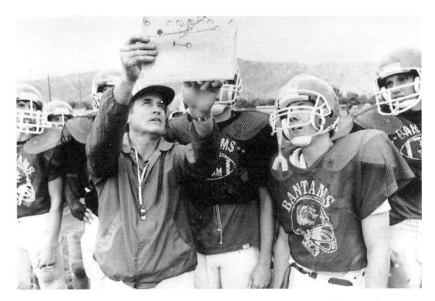

Figure 14.4 Members of a high-school football squad review strategy with their coach.
(Photo: Eric Roxfelt, AB Reportagebild)

(American) football, basketball, track and field, and swimming team (and sometimes baseball, soccer, and other sports as well). The teams wear the school colors and have the school nickname, like the 'Warriors' or the 'Chieftains'. Being a successful member of a team entitles athletes to wear the school **letter** on their varsity jackets, and some athletes have three or four such letters (actually one letter with four separate badges on it). There has been a dramatic increase in female participation in team sports over the past couple of decades: *Newsweek* reported in 1997 that after Congress passed Title IX of the Civil Rights Act of 1972, outlawing discrimination by gender in sports, resources started to be made available to girls' teams. The proportion of high-school girls taking part in team sports had leaped from one in twenty-seven in 1972 to one in three by the mid 1990s. Athletics offers both academically gifted and less gifted students a chance to achieve tremendous popularity among their fellow students. Needless to say, these activities also cut into the amount of time students have for doing their homework, and if a student's participation in sports leads to poor grades, he/she will not be allowed to continue with athletics.

Sports events also entail a number of peripheral activities. The grandest of these is **homecoming**, which refers to the activities surrounding the football team's first home game of the season (in early fall). Classes construct decorated floats, and there is a major **pep rally**, where **cheerleaders** rouse the students to inspire the team to do well in the game.

A **homecoming queen** and a **court** of four other girls are elected (in what amounts to a beauty and popularity contest), and a school dance rounds off the day.

Other extra-curricular activities include language clubs, debating societies, various musical ensembles (besides regular music classes), school newspapers, honor societies (for students with consistently good grades), science clubs, political clubs, and social clubs. These activities are 'sponsored' (in this case, this means 'supervised') by a member of the teaching faculty.

Social activities are also frequent, especially dances or 'proms' (from 'promenade') as the fanciest ones are called. A junior prom is a major occasion for second-to-last-year students and their dates, and the senior prom, held in conjunction with graduation, is a formal ball, with expensive gowns for girls and tuxedos for boys. A prom king and queen are elected, along with a court of four other couples. The prom is usually held at an expensive ballroom with a live orchestra, and groups of couples often compete with each other to arrange the most elaborate dinner parties before or after the prom, sometimes involving such extravagances as plane trips to other cities, for example.

Graduation or **commencement** ceremonies, as they are called, are also formal, with male and female students dressed in **caps and gowns** (the cap is also known as a 'mortar board', which it resembles). The caps and gowns are rented, but students keep the tassel with the school colors that hangs from the cap as a memento, along with their diploma. The student with the best grade point average in the class is called the **valedictorian** and delivers a valedictory (farewell) speech at commencement. The student with the second-best average grades is called the **salutatorian** and gives a speech of greeting. Every year the students and staff publish an elaborately illustrated **yearbook** documenting current students and school activities, with predictions of what future each graduating senior might face.

Foreign students who have spent a year at an American high school often report that the demands made of students are lower there than in the European *gymnasium*, for example. Some of the best high schools are roughly comparable to their foreign counterparts, but the average school presents little challenge to gifted students. On the other hand, there is a spirit of togetherness, a 'school spirit' that is often lacking in schools abroad.

Some exchange students are also surprised at some of the rules that exist in American high schools. One unwritten rule is that teachers are most often addressed as Mr or Ms plus their last name, even in cases where a class or individual students might have very close relations with a teacher. A more formal regulation involves students' freedom of movement. During class sessions the halls (corridors) of the school are supposed to be empty. Exemplary junior and senior students take turns sitting in strategic places as 'hall monitors' to stop and question students who might be caught out in the halls during class time. If the students cannot produce a hall permit signed by a teacher or counselor, they will be sent to the assistant principal's office for disciplinary action.

Some schools have also had dress codes, often mandating skirts for girls and banning jeans for all, for example. Most of these rules have been relaxed in recent years, however. On the other hand, since keeping up with clothing fashions takes so much of students' time and attention and so much of their parents' money, many major public school districts have recently followed the example of some private schools and adopted school uniforms, although these outfits are often less formal than those in traditional private schools. Student response to this experiment has been mixed, but predominantly favorable. It is argued by students and grown-ups alike that if they are not allowed to use clothing to express themselves, pupils will be forced to use verbal and social means to make an impression on others.

CHAPTER 15

Higher Education

History

Post-secondary education started in the British colonies in America in 1636, when Harvard College was established near Boston, Massachusetts (it received this name in 1638 when John Harvard died and left his personal library and a legacy of £800 to the college). It largely trained men (only) for the Puritan ministry, with instruction in traditional subjects given in Latin and Greek. When ideas of the Enlightenment started to permeate teaching at Harvard, a number of its graduates protested and established a college of their own in New Haven, Connecticut in 1701. This later became Yale University.

In the southern colonies, where Anglicanism was the dominant religion, the first college, William and Mary, was established in 1693 to train local men for clerical occupations. Less than a century later, in 1779, this divinity school at William and Mary was terminated, the ideas of the Enlightenment having led to the establishment, instead, of professorial chairs in scientific subjects, law, philosophy, and economics. Thomas Jefferson was instrumental in effecting this shift of emphasis.

In the middle colonies the first colleges appeared in the middle of the 18th century: the College of New Jersey (1746, later Princeton University), King's College in New York City (1754, later Columbia University), the College and Academy of Philadelphia (1755, later the University of Pennsylvania, established by Benjamin Franklin), and Queen's College in New Jersey (1766, later Rutgers University). In 1765 the University of Pennsylvania introduced the first systematic instruction in medicine in the colonies.

All of the institutions mentioned above were private, that is, they were financed mainly by the fees students paid to attend classes. In the second half of the 18th and early 19th century the first state universities began to appear, institutions supported by the state government and charging only minor tuition fees. What was to become the public University of Delaware was founded in 1743, and the universities of Georgia (1785), Pittsburgh (1787), Vermont (1791), North Carolina (1795), and South Carolina (1801) were established after the Revolution. The first to be established in the new territories outside the original thirteen colonies were the University of Michigan (originally Michigania), which dates from 1817, twenty years before Michigan Territory became a state, and Indiana University (1820). Thomas Jefferson founded the public University of Virginia in 1819 and made it the most progressive university in the country at the time.

As was mentioned above (p. 208), the Morrill Act of 1862 granted major tracts of land to all states willing to establish public agricultural colleges. This land-grant system promoted the establishment of some seventy institutions that are now state universities.

The first college to become **coeducational**, that is, to admit women (women students are still often referred to as 'coeds' [two syllables]), was Oberlin College in Ohio, as early as 1833. The first full-fledged college for women only was Vassar, founded in upstate New York in 1861. Universities in the Midwest and West were often coeducational from the beginning, while older institutions back east were slow to change. Radcliffe College was established as a women's college within Harvard University in 1879, but in the early 1970s Harvard College for men and Radcliffe for women in effect merged into a single coeducational and co-residential school, Harvard and Radcliffe Colleges. There was a similar development at Columbia (Columbia College and Barnard College) and other 'Ivy League' (see note on p. 230).

A women's college, Bryn Mawr in Pennsylvania (1885), was one of the first American colleges to offer **doctorate** degrees. Johns Hopkins University in Baltimore, Maryland, was set up in 1867 as primarily a research institution and pioneered the Ph.D. (that is, doctor of philosophy) in America. Older universities followed suit only in the final decades of the 19th century.

Financing

In regard to financing, there are thus two types of colleges and universities: private and public. Of the some 4,200 institutions of higher learning in the country, over half are privately run. The rest are public, operated by state or local authorities. About 13 million of the country's more than 18 million college students attend public institutions. In other words, private colleges are somewhat more numerous but tend to be smaller. About 2,450 of the 4,200 institutions are four-year colleges or universities and 1,750 two-year institutions (see community colleges below p. 232–233). Women account for 56 percent of college students.

Private universities rely on student tuition fees for about 43 percent of their revenues, while public institutions bring in only 19 percent of their money from this source. In the aggregate, public institutions get 36 percent of their funding from state governments and about 4 percent from local governments. For private colleges, direct support from state and local sources is negligible. Private colleges receive 14 percent of their funding from the federal government, and public institutions 11 percent.

Private donations (including private contracts for research done) account for roughly 9 percent of funding for private colleges and about 4 percent for public ones. About 5 percent of private college financing is from so-called **endowments**, that is, large sums of donated and earned money that the college invests in businesses and elsewhere and which yield an annual return in the form of interest. This source is negligible for public institutions as a whole, although some prestigious public universities have sizable endowments. Harvard University (private) had the largest endowment in 2006, on the order of $29 billion (thousand million) and about $20 billion more than the second largest Yale University, $10 billion. Four of the ten largest endowments are at public institutions: University of Texas, University of California (all ten campuses), University of Michigan, and Texas Agricultural and Mechanical University (Texas A&M). At the end of 2008, *The Wall Street Journal* reported that Harvard's endowment had reached as high as $45 billion in the summer of 2008 before losing $8 billion in the stock market slump, a loss that exceeds the value of any other individual endowments with the exception of six universities.

Colleges appeal to their **alumni**[1] (graduates) for contributions. The more prestigious universities normally have more affluent alumni who are able to donate more money than others to their old **alma mater** (nourishing mother) to help sustain or even raise its educational status, which in turn increases their own status as graduates of the school. Alumni gifts amounted to $8.4 billion in 2006. Gifts from non-alumni individuals added another $5.7 billion in 2006, and support from business and foundations added another $4.6 billion in 2006. All private donations totaled $28 billion in 2006. It should be added that voluntary contributions to both state and private institutions of higher learning are in varying degrees deductible when paying state and federal income tax. This means that by giving tax benefits to donors, the federal and state governments indirectly support the finances of private institutions.

From the point of view of the fee-paying student, the most expensive private colleges cost about $30,000 a year for tuition alone, not including other costs such as living expenses and books. This figure is extreme, but even the average charge for private four-year colleges is about $27,000. Public four-year colleges, on the other hand, charge students an average of about $6,400 a year. State universities are much cheaper for residents of the state; out-of-state students can pay three times as much to attend. Dormitory charges are typically over $5,500 a year at private institutions and about $3,700 a year at public ones. Board (food) adds another $4,000 and $3,400, respectively, to those figures.

College students finance their studies in a number of ways: through loans, scholarships, work, and parents. Students can borrow money from the federal government through the Perkins Loan Program (formerly called the National Direct Student Loan Program) or through Federal Family Education Loans, various federally guaranteed student bank loans

---

1   This Latin word presents an insoluble problem to those wishing to avoid 'gendered' language. The masculine form is *alumnus* in the singular and *alumni* in the plural; the feminine forms are *alumna* and *alumnae*. Thus there is no neutral singular or plural form available. Informally, it is becoming increasingly common to use the truncated forms **alumn** and **alumns**, often spelled **alum** and **alums**.

at lower-than-normal interest rates, among others so-called Stafford loans. About one quarter of all freshmen have federally guaranteed loans and about 9 percent Perkins Loans directly from the government.

Scholarships are relatively common in the US. Especially bright and deserving students can be offered a full-tuition scholarship to prestigious private universities. Roughly half of Harvard College freshmen receive sufficient needs-tested funding. Students who are good at sports are often recruited to university teams with the help of partial or full scholarships. Colleges and universities themselves spend more than $10 billion annually on scholarships and (graduate) fellowships for their own students ($6.4 billion from private, $3.7 billion from public colleges). Some 29 percent of all freshmen receive some sort of grant from their college, and 19 percent have a grant from their state.

The state of Georgia distinguished itself early when it comes to providing state aid to college students in the last decade. The implemented Project HOPE, Help Outstanding Pupils Educationally. Students who get good grades in school are basically guaranteed a free college education within the state, including free tuition and a book allowance as long as they keep their grades up. They can even choose a private university in Georgia, although in that case the funding is limited to a set sum (about $3,000) toward tuition. In 1996, 97 percent of freshmen students at the two leading universities in Georgia were studying for free. The money comes from the state lottery. Other states now have similar guarantee programs.

Federal aid is available under two major programs. Pell Grants, also known as Basic Educational Opportunity Grants (BEOG), are needs related (that is, are given to students from families that would not otherwise be able to afford to send their children to college) and the average size is roughly $2,400. About one fifth of all college freshmen have Pell Grants. The Supplemental Educational Opportunity Grants Program also provides grants of up to $2,000 a year, with the stipulation that the amount may not exceed 50 percent of the student's demonstrated need. About 6 percent of all college students are recipients, with grants averaging $770. Over the last five decades, hundreds of thousands of veterans of the armed services have taken advantage of the 'GI Bill (of Rights)' instituted at the end of World War II, which specially earmarked federal funds to help ex-GI's[2] to go to college. There are also generous grants and scholarships available from private corporations and foundations.

More and more college students, almost two thirds in the early 2000s, find it necessary to work at least part-time, and about one third full-time, during the academic term. Juniors (third year, see p. 213 f.) and seniors (fourth year) are more likely to have jobs. Colleges and student unions often offer students part-time employment in dormitories, stores, and cafeterias. Seniors are sometimes employed to serve as tutors for freshmen who need remedial help with English composition or mathematics, for example. Almost 90 percent of all college students work during the summer, most of them full-time. There is also a federal program called College Work-Study (CWS) that provides jobs for students with demonstrated financial need. Some 12 percent of students take part in this program each year.

It is still considered normal for parents to pay for the bulk of their children's college education, and there are numerous savings plans for young couples to embark upon as soon as their children are born. Some colleges offer parents special tuition rates if they start paying in advance, while the child is still a baby. Even for fairly well-to-do families, putting several children through college can be a tremendous financial burden, but one which American parents are normally willing to do their best to bear.

For the last two or three decades America's best graduate schools have relied heavily on foreign, especially Asian, students to maintain their leading position in science and engineering. The National Science Board reported in 2003 that 38 percent of all doctorates in science and engineering are held by foreign-born individuals. Fee-paying foreign students have also represented a welcome boost to the finances of universities and the economy in general, as much as $13 billion in 2003.

---

2   This is a common term for people in the armed forces. It is an application of the initials stamped on materials issued by the government for military use, short for 'Government Issue'. Originally the initials referred only to items made of galvanized iron, a standard category in military accounting.

After the attacks of September 11, 2001, foreign students in the US found it increasingly difficult to renew their student visas, often being forced to abandon their studies midway and return home, and prospective students from abroad started shifting their attention to universities in other English-speaking countries. America's leading universities petitioned the government to stop delaying and denying so many student visas, citing the great loss to US higher education and to the future US economy. In late 2004 Nils Hasselmo, president of the Association of American Universities, reported that the major factors behind declining numbers of foreign students are "visa policy, increased international competition, and perceptions that the United States is no longer a welcoming country".

Control

Although public colleges and universities are more dependent upon state and local governments for support, it should not be assumed that they are substantially less independent than private institutions are. American state universities are run by a publicly elected **board of regents** or **board of trustees** or **board of governors** and a chief executive, called the university **president** or **chancellor**. Once elected, this board is ultimately responsible for spending, curricula, and policy matters, and the state or local government is not directly involved in running the school. Perhaps the greatest danger to the independence of academic institutions, private and public, is the growing amount of research commissioned by private corporations, often focused on attaining useful research outcomes.

Academic standards are set and continuously monitored by regional **accreditation associations**. Being accredited by such an organization is essential for any college wishing to maintain or establish a good reputation.

It is commonly believed abroad that all of the best American universities are private and that public institutions are generally of lower quality. This is not the case. While it is true that listings of the 'top' universities (based on their reputation among university presidents and college deans, for example, or on 'objective' indexes gauging the quality of staff, rigor of curriculum, and other criteria) are dominated by private, often old 'Ivy League',[3] schools and 'newer' ones like Stanford in California (1891) and the University of Chicago (1890), there are some state universities that consistently rank at the very top, including the University of California at Berkeley, the University of Michigan, the University of California at Los Angeles (UCLA), the University of Wisconsin, the University of Texas, and the University of North Carolina. In any specific field, private and public institutions share positions of leadership. In medicine, for example, the public University of California at San Francisco is ranked with Harvard and Johns Hopkins. In law, the University of Michigan and the University of Virginia are often placed alongside Harvard and Yale. It gives some indication of the quality of library resources to note that when Google initiated its huge project of digitizing virtually all books to make them available to the general public, it chose the University of Michigan Library as the core collection, to be supplemented by special collections from the New York Public Library and university libraries at Harvard, Yale, Stanford, and Oxford, England, among others.

Just below the most prestigious institutions, there is excellent instruction and research at a great many colleges and universities, both private and public. At the bottom, the mediocrity is roughly equally portioned out between private and state colleges.

Some states have a two- or three-tiered system of higher education. California, for instance, has three differentiated types of public institutions: the University of California system, with 10 campuses, consists of research-oriented universities that also teach undergraduates culled from the top ten percent of the state's high schools as well as from elsewhere in the country; the California State University system has 23 campuses and, though solid research is carried on, the emphasis is on undergraduate teaching, with a broader selection of students; and then there is the California Community College system (see p. 232 for the concept of 'community college') to provide the first two years of four-year

---

3   This term is used to refer to eight old and prestigious private institutions in the northeast (typically with ivy-covered buildings): Harvard, Yale, Princeton, Brown, Cornell, Dartmouth, Columbia, and the University of Pennsylvania.

Figure 15.1 A.D. Campus of Mt. Holyoke College for Women in South Hadley, Massachusetts. (Photo: Christofer Little, Courtesy USIA)

programs as well as remedial and job-related instruction on 110 campuses. While it is usually considered more prestigious to attend one of the great research universities in the US, it can sometimes mean that some of the professors are less interested in their students than in their research. A small, quality liberal arts college often offers invaluable student/professor relationships.

Structure, Curricula, Activities

The reader will have noticed that we have been using the terms college and university more or less interchangeably throughout this section. 'College' is a generic term in American English; an American undergraduate student is 'in college' whether he/she is studying at a college or a university, and where British speakers refer to going 'to university' or recall something they learned 'at university', Americans say they are going 'to college' and learned this or that 'in college'. It is also common to say that you are 'in school' when you are studying at a university or college.

A college may be an independent institution or a part of a larger unit, a university. Where Europeans, for example, refer to the different 'faculties' of a university, Americans use the term 'college'. A university might comprise a 'college of liberal arts', a 'college of music', and a 'college of social sciences', etc. The word 'faculty' is normally perceived as referring to the teaching and research staff. The head of an independent college is called a **president**. Colleges within a university are headed by **deans**.

Although some institutions which call themselves colleges offer graduate[4] degrees in certain subjects, the conferring of especially doctorates is usually associated with universities. Graduate and professional colleges within American universities are often called **schools**: school of medicine, school of law, school of business studies, school of engineering, etc.

An ever more important form of post-secondary education is the junior college or community college. This is a two-year institution that first appeared in the 1910s, but came into its own in the 1960s and later. The community college is usually run by a municipal or county board of education or other local authority and is relatively inexpensive for residents, typically between $2,000 (for city/county residents) and $3,000 (for non-residents) per year for tuition. It provides the equivalent of the first two years of college, preparing its graduates to go on to a four-year institution (either a college or a university) and start at the junior level (third year). Students can also terminate their studies after junior college, which offers an **associate in arts** (AA) or **associate in science** (AS) degree after two years. Shorter programs result in **certificates**.

This inexpensive alternative to four years away from home at a four-year college is also proving to be perfectly suited to retraining and continuing-education courses needed by local businesses and job-seekers. Working in close cooperation with the business community, unions, and local authorities, the flexible community college can often tailor courses

4   Studies leading to BA and BS (or BSc) degrees are called 'undergraduate' studies. Programs above the undergraduate level are usually called 'graduate' studies in American English and 'post-graduate' studies in British English.

to specific needs more easily than colleges and universities can. Adults can also receive remedial and complementary education to make up for poor results achieved earlier in high school and perhaps improve their scholastic record enough to be accepted at a four-year institution. Some community colleges also offer junior- and senior-level courses on their campuses in cooperation with neighboring four-year institutions, thus enabling students to get a degree from the four-year institution without having to move to that campus.

Counting individuals, but not full-time places, adults over twenty-five now make up almost half of all post-secondary students in the US, a proportion which has nearly doubled since the 1960s. Sixty percent of these students are women, and seventy percent of them work full-time and study part-time, not only at community colleges but also at four-year institutions. Many pursue independent study programs, with only occasional visits to campus, keeping in touch with professors by mail, telephone, and starting in the second half of the 1990s, e-mail and the Internet. The University of Phoenix has been a pioneer in offering online courses and degrees, requiring only occasional visits to its local campuses all over the country.

Admission to junior colleges is usually automatic for graduates of the local high schools. For admission to most four-year institutions, high-school students usually have to take Scholastic Aptitude Tests (SATs) or, especially in the Midwest, American College Tests (ACTs), which measure verbal and mathematical skills. Students wishing to attend elite universities and colleges have to perform well on these tests and have good high-school grades as well. Prospective students are sometimes asked to come in for a personal interview. Application is made to each institution individually, not to a central authority, as may be the case in some other countries. Applicants are normally charged a fee to have their application processed, so students usually limit their choices to a small number of schools. With the help of alumni associations, elite universities actively recruit gifted students from all over the country, especially from minorities in order to achieve a racially and ethnically mixed student body.

American undergraduate programs are based on a **credit** system related to the number of hours spent studying a certain subject. The

normal basic academic degree,[5] the **bachelor of arts** (abbreviated BA or
AB) or **bachelor of science** (BS or BSc), requires 120 *credit hours* (also
called **semester hours, credit units**, etc.). This normally takes four years
or eight semesters[6] to complete, which means that students typically take
15 hours per term. These 'hours' correspond to the number of hours
actually spent in class each week. For typical basic degrees, then, the
system looks like this:

8 × 15 hours = 120 hours in 4 years

There is a major difference between college studies in the US and many
European countries, for example. American students are encouraged to
take many different subjects at a time and never to specialize in one or
two fields only. A typical 15-hour course load consists of five different
subjects, for instance, 4 hours of English literature, 3 hrs of botany, 3 hrs of
psychology, 3 hrs of Spanish, and 2 hrs of music appreciation. Parts of the
first two years of study are usually fairly firmly set by the college,
guaranteeing proficiency in composition writing, for example, but there
are usually a variety of elective[7] science courses to choose from to fulfill
the science requirement (12–14 hours), just as there are a number of social
studies electives available to satisfy that requirement (12–14 hours).

Students are not allowed to start to 'specialize' until their junior (third)
year, when they are expected to **declare a major**. The major field of study
they choose may entail certain other choices, perhaps leading to a **minor**
in another subject. But even seniors do not normally concentrate on one
subject alone, the goal being a **liberal education**, meaning a general
orientation in a broad range of fields.

---

5 A degree is never called an 'exam' as in some other languages. An exam(ination) is a
   test in English.
6 This Latin term, borrowed by English from German, is commonly used alongside
   'term' in American English. Some colleges have three semesters a year, called
   'trimesters' and some four, called 'quarters'. Even with a two-semester system, the
   summer is often used as a third term or half-term.
7 These courses are usually termed 'optional' in British English, but they are not truly
   optional: the student is required to choose a certain number of them.

Examinations are usually administered in the middle of the semester, so-called mid-terms, and at the end of the term, so-called finals. There are exams in each separate subject, usually about five, written in blue-books, special pre-printed stationery with the university emblem. All of these two- or three-hour exams take place in just a few days, and students who fail do not normally have a second chance (or third, seventh, etc. as in some countries). They must take the same or a similar class during the next term if they want to try again. Students who fail to maintain average grades or better are placed on probation and then expelled if they do not improve.

True specialization sets in only in graduate school. The first graduate degree, the **master of arts** (MA) or **master of science** (MSc or MS), usually requires two or three semesters of class work plus a short thesis, which takes another term to write. The **doctor of philosophy** or Ph.D. is normally a four-year program (but often takes longer) leading to a dissertation to be examined by a committee of professors.

Professional schools, like medicine and law, have their own degrees, doctor of medicine (MD) and juris doctor (JD), respectively. Further study can lead to a Ph.D. in medicine and an SJD (doctor of juridical science) in law.

The difference in approach to education is evidenced by European students who have majored in business administration, for example, and enroll in an American graduate school of business. They are surprised to find that much of their instruction is relatively basic, covering material they learned as undergraduates in Europe. In the American system the typical graduate student in business has probably had little, if any, instruction in the field. He/she might have majored in English, for example. Graduate schools in the US prefer having students who have undergone a general liberal education, even if this means the schools have to provide rudimentary instruction in the field of specialization. Some of the best medical schools in the country actively discourage pre-med(ical) undergraduates from majoring in science.

There are even more extra-curricular activities available at colleges and universities than at high schools (see p. 218). Again sports dominate the scene at major universities, with their football and basketball operations assuming astronomical proportions. There have been many scandals involving athletes who are 'helped' to pass their academic courses at universities all over the country, but from the early 1990s there has been a general movement underway among colleges to tighten their control of athletes' classroom achievement. The aim of the reform program was that students who are failing classes should not be allowed to participate in sports and that there should be no separate 'Mickey Mouse' courses and programs for athletes.

Debating is a common form of inter-collegiate competition. Opposing teams are given a subject in advance and allowed to prepare their arguments, but they are told which side they are to argue for only at the beginning of the debate. Needless to say, this type of competition is a good training ground for future politicians. Other activities include drama groups (both for credit and extra-curricular), honor societies (for students with consistently good grades, usually with names consisting of Greek letters), film clubs, jazz clubs, newspapers and journals, etc.

A strikingly American feature of campus life is the prevalence of so-called **Greek organizations**, or **fraternities** and **sororities**. They are called 'Greek' because they have two or three Greek letters as names. They are primarily social clubs, and only upperclassmen (juniors and seniors) can be members (although junior colleges often have these organizations for sophomores). 'Application' is made during a week-long **rush**, when the various fraternities (for men) and sororities (for women) open their doors to prospective members, usually second-semester sophomores. They arrange open-house parties in their large residential houses on or close to campus and try to attract the 'best' future members, often meaning students whose families could be expected to make contributions to the society's house or simply very attractive and gregarious people. After rush, the societies decide which of the visitors they would like to accept and invite them formally to **pledge** the society. The life of a pledge is rendered hellish for a week or two by the members (this demeaning treatment is called 'hazing'), but if the pledge fulfills the requirements and survives **initiation** night, he/she will be invited to move into the fraternity/sorority house for his/her junior year. Certain fraternities and sororities usually cooperate when it comes to arranging parties and dates, and they serve as 'old boys' networks after graduation, often with national affiliations. If nothing else, pledging and initiation do instill a feeling of community among those who have gone through them together.

Most students ignore (or pretend to ignore) the fraternities and sororities. Freshmen and sophomores are often required to live in 'on-campus' student dormitories, because the university is acting to some extent *in loco parentis*, 'in the place of a parent', and is partly responsible for their well-being. This responsibility has been greatly lessened in the past couple of decades, however, and students are granted very broad freedoms nowadays. By their junior year, many students want to move into 'off-campus' private housing, usually sharing an apartment with a couple of friends. Fraternity and sorority seniors often do this too, finding one year of full-blown Greek-society life sufficient.

Much of the excitement of attending college is found outside the classroom. American campuses exude a collegiate atmosphere that is very stimulating to students in their late teens and early twenties. Major campuses attract cultural events and interesting specialty shops and eccentric characters that add color to the surroundings. Also—and here the similarity with other countries is great—the opportunity to get to know other students from different parts of the country and from abroad is probably just as valuable as the formal instruction offered by the professors.

CHAPTER 16

The Education Crisis

Symptoms

As was demonstrated at the beginning of this chapter, there is general agreement in the US today that the schools have been in a state of crisis for some time, even though some progress has been made in the last few years. The problems were documented in a number of national and international reports in the 1980s that placed American students well below their cohorts in other countries. For instance, *Newsweek* reported in 1990 that Hong Kong high-school students did best on a chemistry achievement test involving thirteen countries. England and Singapore placed second and third, while the United States wound up in eleventh place. In physics, Hong Kong ranked highest again, followed by England and Hungary. American students came in ninth. In biology, they were in last place.

The same 1990 article pointed out that only 45 percent of American adults knew that the earth revolves around the sun once a year, and roughly the same percentage had accepted that human beings evolved from earlier species. The *average* Japanese twelfth-grader had a better command of mathematics than the top 5 percent of his/her American counterparts. Average science and mathematics achievement among American eighth-graders in 1999 showed some improvement over 1990, but US pupils were still ranked only in the middle of the 38 nations included in the recurring study.

The picture was bleak in the humanities and social sciences as well. Only one quarter of all high-school students were enrolled in foreign-language classes in the late 1980s. A majority of American students could not locate the world's major countries on the map. In 1988 the National

Geographic Society commissioned a study to test how much American adults knew about geography. One in five could not name a single country in Europe, while one in four could not locate the Pacific Ocean on a map. Nearly half of those tested could not find New York State, and fourteen percent of them could not even correctly identify the United States on a blank map of the world's nations.[1] In a 1989 study called *Crossroads in American Education*, the National Assessment of Educational Progress found that sixty percent of all high-school students could not understand the material they read in school. In the 2006 PISA (Programmed International Student Assessment) tests of the math, science, and reading proficiency of 15-year-olds, the US was not listed among the top twenty countries in any of the skills.

The Bureau of the Census tested the reading ability of 3,400 Americans over twenty years of age in 1986, asking them to answer multiple-choice questions like the following:

Don't allow your medical identification card to

> a) be used
> b) have destroy
> c) go lose
> d) get expired

by any other person.

Thirteen percent of them failed the test, answering 20 or fewer of 26 such questions correctly. Twenty percent of those asked to take the test refused to do so, presumably because they were afraid to reveal their illiteracy.

Even the cream of the schools' crop of scholars has been performing less and less well over the last couple of decades. Scholastic Aptitude Test (SATs, see p. 233) scores in both verbal and mathematical skills declined

---

1   This shocking report should be placed in perspective: the study gave the same world map to adults of all ages in the US and several other countries, asking them to identify 16 countries and bodies of water. Americans and Britons did equally badly, averaging respectively 8.6 and 8.5 correct answers. Italians and Mexicans got only 7.5 right, while Canadians, Frenchmen, and Japanese scored 9.5. West Germans and Swedes placed more than 11 correctly. More alarmingly, among 18–24-year-olds only, Americans came in last, with a mere 6.9 right (young Swedes again placed first, with 11.9).

consistently from 1963 until 1983, when they leveled off. Since then math scores have started to climb slowly, but verbal skills remain relatively stagnant. On the other hand, it should be remembered that far more students have been taking these examinations. The students who are pulling down the national average today correspond to students who, a generation ago, were not even in a position to take the tests. While this fact offers a moral defense in behalf of today's students, it offers little consolation to the country: the economy needs more and more students with high scores and many skills. It was clear from the 1983 report that what had happened over the previous couple of decades was that the educational system, especially at the secondary and post-secondary level, had felt forced to dilute standards in order to educate an ever larger proportion of the population. One lesson of the 1990s seems to be the realization that such dilution of standards—and a concomitant lowering of expectations—may have aggravated the problem in the 1980s. Improved achievement seems to lie down the road of increased expectations on the part of the schools.

Diagnosis and Remedies

A great deal of intellectual energy has been expended over the past two decades to find ways to improve America's schools. They are grappling with both exogenous problems, that is, general societal disorders that hit schools along with other parts of the social fabric, and endogenous, more school-specific, ones.

Crime—especially drug-related—makes up one of the most intractable hindrances to quality schooling. Inner-city problem schools are sometimes patrolled not by senior hall monitors but by armed police officers or security guards. In 2005, some 30 percent of secondary school boys reported carrying guns outside school and about 10 percent on school property; the respective figures for girls were 7 percent and 3 percent. It is, of course, not unusual for guns to be fired either accidentally or on purpose, causing sometimes fatal injury. In 2001 some 9 percent of students reported being threatened or injured with a weapon on school property, about 12 percent of boys and about 7 percent of girls. Playgrounds of even elementary schools can be the sites of extensive drug dealing, especially in big cities, but also in the suburbs and in small towns. Teachers feel intimidated by such a situation and obviously find it difficult to carry on meaningful instruction.

Among girls, teenage pregnancy is a major cause of disrupted schooling. In minority populations like African Americans, Puerto Ricans, Mexicans, and American Indians, 14–18 percent of all births are to teenage mothers (the rate for the entire population is around 10 percent). The rate for African-American teens has improved over the last few years, down to 17 percent in 2005 from 23 percent in the 1990s.

Poverty and homelessness represent another societal ill that hampers the schools. Malnutrition related to poverty has been recognized as a major cause of learning disability. It was estimated in 1990 that every dollar spent on improved perinatal health care and family nutrition would save five dollars' worth of future remedial schooling for poor children. Tens of thousands of children attend school only sporadically because they are homeless, and school districts sometimes refuse to accept them as pupils because their parents have no address in the community. In such cases courts have normally stepped in and ordered such schools to receive homeless children. This is a problem that has plagued children of migrant (often Mexican) workers for many decades, but it now affects a sizable section of the general population.

Television and videos are often mentioned as another external factor affecting schools to some extent, although experts disagree on their true importance. By the time they are eighteen years old, American children have typically spent more time in front of the television than in school. It is generally recognized that the nature of television and video programming, with ever shorter intervals between shifts in scenes and camera angles, has shortened the attention span of children, who then find even twenty- or thirty-minute lessons unbearably boring. Another negative consequence of watching television is that very young children grow used to not understanding what programs are all about. In school they consequently tend merely to accept the fact that they do not understand what is being taught, and they do not bother to ask questions. Scientific studies have also shown a strong correlation between playing violent video games and both desensitization in regard to violence and more aggressive behavior.

Schools have traditionally been seen as a key instrument for creating equality of opportunity in America. In no context have such hopes been higher than for African Americans, nearly all of them descendants of slaves originally brought to the country by force. Yet, despite the documented success of remedial pre-school programs such as 'Operation Head Start', started by the federal government in the mid 1960s, black American achievement later in school continues to lag substantially behind that of whites, and the schools are blamed for their failure. Educators counter that the schools alone cannot turn the overwhelming tide of social and economic conditions that conspire to disable African Americans.

A controversial attempt to establish, if not actual equality, at least equality of opportunity for blacks was mandated by federal and state courts starting in the late 1960s. Since by the 1960s inner-city districts had become almost entirely black as a result of whites' leaving for outlying areas and suburbs, the quality of inner-city schools was far inferior to that of surrounding areas. The schools were *de facto* segregated. To alleviate this problem, the courts ordered all schools in a certain city to achieve roughly the same racial balance as the city as a whole. The only practical means to accomplish this was through **busing**. Children would not automatically attend their neighborhood schools but rather would be bused to other neighborhoods.

This busing caused riots and boycotts in many parts of the country, not least in the Boston area. Private white 'academies' sprang up everywhere, effectively emptying some school districts of their white children. In some places this exodus was so great by the mid 1980s that federal courts allowed the school district to return to a neighborhood system. But in many places busing has proved to be a workable albeit inconvenient way to mix students of different races. At the same time, it is clear that busing, indeed, even schooling, is not sufficient in itself to bring about a general change in relative social and economic status of blacks and whites.

In the summer of 2007 the US Supreme Court found, in a 5–4 decision, that race could not be used as a factor in deciding which schools children attend. This decision, based on cases in Seattle, Washington, and Louisville, Kentucky, in effect put an end to efforts across the country to achieve racial balance. This can be interpreted as fundamentally overturning the landmark 1954 *Brown vs. Board of Education* decision (see p. 156) that initiated attempts to integrate the country's schools. The more conservative leaning of the Supreme Court is a result of new appointments made by George W. Bush.

Turning to more school-specific problems and remedies, we can start with money. The US spends roughly 7 percent of its gross domestic product (GDP) on education, ranking close to the top of OECD countries (on a par with, say, Sweden, and slightly behind Canada, Norway, and Finland, but well ahead of Germany and France). It is more fair to look at public expenditure per student as a percentage of GDP per capita. With this measure, which relates public spending on education to the ability of the country to pay, the US places in the middle of the G7 countries (the world's wealthiest industrial nations) with 20 percent, behind Canada, Italy, and France but ahead of Germany, Japan, and the UK. Many education experts look for an increased role for the federal Department of Education both in evening out regional and state differences in spending and in establishing new national standards of excellence, for instance, a national curriculum and national teacher certification. While more money as such does not automatically mean higher quality, there are obviously many areas in the field of education where increased funds could work wonders.

The state of South Carolina presents a case in point. When the *Nation at Risk* report was published in 1983, South Carolina ranked second to last on school-spending per student, and the state had some of the lowest student-achievement statistics in the country, according to *The Economist*. The governor persuaded the state legislature to raise the sales tax from 4 to 5 percent and spent the added money to overhaul the state's schools. Teacher salaries were raised (from an average of $17,000 in 1984 to $25,000 in 1988), remedial and gifted-children programs were started, and bonuses were offered to schools that performed well. By 1988 South Carolina, though still below average, had led the nation in average improvements in SAT (see p. 233) test scores for four years in a row. Students in the state were taking advanced-placement programs at twice the national average. Truancy went down, and teacher morale was reportedly the highest in the country. President George H. W. Bush said in the late 1980s that he wanted to be 'the Education President', but he also stressed that what is really needed is fifty 'education governors'. The example of South Carolina indicates that he may have been right. Even if there were to be a major increase in federal involvement in education, most of the day-to-day hard work will have to be done at the state and local levels as it has in the past.

President George H. W. Bush's plans to bolster education included two types of schools. **Magnet** schools, which already existed in a number of school districts, are schools offering especially attractive curricula in specialized fields related to students' personal development and/or career opportunities. **Merit** schools, on the other hand, are schools that receive extra money for having achieved certain academic standards; in other words, they participate in a bonus system. This has sometimes been connected with **merit pay** for teachers, a part of the issue of school **accountability** that has been debated for a couple of decades. The idea is that the best teachers would be paid more. The obvious problem is how to determine who those teachers are. It has typically been easier for politicians to raise teacher salaries in general than to get teachers to go along with assessments of their individual performance.

Many states and local communities have followed the lead of Minnesota and introduced the idea of allowing parents to choose which public school they want to send their children to. If a child decides to move from one school to another, state funds are transferred to that school as well. In Minnesota juniors and seniors in high school can even choose to take some of their courses at local community colleges or universities. The rationale is that if state support—about half of all funds (see Figure 14.1 "Financing Public Schools" p. 210)—is tied to the student, the schools will feel a sort of 'market' pressure either to perform well or lose funds. Schools that fail to attract a minimum number of students are closed down or reorganized. In a sense, they 'go bankrupt'. The result of this kind of thinking has been that school principals are starting to do public relations work for their schools, and local curricula are being revised to attract students from near and far, a sort of voluntary busing system that has often led to effective desegregation.

Minnesota's experiments in the early 1990s paved the way for another innovative form of organizing schooling, so-called **charter schools**. These are schools that in a sense 'opt out' of the usual system: they tear up union contracts, eliminate bureaucratic rules, and generally do whatever is thought to be necessary to improve their students' chances of succeeding. Teachers, principals, and parents are free to experiment—and, of course, to run the risk of failing. Most states that allow charter schools (and more than half of all states now have some) impose at least initial limits on the number or percentage of schools that can participate in this experimental scheme. Charter schools come in all shapes and sizes, so to speak, and while there have been many dramatic local improvements, it is still too early to generalize about their success or failure. By 2005, there were more than 3,000 charter schools nationwide, about 3 percent of all schools, with about 2 percent of all students.

Conservatives would like to go one step farther and give each student a voucher representing a standard amount of money spent per pupil for public schools. Families would then be able to use this voucher toward their children's tuition at a public or private school of their choice. A 1990 Brookings Institution study suggested that all local and state school boards and superintendents be done away with, leaving each individual school an autonomous institution that would have to compete with others for students and funding. In 1990 Milwaukee, Wisconsin, became the first city to allow substantial numbers of students to attend private schools using vouchers funded by public tax money. A five-year study of this system run by the University of Wisconsin showed that vouchers produced no appreciable affect on student achievement.

Another form of privatization has been attempted in places like Baltimore, Maryland, and Hartford, Connecticut. Here local school boards have hired private companies to provide schooling. Although this was much touted by conservatives in the mid 1990s as the key to success in American education, the results were generally disheartening. The largest supplier of for-profit schools using public funding is Edison Schools Incorporated. The company produces annual reports that show considerable gains among its students, but independent analysts, at Arizona State University and Western Michigan University schools of education, for example, have found that its glowing results rely heavily on skewed readings of figures. The results are mediocre in general, with some high spots, and Edison's involvement in schools across the country typically leads to stormy controversy.

Teachers' associations have been ambivalent toward this application of market-thinking to the field of education. Critics argue that it takes aim at brighter students primarily, even 'skimming the cream' off the student body in troubled schools, leaving weaker students behind in even worse straits. On the other hand, many teachers who have experienced the creation of magnet schools, local curricular autonomy (often called **local empowerment**), and charter schools have changed their minds, having found that the new incentive spurs previously mediocre schools to pull themselves up by their bootstraps.

Business leaders generally agree that whereas the entry-level qualification for most jobs used to be a high school diploma, employers now generally expect at least two years of college.[2] As American business firms find it more and more difficult to recruit properly qualified workers, they have started to donate money and equipment to schools at all levels. For years companies have been forced to spend huge sums anyway on teaching new employees basic skills on an in-house basis. Private corporations also spend hundreds of millions of dollars in direct support of public schools. Programs include awards for imaginative curricular innovations and direct purchase of equipment. Computer manufacturers give large numbers of computers to schools, obviously with the dual purpose of doing good and establishing their products.

The National Commission on Excellence in Education made several concrete recommendations in its 1983 report. It criticized the fact that so many high schools allowed students themselves to choose up to fifty percent of their curriculum. Too many students opted out of classes that might challenge them. In *Nation at Risk*, the commission recommended 'five New Basics' (echoing the 3R's) as a minimum requirement for all four-year high schools:

a) 4 years of English
b) 3 years of mathematics
c) 3 years of science
d) 3 years of social studies
e) 1/2-year of computer science

2 Employers admit that it is not so much the specific knowledge possessed by college and junior-college graduates that makes them suitable workers, but rather their proven discipline and ability to concentrate and apply themselves to a task. Specific skills are learned on the job anyway.

For students intending to go on to college, this curriculum should be supplemented by two years of a foreign language, building on the semesters already taken in junior high. The commission also recommended that colleges raise their admission standards to send a signal to high school students that they will have to work harder to be accepted.

This recommendation was followed by a great many states. Many others increased the requirements, but modified the New Basics to include only two years of science and mathematics. Altogether 42 states adopted one plan or the other. The improvements were dramatic in both cases: between 1982 and 1994, the percentage of high school graduates successfully completing this modified requirement more than doubled, and the percentage of students completing the equivalent of the more stringent New Basics programs more than tripled. By the early 21st century, the proportion of students studying foreign languages in the schools had doubled, from one quarter to nearly one half.

Another strong recommendation of the commission had to do with the time spent in school. The study compared academic upper secondary schools in Europe with those in the US and found that European students spent up to 8 hours a day and 220 days per year in school, whereas American students typically spent only 6 hours a day for 180 days. The commission recommended 7-hour days as a minimum and a 200–220-day school year. By the start of the 21st century, figures from the OECD indicated that American schools offered roughly 30 percent *more* teaching hours at the upper secondary level than the average European country.

A major international study of literacy from the early 1990s found a correlation between more instructional time and better achievement. This study, carried out by the International Education Association, placed the US right next to the top among fourth-graders and ninth-graders alike. Finland scored ahead of all others, but the American students outperformed their counterparts in, for example, Germany, Sweden, and Denmark. Students from poor American families did less well than their wealthier peers, but the average reading performance of the most economically disadvantaged American group never fell significantly below the OECD average. The National Assessment of Education Progress (NAEP) could report in its latest long-term study from 2004 that reading scores increased for 9-year-olds and mathematics scores increased among both 9- and 13-year-olds.

Studies evaluating skills in science and mathematics have proved disheartening, however. The 2006 OECD Program for International Student Assessment (PISA) study of 15-year-olds in 40 countries gave the US below average scores in science literacy and mathematics literacy. The US placement in the former field was 21st and in the latter 25th. The top scorers internationally are countries like Finland, with an exceptionally homogeneous population and negligible immigration, but a country as culturally diverse as neighboring Canada outscored the US as well, with placements close to the top on all counts.

American textbooks tend to be diluted and bland, often as a result of textbook authors' anticipating ever lower standards among students, but sometimes because their authors have tried to avoid controversy. Large conservative states like Texas can often influence what science books say about evolution or how history is told, for example, by boycotting certain textbook publishers. In the fall of 2004, for example, a standard social studies textbook was removed from Texas schools because its presentation of marriage failed to expressly state that marriage is a union between a man and woman. Since textbook publishers do not want to have different editions of books for different sections of the country, the effect of such a boycott can be national in scope.

A final recommendation deals, not surprisingly, with teachers. Too many American teachers are recruited from the bottom quarter of graduating high school and college classes, and over forty percent of their training as teachers is devoted to education courses, thus limiting their competence as regards the subject matter they teach. Qualified teachers continue to be in chronically short supply, and the situation has become critical especially in mathematics and science. Teacher salaries need to be raised.

The most significant legislation in education in decades was signed by President George W. Bush in January 2002. A major bipartisan effort, the act is called **No Child Left Behind**, and the White House sums up its main objectives as:

1. Increase Accountability for Student Performance: States, districts and schools that improve achievement will be rewarded. Failure will be sanctioned. Parents will know how well their child is learning, and that schools are held accountable for their effectiveness with annual state reading and math assessments in grades 3–8.

2. Focus on What Works: Federal dollars will be spent on effective, research based programs and practices. Funds will be targeted to improve schools and enhance teacher quality.

3. Reduce Bureaucracy and Increase Flexibility: Additional flexibility will be provided to states and school districts, and flexible funding will be increased at the local level.

4. Empower Parents: Parents will have more information about the quality of their child's school. Students in persistently low-performing schools will be given choice.

These broad objectives were channeled into seven "performance-based titles":

   I. Improving the academic performance of disadvantaged students
   II. Boosting teacher quality
   III. Moving limited English proficient students to English fluency
   IV. Promoting informed parental choice and innovative programs
   V. Encouraging safe schools for the 21st Century
   VI. Increasing funding for Impact Aid
   VII. Encouraging freedom and accountability

No Child Left Behind signals a new era in federal involvement in education. The greatest impact has been the introduction of mandatory testing of reading and math skills in grades 3–8, although, in keeping with educational tradition, the design of these annual tests and the standards to aim for are left to the states to decide. In addition, a sample of students in each state is to be assessed annually using the National Assessment of Educational Progress (NAEP) 4th and 8th grade examinations in reading and math. This clearly increases the accountability of schools and state educational authorities, although critics maintain that teaching has predictably become more "test-driven" than "learning-driven" since the sanctions on poorly performing schools are severe. If a school fails to make progress toward minimum standards three years in a row, disadvantaged students will be allowed to use federal funds to transfer to a higher-performing public or private school. States that do not continue to improve will face cuts in federal funding for administration of schools. School superintendents and principals need to worry about their jobs if their districts or schools are not performing better from one year to the next. Some very good schools face a difficulty of not being able to "improve" continuously. There have also been some unintended counterproductive effects of these threatened sanctions already: realizing that many of their schools would find it difficult to show improvement, Ohio educational officials deliberately lowered the standards of achievement for students in that state. Although the basic intentions of No Child Left Behind are nearly universally approved, many classroom teachers experience a huge gap between the glowing wording of the Act and the resources made available to schools to meet demands for improved outcomes.

One non-profit, donation-based organization has had a significant impact on schools in the most deprived areas of the country, **Teach for America**. Started in 1990 by a Princeton graduate student, Wendy Kopp, the organization recruits top students graduating from the best universities in the country to commit to two years of teaching in poor schools, regardless of what they majored in. By 2008 the program had become so successful that as many as 12 percent of students graduating from elite universities were applying for the two-year experience, although only a tiny fraction could be accepted for the some 6,000 places. These young idealists certainly make a difference in the schools, and their own future careers both within and outside education clearly benefit from the experience. One alumna of the program has gone on to tackle the job of improving one of the worst-performing schools systems in the US, in Washington, D.C. She is directly responsible to the mayor of the city in her work and has considerable power to hire and fire teachers and to reorganize schools.

Other idealistic recent college graduates can also benefit in a different way from working in schools in poor US communities for a period of two years in **Americorps** or by taking part in projects in the **Peace Corps**—a federal organization created by President John Kennedy—to help struggling communities around the world. Under federal programs, these college graduates can cancel a major portion of their student loans by volunteering to perform such community or international service.

It is worth noting that most Americans do not seem to place academic excellence at the top of their list of priorities. A Gallup Poll commissioned in 1996 by the Phi Delta Kappa educational honor society showed that 60 percent of US parents would rather have their children get average grades and be active in extra-curricular activities than have them bring home all-A report cards; only 28 percent would rather have it the other way around.

In higher education for the last two decades there has been much concern about the general level of freshmen when it comes to basic skills, especially writing. In the late 1970s and 1980s a wave of reform swept the nation's campuses. The idea of a common core curriculum was widely accepted, largely a reaction to tendencies toward excessively vocation-oriented courses. The idea was to resuscitate the ideal of a liberal education, including in the curriculum basic concepts such as critical thinking, scientific method, problems of democracy, peace studies, the environment, etc. A movement called **Writing Across the Curriculum** (WAC) stressed the importance of students' being required to write compositions in whatever field they happened to choose, instead of, as was increasingly the case, merely taking multiple-choice or short-answer exams. Starting in the mid 1970s the (San Francisco) Bay Area Writing Project started gathering teachers at all levels—from kindergarten through graduate schools—and from all over the country (and eventually the world) to swap ideas about the teaching of writing. The so-called 'process-oriented' approach to written composition spread from there across the US and to many other parts of the world.

In the late 1980s a great debate arose over just what should be included in the core curriculum in terms of cultural understanding. Traditionalists deplored the fact that most students were completing college with little knowledge of the pillars of Western society, while others, especially on the west coast, felt it was time to open the door to other—for example, Asian and American Indian—cultural traditions, stressing the pluralism of American society. This debate and the parallel discussions about political correctness regarding gender, race, and sexual orientation, for example, have colored American campus life for more than a decade now.

On average, American schools are not of top quality, but there are many excellent institutions at all levels. While in the recent past too many schools at all levels had given in to external and internal forces and lowered their standards to accommodate greater numbers of students in a commendable but failing and even self-defeating effort to make access to education truly universal, gains made in the last few years have shown that mass education can be combined with high demands. Indeed, a key lesson of many local projects and even of the general upward climb of American schools today seems to be that underprivileged children and poor achievers can learn if they perceive that the adult world *expects* them to learn. The movement toward crisis identified more than two decades ago has in some ways been reversed, although a great deal remains to be done to raise the weakest students to acceptable levels. Reaching that goal fully will probably require the continued and even expanded participation of the federal government and will most certainly involve imaginative innovations in local empowerment. The zeal of teachers from organizations like Teach for America will certainly be needed, but the question is whether the quality of an entire educational system can be expected to be dependent on the passion of young teachers. Finding ways to provide quality education for all students will remain a major challenge to the United States, as to the rest of the world, for many decades to come.

SUGGESTED WEB SITES

Department of Education, National Center for Educational Statistics
www.ed.gov/NCES

Educational Resources Information Center
www.eric.ed.gov

American Association of School Administrators
www.aasa.org

American Federation of Teachers
www.aft.org

National Education Association
www.nea.org

Organization for Economic Cooperation and Development
www.oecd.org

Council for Aid to Education
www.cae.org

Non-profit organization to bring college graduates into schools
www.teachforamerica.org

PART V

Challenges

CHAPTER 17

Introduction

Journalists often hear the complaint that they spend too much of their time writing about negative things. They argue in their defense that, in order to be considered 'newsworthy', events have to be unusual, different from what happens every day. Such events tend to be disasters, wars, social upheavals, etc. This journalistic problem has been especially noticeable in Third-World countries over the last couple of decades, where many people have complained that the rest of the world, hearing only these depressing reports about them, mistakenly believe that life in their countries consists of endless misery. Little is heard about the joy and the pride their people might feel about their culture or about advances being made on a large or a small scale.

Similarly, any discussion of the 'social issues' of a country will necessarily be negative, problem oriented. In the case of the United States, Americans traveling abroad sometimes find that people they meet have a somewhat distorted picture of what life is like in the US, a picture dominated by crime, poverty, homelessness, racial strife, etc. These travelers find it difficult to convince foreigners just how 'normal' everyday life actually is for the overwhelming majority of Americans. Residents of Northern Ireland experience a similar problem in getting people to recognize that they do not spend their days dodging bullets and bombs.

There are two ways of dealing with this type of negative bias. A number of Third-World nations have tried to counteract the one-sided images the world has of them by establishing official news agencies which in effect censor reports from their countries. Some Americans react in a similar way to problem-oriented presentations of their country, trying to play down the difficulties the US faces, even to the point of denying their existence.

Figure 17.1 Many American families are sometimes forced to turn to the authorities and charities for help in distress. (Photo: Courtesy USIA)

Others are distressed more by the problems themselves than by the way they are dealt with in the mass media at home and abroad; they argue that, while it is important to maintain some balance in how a country's weaknesses are covered, it is wrong to pretend that they do not exist.

The following brief survey of social issues, like the rest of this book, subscribes to the latter view. While every attempt will be made to remind the reader of the sometimes limited scope of various problems and to represent differing views on how those problems should be solved, this overview will examine some of the serious problems that are—and should be—an embarrassment to the world's richest nation. Homelessness, for example, may be statistically 'marginal'—affecting less than one percent of the population—but it is nevertheless a real and relatively new phenomenon that blights the lives of hundreds of thousands of people and that even the most casual visitor to nearly any major American city cannot fail to be moved by.

CHAPTER 18

Poverty

The United States is obviously not a poor nation. Indeed, due to its size, human and natural resources, and industrial productivity, in absolute terms it is far and away the wealthiest nation in history. The very fact that hundreds of thousands of people from all over the world make unbelievable sacrifices merely to get into the country—even to be poor there—suggests that even the poorest Americans have more 'wealth' than millions of other people on earth.

Yet wealth is undeniably relative. The tremendous riches of the American nation as a whole are small compensation to the millions of inhabitants—citizens and non-citizens—who live right next to, but are light-years away from achieving, its plenty. How many poor people are there in the US? Who are they, or rather, what sorts of people are most likely to be poor? What is being done to relieve and eliminate poverty? What are its consequences and what chances does an individual have of breaking out of its vicious circle? These are the questions we will touch upon in this section.

In 2007 some 37.3 million Americans (12.5 percent of the population —up from 11.3 percent in 2000) were living in poverty according to official statistics. The level of poverty was then calculated to be roughly $21,386 of cash income per year for a family of four (various non-money forms of support, such as food stamps, rent subsidies, medical care, are thus not included in this figure). The number of people living in poverty was nearly 40 million in 1960, 43 years earlier. In 1960 forty million people represented fully 22 percent of the entire US population. This fact—and a book by Michael Harrington called *The Other America*—shocked the Kennedy and especially the Johnson administrations into declaring a

'War on Poverty' in the early and mid 1960s. This 'war' consisted of massive increases in welfare and job-training programs, and it seems to have worked: by 1969 the proportion of poor people was down to 12 percent, and it continued to fall until the end of the 1970s, even through the difficult years of the Ford and Carter administrations (which had to deal with the inflation triggered by the Vietnam War and inflamed by the oil crises of that decade). The Reagan administrations of the 1980s were less willing to spend federal funds on such programs, however, and by 1983 the poverty figure had risen to 15 percent. Although the 1980s ended with a slightly lower rate, the figure reached 15 percent again in 1993 before coming down again. The Reagan and George H. W. Bush decade, with its conservative emphasis on market solutions to social problems, resulted in more people joining the ranks of the poor, while wealthy Americans grew richer, with the top quintile (fifth) of the population increasing its share at the expense of the other four quintiles. Comparing the top and bottom fifths, we find the lowest quintile dropped from 4.3 percent of all household income in 1980 to 3.4 in 2007, while the top quintile grew from 43.7 to 49.7 of all household income over the same period. In other words, this accumulation of income in the hands of fewer individuals continued through the Clinton and George W. Bush presidencies, but after 1993, poverty rates fell, probably owing to the unprecedented prosperity of the American economy throughout the Clinton years, only to start to rise again in 2001.

Poverty has predominantly been an urban phenomenon that afflicts the core areas of America's major cities, areas abandoned since the 1950s and 1960s by those who could afford to move to the suburbs. But by 2007 poverty rates had declined somewhat in central cities, with an average rate in metropolitan areas just below the national average at 11.9 percent. Within those metropolitan areas, the central cities had well above average poverty rates of 16.5 percent, and the suburban areas 9.0 percent, up slightly from 8.9 percent in 2002. In other words, a small but slightly growing percentage of poor people are now suburbanites (see 'urban sprawl' p. 26 and "minorities in suburbs" p. 86). The remaining poor people live in rural and small-town areas outside the major cities, with an above average rate of 15.4 percent. They are often families with two parents, one of whom may have a full-time job. Working full time at the official minimum wage of $7.25 (2009) amounts to an annual income of less than three quarters of the official poverty level for a family of four.

The most striking feature of American poverty is the tremendous number of children victimized by it, although great improvements have occurred in recent years. Rates have dropped from roughly a quarter of all children in America lived in poverty or near poverty in the early 1990s to about 18 percent in 2007, though that percentage is again on the rise. More than half of these children are the sons and daughters of single mothers, women whose men have abandoned them. Looking at the entire population, about 28.3 percent of all children in such families grow up under the poverty line, a figure that is increasing steadily. If we add a further dimension of skin color, we find that almost 40 percent of all children in families headed by a black female live in poverty, a figure that is has come down rapidly from over 60 percent in the early 1990s. For Hispanic single mothers, the figure is virtually the same as for black single mothers. In general the percentage of African Americans who are poor is more than three times the percentage of (non-Hispanic) whites, respectively 24.5 and 8.2 percent in 2007. Hispanics have a general poverty rate of 21.5 percent. For Asians the rate is around 10.2 percent.

The number of single-parent families is growing. In fact American families are generally getting smaller (as are families in most industrialized countries). In 1790 the average family consisted of more than seven persons; more than two hundred years later the figure is fewer than three. More and more people, both young and old, live alone these days.

But it is among African Americans that the problem of the single-parent family is most aggravated: some 70 percent of black poverty is related to female-headed families. This pattern has commonly been seen as a heritage of slavery, since slave families were often broken up, with members being sold to different owners, but modern research has shown that the African-American family survived slavery relatively well. The break-up of the family is rather to be traced to the strains of the great migration to the Northern cities. Generally speaking, however, it seems probable that male slaves were socially emasculated by slavery and the system of segregation that replaced it. Today's black men still suffer from poor self-esteem and have few positive role models to follow, sensing at an early age that there is a 'ceiling' to what careers they might aspire to. The result has often been the sort of exaggerated 'macho' behavior which is not conducive to stable family life (see 'Million Man March' p. 79).

A Welfare Revolution

Some of the blame for the wide prevalence of fatherless families, however, must go to the structure of the very programs that were devised to help the poor. From the 1960s until the late 1990s many welfare rules inadvertently encouraged fathers to leave their families. The best-known of these is AFDC, Aid to Families with Dependent Children, which is normally not available to families with a male provider present. Many fathers thus 'helped' their families by moving out in order to render the family eligible for welfare benefits. Even a man with a full-time but poorly paid job could often bring in more money by putting his family on welfare than by staying on to head the household. Conservatives and liberals alike were dismayed by the fact that so many families seemed to be locked into permanent poverty and dependence on welfare payments. Many attempts were made over the years to reform various welfare programs so as to encourage (especially black) men to stay with their families, but the problem remained a major feature of the welfare system until 1996, when a major reversal was set in motion.

On August 22, 1996 President Clinton signed into law the **Personal Responsibility and Work Opportunity Reconciliation** Act. The new legislation was designed to 'put an end to welfare as we know it' by replacing programs unrestricted like AFDC with **Temporary Assistance for Needy Families, TANF.** Under this system welfare recipients are normally no longer able to receive benefits for more than a lifetime total of five years, and, if able, they are required to take part in community work programs within two years of signing up for assistance or they will be cut off. Funding for the program is in the form of a **block grant** to the states, meaning that the federal government provides a block sum of money with only general guidelines and leaves it up to the states to devise plans to comply with them. States are rewarded for taking people off the welfare rolls and putting them to work, and they will be penalized if they fail to produce results. The original law required states to have moved 25 percent of welfare families off of welfare into work by the end of fiscal 1997 and 50 percent by the end of fiscal 2002. Single minors with children are required to live in an adult-supervised environment and attend training courses in order to receive benefits. At the same time, rules for collecting child-support payments from delinquent parents (usually 'deadbeat dads' as they are called) have been stiffened, and some provision has been made for increased availability of day care and other necessary services for single parents who are required to work.

Generally speaking, the 1996 law provided for 'workfare' not 'welfare', a slogan that had been in circulation since the early 1970s but which few politicians had ever dared to act upon. A pioneer in this respect was Republican Governor Tommy Thompson of Wisconsin in the early 1990s, who launched a program called 'Wisconsin Works'. This program was the forerunner of many features of the national plan, and it could boast a 55 percent reduction in the welfare rolls after just a few years. Supporters maintain that roughly 75 percent of those leaving welfare in Wisconsin have found jobs in the private sector, while critics claim that even those now working are in greater poverty than before the reform and that many people leaving the welfare system are now living in shelters for the homeless in even greater misery.

While nearly everyone agrees with the lofty aims of the Personal Responsibility Act, many experts are seriously concerned that it is so seriously underfunded and flawed that it will in fact lead to an increase in poverty. One major problem involves the job skills of traditional welfare recipients: they are overwhelmingly young minority women with only high-school education or less, and their prospects for landing a regular job are extremely poor. The jobs that the states are to provide them with under the law are so poorly paid that many families will face cuts in their income as a result. Furthermore, day-care service is very poorly developed in the US and funding for new facilities is sorely inadequate. By 2001, well into the new system that took effect in 1997, the federal government had doubled its spending for child care, but demand still outpaced the supply of new places. One perverse effect of the 1996 legislation has led to poor working families' being placed at the bottom of the waiting lists for day-care services, as priority has been given to single mothers coming off of welfare.

One example of ambivalence among lawmakers involves one of the most controversial provisions of the welfare revolution—the exclusion of immigrants who are not citizens, even legal ones who have always played by the rules, from government benefits. Those in need of such support are overwhelmingly elderly or disabled people whose only income has been government assistance in the form of Supplemental Security Income. Immediately after his re-election in 1996 President Clinton promised to reinstate this support money, and by the spring of 1997 he had managed to gain the backing of congressional leaders for this as well as for restoring funding that had been cut from the food stamp program (food stamps are vouchers that can only be used for the purchase of food—about one American in ten uses food stamps). The public outcry, and the protests of governors whose states were home to thousands of legal aliens, had made it difficult for the Republican-dominated lawmakers to follow through with their cuts.

The welfare reform law also removed the requirement that poor people have to be receiving family assistance payments in order to qualify for free basic medical care under the **Medicaid** program. Old-age retirees are covered by a program called **Medicare**, and veterans of the armed services have their own excellent medical care programs under the Veterans' Administration. Some 45 million Americans, many of them in families headed by one or two full-time workers, had no health insurance in 2007. This figure corresponds to 15.3 percent of the population. As the economy turned downward in the fall of 2008, these figures were assumed to be on the rise. The establishment of a nationwide health-care system was one of the main campaign promises of President Barack Obama. His projected program would not be a government single-payer system but would instead retain a role for insurance companies.

The greatest concern was that the new workfare programs were put in place during a period of record low unemployment and economic prosperity; what would happen when the economy turns downward and the long-term safety nets are no longer strung up? These and similar arguments were what made politicians reluctant to enact workfare in the past, and President Clinton was aware of the risks involved when he signed the bill in 1996. He seemed to want to eat his cake and have it, too, as he faced re-election in the fall of 1996, signing the bill and yet promising to work for measures to cushion its effects in his second term. Nevertheless, as the economy began to turn alarmingly downward in the final year of the George W. Bush administration, observers feared there would be a new wave of welfare seekers with no welfare available under the new rules.

Life in Poverty

What are the consequences of being poor in the United States? We have already stated that American poverty is rarely as abject as the misery experienced by hundreds of millions of people in the Third World. But the problems poor Americans face are nevertheless serious, mainly in terms of their health, education, and quality of life in relation to their more affluent countrymen.

Many Americans are overweight, even among the poor, a fact which might suggest that they simply eat too much. But the type of obesity that poor—and many not-so-poor—people often suffer from is rather a form of malnutrition; they eat the wrong kind of food. Their lack of nutritional awareness leads parents to serve meals made up of canned beans, cheap hot dogs, and pasty white bread, fare made more attractive to children by the addition of potato chips and soda pop. Perhaps surprisingly, studies have shown that poor families living on food stamps in fact purchase more healthful food, within their means, than do average families. But a major study by the Food Research and Action at the turn of the century also found that some 4 million children under the age of twelve—one eighth of all such children—sometimes have to go without food and that another 9.6 million are at risk of going hungry.

Malnutrition, inferior housing, and lack of preventive health care lead to sickness. The 4 million children who suffered from hunger in the Food Research and Action Center study were found to have sickness rates two to three times those of other children. Around the turn of the new century low-income people averaged about 28 days of disability per year as compared with 13 for middle-income and 10 for high-income earners. The US as a whole had an infant mortality rate of 6.3 deaths per thousand births in 2006, which is comparable to other industrialized countries (although its rank in 33rd place in 2006 according to the United Nations

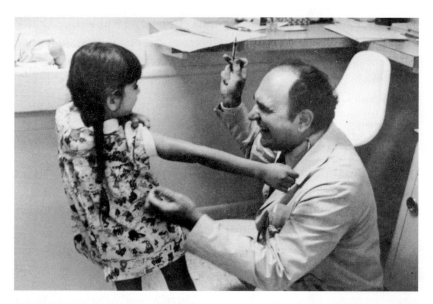

Figure 18.1 Lack of preventive health care in inner cities lies behind higher rates of sickness and infant deaths. (Photo: Suzanne Szasz, Courtesy USIA)

surprises many Americans), but the figure is twice as high among African Americans in general and some inner-city areas have rates usually associated with Third-World countries, around 25 deaths per thousand births. These drastic figures are largely ascribable to lack of pre-natal care, poor nutritional awareness, and substance abuse among indigent women.

Malnutrition also affects children's performance in school, as do overcrowded or unsettled living conditions. Since a high school diploma is a bare minimum for entry into almost any decently paid job (more and more employers now demand this plus two years of college), a combination of inferior schools and home conditions not conducive to studying tends to doom those born into poverty to lead the rest of their lives in poverty. In some inner-city areas the high-school dropout rate is over fifty percent (compared with just under 10 percent nationwide). It is easy to understand why so many poor teenage boys yield to the temptation to escape into drug abuse or to make a fast dollar by dealing in narcotics and why many mothers are forced to look the other way when their children bring home drug money. For girls the temptation has been to

266

have a baby as soon as possible in order to qualify for their own welfare checks. Thus the cycle of poverty is perpetuated.

It must be remembered that most welfare recipients would much rather earn their own living and that most poor people do not turn to crime to escape their plight. Indeed, living in the middle of it and being its primary victims, the poor loathe crime even more than other groups do.

It should also be reiterated that the great majority of Americans do not live in poverty. Most of them are greatly concerned that so many of their fellows do. Roughly half of all Americans—and 70 percent of the wealthy —take part in some form of volunteer work to help others, on average over four hours per week, and the average annual contribution to charities is 2.5 percent of household income—and over 6 percent among the lowest income families.

CHAPTER 19

Homelessness

No one can visit the United States without noticing the large number of people who seem to be without a home. The most obvious ones are those who push all their earthly belongings before them in a shopping cart or carry their possessions in overloaded backpacks or shopping bags. Such people often wear several layers of clothing, partly to protect themselves from the cold, partly to lighten their packs. Those in the direst situations are former mental patients who live from hand to mouth, making the rounds of trash cans and dumpsters, panhandling, eating in soup kitchens, sleeping under bridges and viaducts, crouching over hot-air vents in sidewalks. But that product of the 1980s, the bag lady, is just one of a number of types of homeless people. Who are they, why do they have no place to live, and how many of them are there?

There is no general agreement about how many homeless Americans there are. Nearly everyone agrees that they rather suddenly became visible —first in urban areas, later in small towns—in the early and middle 1980s. The National Law Center on Homelessness estimates that some 750,000 people are homeless in the US on any given night and between 1.2 and 2 million experienced homelessness sometime during a year. The first Clinton administration relied on another survey from 1990 that looked at life-time and five-year rates and found that 7 percent of those surveyed had gone without a roof over their heads sometime in their lives and 3 percent had been homeless sometime between 1985 and 1990. This study was largely corroborated for the following five-year period. Several studies from major cities have each found that about 3 percent of their respective populations use community shelters sometime during a year. The actual figures are much higher if adjusted for two other groups: the hidden homeless who live in dumpsters and cardboard boxes and never go to shelters and the many people, especially families, who squeeze into temporary quarters with friends or relatives when they lose their homes.

Who are the homeless? A 2000 study run in 25 cities for the US Conference of Mayors determined that the homeless population in cities was made up of 44 percent single men, 13 percent single women, 36 percent families with children, and 7 percent unaccompanied minors.

The same Conference of Mayors study found that 50 percent of the homeless are African American (trending downward), 35 percent non-Hispanic white (trending upward), 12 percent Hispanic (trending upward), 2 percent American Indian, and 1 percent Asian. Some 37 percent are substance abusers, and 15 percent are veterans. As many as a quarter of homeless adults in cities have jobs. In rural areas most homeless people are white.

A major triggering factor of homelessness is domestic violence. A 1997 study by the National Coalition for the Homeless found that between 25 and 30 percent of homeless women and children were fleeing abuse in their former homes. A Ford Foundation study from 1990 estimated that as many as half of all women and children without a home were victims of domestic violence.

Of course there have always been drifters and hoboes in America, but prior to the 1980s they were limited to 'skid row' areas of cities. Something —or some combination of circumstances—created a new phenomenon around 1982. One factor that has often been mentioned as being seminal in this context is the wholesale emptying of mental institutions that took place in the United States starting in the late 1950s and accelerating in the 1960s and early 1970s. Many people quite rightly reacted against the way hundreds of thousands of patients were being treated in overcrowded, understaffed, and inhuman institutions, and it was felt that many of these patients would be able to adapt to life in society if they were given a proper chance. The success of places like Fountain House in New York City inspired other 'halfway houses' that softened the transition from life in psychiatric hospitals to more or less normal life in society. Community care centers were planned to provide out-patient service. Institutionalization was rightly seen as a violation of basic human rights, but now few people doubt that, to rectify the situation, the gates were opened too wide, too quickly: in the space of just a few years hundreds of thousands of patients were left to their own devices with little or none of the promised help from the state and local authorities, who were often strapped for funds in the wake of the oil crises of the 1970s.

While roughly 22 percent of homeless people in the cities indeed are mentally ill, the Federal Task Force on Homelessness and Severe Mental Illness claimed in the 1990s that only between 5 and 7 percent of these mentally ill homeless persons should be placed in institutions. Most of them would be able to cope in society with appropriate community support.

The two main causes of homelessness are in fact the self-evident ones: poverty and the lack of affordable housing. Poverty has been dealt with above; it should be sufficient to say here that real wages have declined over the last couple of decades for those at the bottom of the income ladder, placing more and more individuals and families just a few paychecks away from homelessness.

Why is there such a shortage of affordable housing for low-income families? One major cause is the chain reaction created by the process of

Figure 19.1 A Bag Lady. (Photo: Örjan Björkdahl, Pressens Bild AB)

gentrification that started in the 1970s. The late 1940s saw the beginning of what is usually referred to as 'suburban sprawl' (see p. 26 and p. 86): cheap housing loans and, especially, massive highway construction encouraged working families to move away from inner-city areas and settle in the nearby suburbs. By the late 1960s those who could afford to do so had moved out, leaving the central sections of the big cities to the poor. Property in such areas lost its value and was not kept up. Slums resulted.

In the 1970s real estate investors discovered that properties in inner-city neighborhoods could be bought for a song, thoroughly renovated, and sold to wealthy buyers at a handsome profit. The new 'gentry' started moving back into the cities, and former slums became chic addresses. The previous residents could not afford to stay on and were displaced.

This displacement was at first moderated somewhat by the existence of low-income housing projects supported by the federal government. However, the Reagan administrations cut the funding of such projects during the 1980s (federal housing expenditure was cut from 7.5 percent of the federal budget in the late 1970s to 1.5 percent in 1988), and new low-cost dwellings more or less ceased to be built, leaving hundreds of thousands of people with nowhere to live. Ironically, the more the economy prospered, allowing the upper middle-class to gentrify urban neighborhoods, the more the poor were forced out of their slum dwellings and into the streets.

What has been described above represents the upper and lower extremes of a greater housing problem in the US. Ever since the 1930s, when cheap mortgages and the income-tax deductions for interest payments were introduced, Americans have grown accustomed to owning their own 'single-family detached' dwellings, or, in other words, 'homes'. It has come to be assumed that a working- or middle-class family will naturally go through only a short period of apartment living and then purchase a house of their own.

But two factors started to change that picture in the latter half of the 1980s: on the one hand, President Ronald Reagan's tax reform limited the deductibility of interest payments (this has since been restored in full, although there are general dollar limits on deductions for higher income brackets), and, on the other hand, house prices rose dramatically in many burgeoning metropolitan areas. Home ownership rates declined for a few

272

years (although they are still two or three times higher than in most European countries, for example) as young first-time buyers found that they had been priced out of the market. They stayed in their apartments instead, effectively taking these rentals out of circulation, and the 'odd family out' was in many cases left to shift for itself, to live in cheap motels, charity shelters, cars, parks, or the streets. The winners were the 'pippies' —'people inheriting parents' property', which they could either live in or sell in order to finance a new home.

Housing prices continued to rise throughout the first few years of the 21st century, but this price increase proved to be a 'bubble' that began to burst in 2005, with substantial drops in house sales. When the burst bubble was analyzed in 2008 it became clear that predatory lending on the part of mortgage companies and banks—that is, aggressive lending of mortgage funding to individuals and families that clearly would not be able to keep up their monthly payments once the adjustable interest rates began to rise rapidly—was creating unprecedented numbers of mortgage foreclosures and leaving millions of home-owners with 'upside-down' mortgages, that is, home-loan debt amounting to sums that are considerably higher than their home is worth on the market. These predatory lenders, working under virtually no regulation from government, made huge amounts of money for years by selling their mortgages to companies that repackaged them in bundles to be sold to investors for even more money. This finance bubble burst a couple of years after the true market value of houses fell precipitously starting in 2005, causing widespread bank failures. These bank failures largely froze the credit market not only in the US but elsewhere in the world and plunged most world economies into severe recession, if not depression. All of these forces conspire, of course, to put more families in the streets.

Apart from shelters and soup kitchens there are many private and public attempts to alleviate the plight of the homeless. One fairly common private solution that kills two birds with one stone is that of home-owners converting their garages or other utility space into living space and then renting the room to persons or families in need of cheap housing. The home-owner gets needed income to pay the mortgage while poorer families at least have a roof over their heads. This is a new suburban version of the old boarding house.

Some city governments have stimulated low-cost housing construction by offering low-interest loans to developers and by liberalizing building codes. For a 1,000-apartment development scheme New York City attracted about thirty percent of its funds from private corporations, which could use their contributions as federal tax write-offs. Similar programs have appeared in Los Angeles, Kansas City, and San Francisco.

One general movement from the mid 1990s has entailed improvements for some families but at the same time forced others into life on the streets. In the 1960s low-cost housing was often made available in the form of high-rise apartment projects, but these large-scale building complexes normally developed into dilapidated, drug-ridden high-crime neighborhoods within just a few years. However, in 1993, early in the first Clinton administration, legislation was passed—called HOPE VI—to begin to tear down these predictably rectangular apartment buildings and to replace them with attractive small three- or four-family units of various shapes and colors and with tiny yards. The poor families who are fortunate enough to land a home in these new public housing areas mingle with the working-class and even middle-class neighbors who are encouraged to share in this new type of mixed-income community living. The feeling of pride among poor families has thus far led to a dramatic shift away from crime, drugs, and graffiti in these new projects. One problem is, of course, that such small-scale architectural solutions do not provide enough housing units, and a majority of the former apartment-dwellers have had to move out of the neighborhood, often into temporary housing or homelessness. Another problem that was discovered in 2008 is that these mixed-income housing areas outside the city centers turned out to be the sites of a surprising increase in crime (see p. 279 under "Crime"), probably related to a large number of former prison convicts completing their sentences and rejoining their families, now in the new mixed-income areas.

Churches have been extremely active in renovating old and building new homes for the needy. Various programs involve the concept of 'sweat equity', that is, the poor family works on renovating or constructing a home with the help of church and community volunteers, often with some support from the local government. The 'sweat' of their work becomes a part of their 'equity' or 'investment' in the house or apartment. Generally speaking, churches and other volunteer groups have been extremely active in helping the homeless, by providing soup kitchens, temporary shelter, and counseling, often in cooperation with local city authorities. President George W. Bush went on record in 2001 as wishing to see a greater role played by churches and other volunteer organizations in alleviating the burdens of poverty and homelessness. He wanted federal and state funding for such purposes to be channeled through volunteer groups.

Some major cities, like New York and Chicago, have shifted in recent years to programs offering **Care Not Cash** to the homeless. Money is not given to homeless people directly, for fear that such money will wind up fueling substance abuse, but rather invested in housing and shelters and detoxification centers. The city of San Francisco, with huge numbers of very visible homeless people in its civic center area, is trying to enact similar measures, no longer providing $500 per month to a homeless adult but a place to stay and $60.

Health care is obviously a major problem for the homeless. The life expectancy of a homeless person is approximately 46 years. To provide direct health-care services to the homeless in the streets, James Withers, a physician, and a formerly homeless partner, Michael Sallows, started the non-profit Operation Safety Net in Pittsburgh, Pennsylvania, in 1993. This was to be the seed of the Institute for Street Medicine, starting in 2005, an organization that stimulates and coordinates similar efforts in many big cities in the US and other parts of the world.

The most tragic victims of homelessness are children. Apart from the obvious health problems associated with living outdoors, the most serious effect of not having a place to live is the fact that children's schooling is often severely hampered. The National Coalition for the Homeless estimates that some quarter of a million homeless children attend school irregularly or not at all. Homeless families often find that local school boards are unwilling to recognize the right of their children to attend schools, because the family has no 'residence' in the community. Even if the children are accepted as pupils, they find it difficult to keep up with other kids who have a place to study and a secure place to sleep. A Harvard University study of homeless pupils in Massachusetts schools found in the early 1990s that some forty percent of them were failing or doing below-average work, fifty percent had repeated a grade, and twenty-five percent were in special-needs classes. These problems—which, as mentioned above (p. 242), have been faced by families of migrant workers for generations—are now plaguing a large number of working families that were only recently a part of the mainstream. In some cities local shelters for the homeless, run by the YWCA (Young Women's Christian Association), for example, offer schooling on the premises. This solution has been rejected by other cities, however, because it means isolating the homeless from the rest of the community.

Another major problem involving children without a home is that of the runaway child. Hundreds of thousands of children under eighteen run away from home, and they can be seen all over the country, even though glamorous centers like New York City, Los Angeles/Hollywood, San Francisco, and Miami and Ft. Lauderdale attract the greatest numbers. These children do not normally run away just to experience the thrill of street life, however: in the overwhelming majority of cases they leave home because they have been subjected to physical, sexual, or psychological abuse by one or both of their parents. Police report that in a majority of cases where the parents of a runaway are contacted, they are unwilling to take the child back.

Life in the streets is far from glamorous. Most young runaways soon fall victim to crime, drug abuse, prostitution, and violence connected with dope and sex. Both boys and girls are most in demand among the largely middle- and upper-class buyers of sex when they are in their early teens or even before puberty. By the time they reach sixteen or seventeen they are often seen as 'too old' and are rejected. Drug dealing and other criminal activity is usually all that remains for them then. As many as five thousand teenagers wind up in unmarked graves every year.

Perhaps the grimmest manifestation of the growing market for sex with children is the alarming number of children being kidnapped across the country. Although the great majority of America's thousands of missing children have been unlawfully seized by the parent who lost custody of the child in a divorce, shocking numbers of infants and small children are abducted from their parents and either sexually abused and murdered or sold into so-called 'white' slavery. It is not without reason that American parents are strongly advised to hold on to their children in crowded places like airports or shopping malls. American post offices and even check-out counters at supermarkets show pictures of vanished children, photos now sometimes enhanced by computers to show what a child whose picture was taken years ago probably looks like at present. In 1988 one bereaved father started a nation-wide television program where individual cases are highlighted and often cleared up. Needless to say, any abduction by a stranger—even if there is ultimately a happy ending— entails irreparable psychological damage to the child involved.

It must be remembered that the issues discussed here—the plight of children and the housing situation—are statistically 'marginal', and they should not be magnified to typify American society. The vast majority of American children are loved by their families, and the American housing stock far excels that of most countries. Nonetheless the problems addressed here are clearly more aggravated in the United States than in many other comparably 'advanced' countries (although many European cities now face similar problems), and the situation is also much worse than it was in the United States just two decades ago. The problems are all the more alarming because they are occurring in a nation that purports to lead the world in offering equal opportunity to all its citizens.

CHAPTER 20

Crime

The United States has long had a bad reputation for crime and violence, a notoriety that contains an element of fascination. The 'Wild West' has provided a mythical backdrop to hundreds of adventure stories and movies about notorious crooks, despite the fact that statistics give very little support for there ever having been such wide-spread violence[1]. Likewise, the days of Prohibition, when the manufacture, sale, and transport of alcoholic beverages were forbidden by the 18th Amendment to the Constitution in 1920, only to be permitted again by the 21st Amendment in 1933, gave rise to a wealth of stories about ubiquitous mafia violence in Al Capone's Chicago, for example. Various crime syndicates did terrorize certain cities in the 1920s and violence often did accompany dealings in illicit liquor, but, again, legends have tended both to glamorize and to magnify the extent of the gore.

The dastardly deeds of Billy the Kid and Al Capone pale, however, in comparison with the amount of bloodshed being witnessed in certain American cities today. With gunshot wounds now the leading cause of death among 15-to-24-year-old African-American males and with a per capita incidence of rape that is thirteen times that of Britain, the United States can now be said to deserve its reputation for violence. At the same time, as we will see below, the US does not deserve its reputation as a

---

[1] In *Legends, Lies and Cherished Myths of American History* (William Morrow and Co., 1988), Richard Shenkman points out that Dodge City produced only five killings in 1878, its most violent year. The five most notorious Kansas towns of Abilene, Dodge City, Ellsworth, Wichita, and Caldwell witnessed only forty-five murders between them from 1870 to 1885, a figure that is only slightly higher than that of small towns elsewhere.

generally crime-ridden country, and improvements have been dramatic over the last decade, even as regards violent crime.

According to the 2007 *Crime in the United States* report, murders have continuously declined in the country since the peak in the early 1990s: in 1991 the rate was 9.8 per 100,000 people and in 2007 it was 5.6 per 100,000, a drop of about 43 percent. The homicide rate has remained stable throughout the first decade of the new century. Robberies also peaked in 1991, at 272.7 per 100,000, and dropped to 147.6 in 2007, a 46-percent decline. Figures for forcible rape are similarly down 30 percent, peaking in 1992 at 42.8 per 100,000 and coming down to 30 in 2007. These improved figures are probably due to a combination of increased policing and, especially, a general drop in the number of young men aged from the late teens to about thirty.

A surprising and disturbing new pattern was reported in *The Atlantic Monthly* magazine in 2008, however. A criminologist working in Memphis was analyzing the increasing incidence of crime in outlying areas of that medium-sized Tennessee city, while his wife, a sociologist, happened to be working on statistics concerning so-called Section 8 vouchers, support for low-to-medium income housing provided by the federal government to move large numbers of working poor people into somewhat higher-income neighborhoods (see "Homelessness" p. 269). The couple saw a strikingly similar pattern between a new crime wave in formerly calm areas and the introduction of relatively poor families from previous homes in slums and urban housing projects. When they checked other medium-sized cities across the country, they found a similar pattern. A partial explanation for the increase in crime was found in convicted felons who had served their prison term and rejoined their families in the new and slightly more affluent parts of the cities. Many returned to a life of crime, and many practiced new criminal activities learned while in prison. This is of course a perverse effect of well-meaning efforts on the part of the federal authorities to break up crime-ridden inner-city neighborhoods.

The average American has grown to be highly crime-conscious: crime and drugs rank consistently high when citizens' major concerns are polled, although the recent drop in violent crimes in big cities has alleviated some of this fear. Sometimes precautions are out of proportion to actual dangers: colleges strictly advise women students not to walk alone after dark, and campuses offer free 'group walks' where women students are accompanied home from the library, for example, by male and female volunteers, despite the fact that campus assault rates are extremely low. Generally speaking, women are more concerned about being victimized by a stranger in a public place than are men, even though men are much more likely to be attacked than women. Instead, women have much more reason to fear people (overwhelmingly men) they know: nearly 30 percent of all female homicide victims were known to have been killed by their husbands, former husbands, or boyfriends.

Violent crime is not uniformly prevalent. Indeed, roughly half of all urban crimes are committed in only three percent of police patrol points, and people in poor neighborhoods are crime victims far more often than those in middle- and upper-class areas (although domestic violence against women cuts straight across class and neighborhood boundaries).

There are two common denominators in most of the depressing figures presented above: drugs and guns. Drug abuse has blighted American society for over three decades now. In homicides where the circumstances of the crime were known, about 5.3 percent were drug-related in 2006; this figure was down from a high of 7.4 percent in 1989 but was considerably higher than for 2005 (4 percent). The number of heroin addicts at the start of the 21st century was just over 200,000, more than three times the number in 1993; this number has remained roughly the same through the first decade of the century. The average age of heroin addicts is dropping sharply—at the turn of the new century average first-time users were just over 21 years old, down from 25 a decade earlier. The number of abusers of cocaine, including crack, and marijuana has declined steadily since the peak years in the late 1970s and early 1980s. Among teens between the ages of 12 and 17, illicit drug use in the last month has declined steadily throughout the first decade of the century, coming down from 11.6 percent overall and 8.2 percent for marijuana in 2002 to 9.5 percent overall and 6.7 percent for marijuana. Back in 1978 as many as 37 percent among high-school seniors (age 17–18) had used marijuana sometime in the last month.

To place these figures about substance abuse in perspective, however, it should be pointed out that nicotine is officially considered one of the most addictive substances, with roughly 90 percent of casual tobacco smokers becoming addicted, a rate considerably higher than for casual users of crack. Moreover, the cause for the greatest concern among parents in the US is alcohol abuse among teenagers. Nearly everybody knows some teenager who was killed in an auto accident involving drunk driving. Alcohol-related accidents are the leading cause of death among American teenagers. All told, roughly 40 percent of all fatal traffic accidents in 2005 involved a driver with alcohol in his/her blood. This percentage has been roughly the same for a decade but is considerable improvement over the 50-percent figure for 1990.

Nevertheless, dealing in drugs, especially crack, has been a major factor in accounting for the high levels of crime in certain localities over last couple of decades. Some poor neighborhoods have been more or less taken over by drug dealers, leaving many residents so frightened that they cannot leave their homes after dark. There have been a number of examples of neighborhoods like this that have been 'taken back' from the dealers as a result of residents' forming vigilante groups to patrol their streets, reporting to the police any drug deals they spot. In extreme cases vigilantes even close off their area to outsiders. Such citizen action is at odds with constitutionally guaranteed rights of freedom of movement, but local support is nonetheless overwhelming in most cases.

Another factor in accounting for violent crime is access to guns. Here, too, there is a conflict between perceived constitutional rights and public security. The right to bear arms has long been interpreted by many Americans as a constitutional right, although many others maintain that the article in the Bill of Rights that is purported to guarantee this right must be read in the light of 18th-century society (see p. 155). For a tiny minority of militant Americans, including those who are members of illegal and secret militias and other paramilitary groups, any federal or state action to limit access to firearms is interpreted as merely the first step in a series of pernicious plans by government to strip them of all Constitutional freedoms. Be that as it may, the United States is unique among Western nations regarding citizens' access to guns.

In the mid 1990s it was estimated that there were some 240 million guns, 40 million of them handguns, in private hands in the United States. There are roughly 70 million legal private gun owners, 12 million of them women. In the mid 1990s *Time* reported that Americans were buying guns

Figure 20.1 Crackhouse Raid. (Photo: Scott Applewhite, AP, AB Reportagebild)

at the same rate as fax machines, 2 million a year. Most regulation of purchases takes place at the local and state level. In many states, for example, handguns are allowed, but it is illegal to 'conceal' them in a car or on one's person, although laws against concealed weapons are rapidly being appealed. There are great differences from one state to the next. New York state has rigorous controls of gun purchases and use, while Texas has very lax control. In the debate between advocates of strict gun control and their opponents, the latter often point out that New York's stringent regulations have not been able to prevent the some 1,000 murders per year in that state and are therefore useless. The counter argument is that 96 percent of these killings involve illegal guns brought in from out of state, and that federal action must be taken to curtail purchases across the country. In 2008 the US Supreme Court overturned the gun controls in Washington, DC, as being too far-reaching, but at the same time the court confirmed that various levels of government do have the power to enforce reasonable restrictions. Just what is meant by reasonable will no doubt be the subject of heated debate in coming years.

Support for some form of gun control is strong in urban areas and weak in rural. In 1994 the most serious national restrictions involving handguns were instituted by law: the Brady Law, named after its champion James Brady, the former press secretary to President Reagan who was crippled for life by gunshot wounds in connection with an assassination attempt against the President, requires a waiting period of five days for any gun purchase, during which time the store is required to check with authorities that the would-be buyer is not a convicted felon, a drug addict, or mentally ill. Another law from 1994 banned the purchase and possession of several categories of assault weapons. Even with checks on purchasers, however, the number of guns in circulation will continue to spiral upwards. More and more honest citizens are buying legal handguns to protect themselves from criminals, who, of course, will always have access to illicit weapons—often stolen from those honest citizens. A 1996 law prohibited the licensing of anyone to use guns if that person has previously been convicted of even a misdemeanor (a less serious crime than a felony) involving domestic violence. This ban affected the jobs of many of the some 700,000 federal, state, and local law enforcers across the country: they were stripped of their weapons and given administrative duties only.

In the new millennium, gun-control advocates are focusing on extending Brady identity checks to gun shows, a move supported even by President George W. Bush, although he would like these checks to be instant checks only, with no waiting period. A bi-partisan bill was put forward by Senators John McCain and Joseph Lieberman in 2001 to require full checks at gun shows, but it failed to pass. A few states have passed their own legislation requiring background checks for sales at gun shows, but there is as yet no federal regulation. President George W. Bush showed from the outset of his administration that enforcement of existing federal restrictions would be eased: he shortened the storage period for Brady identification checks from ninety days to twenty-four hours, and he terminated funding for government 'buy-back' programs in which people could be paid for guns they handed in to the authorities, with no questions asked. In 2004 Congress failed to meet the deadline to simply renew the law banning assault weapons, even though President George W. Bush professed in his re-election campaign to support such a renewal and background checks, even at gun shows, a clear move to the political center.

Another line of action for gun control took its cue from successful lawsuits against tobacco companies in the late 1990s: victims of shootings, both accidental and deliberate, have sued gun manufacturers for what they perceive as the producers' share of responsibility for the abuse, in the form of weapon design and targeted advertising. State and federal courts, however, have generally been reluctant to assign this role to firearms producers.

Criminals are punished in America. The United States has the world's highest incarceration rate, about four times the international average. The Pew Center on the States reported in 2008 that, for the first time, one adult in 100 was locked up in jail or prison. Federal, state, and local authorities can hardly complete construction of new facilities (some of them in private hands) before they become overfilled. The prison populations are out of all proportion in racial terms: in 2006 one in fifteen African-American adults were in prison. The figure was one in 36 for Hispanic men. For black men between the ages of 20 and 34, the figure was a striking one in 9. Among women between the ages of 35 and 39, only one in 355 whites but one in 100 blacks were behind bars. Roughly 7 percent of all state and federal prisoners are women. In the middle of the first decade of the 21st century, state prisons were operating either at capacity or 16 percent above capacity and federal prisons were either at capacity or 39 percent above capacity. Some 7 percent of state budgets, or $44 billion, went to corrections, the highest budget item following health care, education, and transportation. That represents an increase of 127 percent, adjusted for inflation. One in nine state government employees works in correctional activities.

The judicial system is equally overburdened: the average time available for preliminarily dealing with arrests in metropolitan courts can be less than five minutes. Although the Constitution guarantees all citizens the right to a trial by a jury of their peers in criminal cases (and in some civil cases), shortage of time has made 'plea bargaining' almost the rule: counsel for the defense and the prosecutor agree on a lesser charge for the crime in return for a plea of guilty, thus eliminating the need for a time-consuming jury trial.

The prison population represents only about one quarter of all people under correctional supervision: three quarters of them are supervised in the community, on probation, or on parole from prison. About 60 percent of all inmates in federal correctional facilities were there for drug-related offenses at the turn of the century. Over 80 percent of the increase in the federal prison population from 1985 to 1995 was due to drug convictions. The tremendous rise in the number of convicted drug offenders, coupled with the crippling costs of building and maintaining new prisons, has led many Americans—including government officials—to question the efficacy of US drug policies based on policing and cutting off supplies from abroad. As many as one quarter of all prisoners who served time for non-violent drug offenses return to society and commit violent drug-related crimes, probably having been initiated into such a life style during their time in prison. States are beginning to learn this lesson. Even Texas, which in 2007 replaced California as having the largest prison population and is notorious for its executions of prisoners, is beginning to expand its drug treatment programs and non-incarceration penalties for nonviolent crimes. Advocates of less punitive drug policies point out that the World Health Organization recently found that the US and New Zealand were at the top of the list in terms of percentage of the population that had tried marijuana, at about 40 percent. The rate for the Netherlands, in the same survey, was half that of the US. The Dutch Minister of Health explained that their liberal policies have succeeded in making marijuana seem boring.

Incarceration rates have accelerated even more as a result of legislation passed in the mid 1990s. In many cases mandatory sentencing laws now limit judicial discretion in determining who should go to jail and for how long. Nearly half of the states and the federal government now subscribe to a 'three-strikes-and-you're-out' (the term comes from baseball) policy: anyone convicted of a third felony is given a life-time sentence (in California this is regardless of the seriousness of the felonies as such—one California man got a life sentence for stealing a pizza, his third serious crime; almost all other states that have three-strikes policies limit the felonies to violent crimes for all three strikes, however). On top of this, many states are adopting 'truth-in-sentencing' laws that lengthen the actual stay in prison to around 85 percent of the stipulated time instead of the 40–60 percent that was common earlier. These tough sentencing policies are increasingly being called into question, and recently federal courts have intervened in cases where 'three-strikes-and-you're-out' provisions have put relatively minor felons in prison for life, declaring the punishment unconstitutional.

There were virtually no executions of convicts from 1968 to 1976. The US Supreme Court declared in 1968 that the death penalty, as it was then implemented in most states, was unconstitutional. While some justices went so far as to argue that it was a form of 'cruel and unusual punishment' and, as such, was expressly forbidden by the Constitution, the majority opinion was that capital punishment was constitutional but was being applied unfairly and without 'due process', since most of the people who were executed were from minorities, especially African Americans. This decision led to a *de facto* ban which reflected the mood of the country in the early 1970s, but in the latter half of that decade more and more people began to demand a return to capital punishment. By the 1980s many states had modified their statutes to conform with the guidelines implied by the Supreme Court decision. In the quarter century since executions were resumed in 1976, well over 1,000 prisoners have been put to death, the overwhelming majority in Southern states (one third of them in Texas alone). Timothy McVeigh, who killed 168 people when he bombed a federal office building in Oklahoma City in 1995, was put to death by the federal government in June 2001, the first federal execution since 1963.

Three quarters of all states now have the death penalty for some crimes, as does the federal government. More executions can be expected in the future, as the more than 3,000 death-row convicts all over the country exhaust their avenues of appeal. Furthermore, these avenues were limited in number by a 1991 Supreme Court decision. The American Bar Association, the professional organization for all US lawyers, has repeatedly called for a new halt to the death penalty owing to the racial imbalance in its application, basically the same reason the Supreme Court gave when it stopped all executions thirty years earlier. Amnesty International has frequently criticized the United States and individual states for their laws calling for capital punishment.

In 1991 a non-commercial California television station, KQED in San Francisco, sued in court for the right to broadcast a videotape of that state's first execution in the San Quentin gas chamber since the 1940s. The station argued that newspapers were allowed to send reporters to witness executions and it was only right for broadcast media to be allowed to do the same; the public had a right to see what the results of the state's capital punishment legislation actually were. The proposed broadcast was to be in accordance with the wishes of the convict himself and was seen by many people as a potent argument against capital punishment, but critics nevertheless feared that the execution would simply become a gruesome public spectacle. The court turned down the request on grounds that a broadcast could endanger the lives of the executioners and stir up unrest in the prisons.

In January 2000, Illinois governor George Ryan declared a 'moratorium' on executions in his state, not because he did not believe in the death penalty but because of a series of cases in which prisoners on death row were proven innocent after their cases were reopened, sometimes with the introduction of DNA evidence in their favor. Amazingly, the series of reversed convictions was triggered not by state authorities but by the investigative work of a group of journalism students working under Professor David Protess at Northwestern University, outside Chicago. Their journalism class projects eventually led to new trials that freed innocent men who had spent years in prison as a result of shoddy legal defense and careless trial courts. The Illinois example prompted a reconsideration of capital punishment among Americans, resulting in a narrowing of the majority of citizens who still advocate the death penalty.

An alternative method for dealing with violent criminals is the Victim-Offender Reconciliation Program, VORP. Available from some 300 local centers in several parts of the country (as well as internationally), the scheme arranges for criminal offenders to voluntarily meet the victims of their crime face to face. The confrontation generally leads to a realization on the part of the criminal of the consequences of his or her offense. Damages are sometimes paid directly to the victim, or, especially if the offender is poor, a scheme is arranged for him or her to work off the damages instead. Many offenders prefer a jail sentence to having to meet their victims, but among young criminals who do take part in VORP about 90 percent turn away from crime.

When it comes to law enforcement, many metropolitan areas have tried to bring their police departments into closer contact with citizens in two ways. First, in new recruitment of police officers priority has been given to minority groups represented in the various neighborhoods, with an eye to reducing racial or ethnic tension. Second, 'neighborhood-oriented policing' or 'community patrols' have been reinstituted, so that residents recognize the police officers walking the local beat. Both of these measures tend to build up trust in the police force among the citizenry and, conversely, to instill in police officers a respect for the residents as individuals. These moves have decreased the risk of undue force being used in arrests, although complaints of police brutality are still common, especially in big-city areas. The vicious and protracted beating of an unarmed black man stopped for speeding by four Los Angeles police officers in early 1991 happened to be videotaped by a man on a balcony across the street. The incident prompted the US Attorney General to order the reopening of some 16,000 cases of alleged police brutality nationwide.

Starting in the mid 1990s police departments in major cities began to take neighborhood policing one step further: they opened local offices in strategically placed commercial establishments—McDonald's restaurants, for instance—in order to be where people are. Another strategic change that has led to dramatic reductions in crime in major cities like New York is known as 'no-tolerance policing'. This means that young teenagers are arrested and punished for minor offenses, petty crimes that used to be 'tolerated' or ignored but which often lead to more serious criminality if not stopped early.

To help the some 15 million at-risk children in the US to lead an honest life, President Clinton mustered an impressive array of leaders in Philadelphia in April 1997 to launch the Presidents' Summit for America's Future. It was chaired by the African American Colin Powell, former commander of U.N. forces in the 1991 Persian Gulf War, and later to serve as President George W. Bush's first secretary of state. The Summit was attended by all living former Presidents (except Ronald Reagan, whose illness made an appearance impossible), the then Vice-President Gore, thirty state governors, scores of top leaders from corporations and from religious and charitable organizations, as well as television celebrities. The idea behind the Summit was to marshal millions of individual citizens to serve as mentors to young children who have little or no contact with the non-criminal adult world. Corporations like McDonald's, Coca-Cola, Kmart, and Timberland pledged large sums of money and paid time-off from work for their employees to participate in mentoring and tutoring activities. The AFL-CIO, the central trade union organization in the US, provided school-to-work experience for high-school students. The National Football League Players' Association pledged to focus their help on Indian children and teenagers. In a sense, the Summit is a continuation of the one-on-one mentoring stimulated by the Million Man March in Washington a year and a half earlier (see p. 79). The express goal of the Summit was not to replace government programs with volunteer charity work but to form a new partnership between government, business, and other organizations to combat a major problem. Corporations gain goodwill and non-profit organizations, like Big Brothers/Big Sisters and Boys Clubs and Girls Clubs, gain major new sources of funding. This initiative can be seen as a step on the part of President Clinton to make good on his 1996 election promise to cushion the effects of the drastic new welfare laws he signed (see p. 262). The Presidents' Summit led to the establishment of a still-thriving umbrella organization called 'America's Promise: The Alliance for Youth' headed by Colin Powell and involving hundreds of major corporations in community programs to fulfill five promises: caring adults, safe places, healthy start, marketable skills, and opportunities to serve. While it may be tempting to question the motives of some of the participants in this long-term campaign, it would be surprising if such a massive—and peculiarly American—mobilization did not have a considerable effect on the generation that is otherwise at-risk of becoming criminals. If these various measures prove to be successful— and prison populations begin to decrease, the greatest savings will be not in terms of dollars but in terms of human suffering.

SUGGESTED WEB SITES

Urban Institute
www.urban.org

Economic Policy Institute
www.epinet.org

Conservative Web site
www.townhall.com

American Medical Association
www.ama-assn.org

American Bar Association public resources
www.abanet.org

American Public Human Services Association
www.aphsa.org

UNICEF
www.unicef.org

National Governors' Association
www.nga.org

World Health Organization
who.org

UN Population Information Network
www.un.org/popin

Centers for Disease Control, National Center for Health Statistics
www.cdc.gov

Mothers Against Drunk Driving
www.madd.org

National Coalition for the Homeless
www.nationalhomeless.org

Brady Campaign to Prevent Gun Violence
www.bradycampaign.org

National Rifle Association
www.nra.org

Gun-Owners of America
www.gunowners.org

Pew Center on the States Research Center
www.pewcenteronthestates.org

Bureau of Justice Statistics
www.ojp.usdoj.gov/bjs

Victim Statistics from the Office for Victims of Crime
www.ojp.usdoj.gov/ovc

Victim-Offender Reconciliation Program
www.vorp.org

Death Penalty Information Center
www.deathpenalty.org

Amnesty International
www.amnesty.org

America's Promise: The Alliance for Youth
www.americaspromise.org

INDEX